TOWARDS A THIRD THEATRE

TOWARDS A THIRD THEATRE

Eugenio Barba and the Odin Teatret

Ian Watson

With a foreword by Richard Schechner

London and New York

First published 1993
Paperback edition published 1995
by Routledge
11 New Fetter Lane, London EC4P 4EE

Simultaneously published in the USA and Canada
by Routledge
29 West 35th Street, New York, NY 10001

Typeset in 10/12 pt Baskerville

Printed in Great Britain by T. J. Press (Padstow) Ltd,
Padstow, Cornwall

British Library Cataloguing in Publication Data

A catalogue record for this book is available from the
British Library

Library of Congress Cataloguing-in-Publication Data

A catalogue record for this book has been requested

ISBN 0–415–12764–5

CONTENTS

FIGURES

PLATES

FOREWORD
East and West and Eugenio Barba
Richard Schechner

During the twentieth century, Western theatre artists of great accomplishment and influence have in fact and fancy "gone East." The list is long, and a sample from it serves to make the point: Antonin Artaud, Bertolt Brecht, Peter Brook, Jerzy Grotowski, Ariane Mnouchkine, and Eugenio Barba. Sometimes the encounter, though brief and partial, was decisive, as was Artaud's epiphany while experiencing Balinese dance-theatre in Paris in 1931. Sometimes the meeting snapped into focus a theory already in formation. It did for Brecht who, at a banquet in Moscow in 1935, watched Mei Lan-Fan rise from his place at table and – without costume, lighting, or makeup – demonstrate a *dan* (female) role from the classic Chinese theatre, thus embodying in a definitive way what Brecht called *verfremdungseffekt*.[1] Sometimes the journeys East were part of a worldwide, decades-long quest or pilgrimage in search of "universal theatrical truths," as with Grotowski. Sometimes the Asian encounter is a pearl (more cultured than natural) in a necklace of theatrical attainments, as was Brook's *Mahabharata*. And sometimes a theatre absorbs and expresses an Asian-European syncretism as do the spectacles of Mnouchkine's Theatre du Soleil. But no Western theatre thinker and worker – in an attempt to understand and grasp concretely what it means to be an actor – has investigated Asian techniques, theories, and practice as systematically as has Eugenio Barba.

Whether or not Barba's relationship to Asia (and that of the other artists mentioned) is "orientalist" is a question to be discussed. But whatever the answer to that inquiry, Barba's *opus* – his actor training and directing with the Odin Teatret, which he founded in 1964, his theatrical barters in Latin America, Europe, Africa and Asia, his investigations and demonstrations at the several meetings of ISTA (the International School of Theatre Anthropology), and his writings – constitute a most serious, extensive, and systematic attempt to understand the "nature of acting." Barba's "reports" on his investigations, most clearly presented in English in *The Dictionary of Theatre Anthropology* (1991, co-authored with Nicola Savarese), deserve to be studied alongside Bharata's *Natyasastra*, Zeami's *Kadensho* and other treatises, and Stanislavski's *An Actor Prepares*.[2]

Barba's investigations have taken two parallel and often intertwined paths, one theoretical one practical. He states that

> different performers, at different places and times and in spite of the stylistic forms specific to their traditions, have shared common principles. The first task of theatre anthropology is to trace these recurrent principles [which are] nothing more than particularly good "bits of advice."
>
> (1991:8)

This kind of statement (Barba makes it frequently in print and in person), averring the transcultural if not universal "principles" of good acting, gets him into trouble with some scholars – especially anthropologists, feminists, and post-colonial historians and theorists. Furthermore, Barba says that Western performers are not up to their Eastern colleagues:

> Contemporary Occidental performers do not have an organic repertory of "advice" to provide support and orientation. ... The traditional Oriental performer, on the other hand, has a base of organic and well-tested "absolute advice," that is, rules of art which codify a closed performing style to which all the performers of a particular genre must conform.
>
> (1991:8)

Of course, this assertion is about only the *best* Asian traditional performers, not the hacks or ordinary ones. But what interests Barba is not the performers themselves but the practices and principles of training and performance. These are codified in the East while they are for the most part *ad hoc* in the West.

Barba's theoretical assertions are the result of a series of practical investigations into such topics as "pre-expressivity," "energy," "dilation," and "opposition" conducted at ISTA, which from its inception in 1980 to this point has been convened only in Europe, where Barba and his Western stalwarts are joined by Asian artists from India, Bali (Indonesia), China, and Japan. Although many Asian performers have participated in ISTA, Barba developed a special working relationship with the world's leading woman odissi (India) dancer, Sanjukta Panigrahi. Barba also involves in ISTA some of his longtime Odin co-workers – Iben Nagel Rasmussen, Julia Varley, and Roberta Carreri chiefly.

Barba speaks of ISTA as the place where "masters of both Eastern and Western theatre compare work methods, and reach down into a common technical substratum ... the domain of pre-expressivity" (1988a:128).

> Theatre anthropology postulates that there exists a basic level of organization common to all performers and defines this level as *pre-expressive* ... the level which deals with how to render the actor's energy

scenically alive, that is, with how the actor can become a presence which immediately attracts the spectator's attention.

(1991:187–188)

The acquiring through training of certain bodily tensions and oppositions, certain ways of moving, vocalizing, and gesturing leads performers to their "extra-daily" bodies, their special non-ordinary performing bodies. These tensions and oppositions are the continuous source of energy which, both for performers and spectators, constitute the pre-expressive which

> is at the root of various performing techniques. [Theatre anthropology postulates] that there exists, independently of traditional culture, a transcultural "physiology". In fact, pre-expressivity utilises principles for the acquisition of presence. ... The results of these principles appear more evident in codified genres where the technique which *puts* the body *in form* is codified independently of the result/meaning.

(1991:188)

Or to put it more simply, what makes a Jeremy Irons "interesting" is the same thing that draws the spectator to Panigrahi: a way of using the body, of moving through space, of gesturing, speaking, and making contact separate and prior to any "characterization." This way of using the body can be learned. Codified performance genres – kabuki, ballet, odissi, for example – bring into view more directly these practical principles of pre-expressivity, these "bits of advice," than does training that emphasizes "intentions, feelings, identification with character, emotions ... that is, psycho-technique" (1991:187).

Barba is somewhat unfair to Western performing arts because he compares Western "spoken drama" to Asian genres that are theatre-dance-music. The term "spoken drama" is from the Chinese *huaju*, a word signifying the Western theatre adopted/adapted at the turn of the twentieth century by the Chinese from Europe (at first not directly but via Japan). A similar modernizing tendency was occurring across Asia, from Japan to India and Indonesia. The Chinese modernizers, like their counterparts elsewhere in Asia, were attracted to a European drama that used daily speech and daily social behavior as media of expression. Asian progressive thinkers wanted for themselves a theatre of modern, radical ideas, akin to what they saw in the plays of Ibsen and Shaw. Many Asian radicals felt that their own traditional theatres were reactionary and feudal. Some theatre workers wanted to modernize the traditional genres or incorporate traditional ways of representation into modern theatre; a few wanted to get rid of the old ways entirely. Exactly how to relate the traditional genres to the contemporary remains a very burning issue in much of Asia. Barba might have come up with a different theoretical model had he examined the performance systems of ballet or modern dance, looking at the dance-dramas of Martha Graham or the ironic and exquisitely staged works of Pina Bausch. And he might have had a different East–West dialogue had he invited not only Panigrahi to ISTA but theatre artists such as K.S. Karanth and Amal Allana (India), Rendra and Putu Wijaya (Indonesia), and Suzuki Tadashi and Kazuo Ohno (Japan) too.

Barba's theory is not that there is a universal theatrical behavior, nor that diffusion back in history has linked Asian and Western performing arts (though Barba does argue for the existence of "Eurasian theatre"[3]), but that accomplished performers in different cultures have independently discovered the "secret" of "energy" – the actor's fabled "presence" – and in doing so have come upon similar principles of "pre-expressive" behavior. Barba's foremost principle – one seen in his directing, his training methods at the Odin, and in his work at ISTA – is, in fact, dialectical: "If we really want to understand the nature of dialectics at the theatre's material level, we have to study Oriental performers. The opposition principle is the base on which they construct and develop all their actions" (1991: 176). Barba shows how the Chinese actor, for example, in wanting to look at a person to his right will begin the action by moving, ever so slightly perhaps, in a direction other than to the right. Then, at a decisive moment, the actor turns suddenly to the right.

> According to the opposition principle, if one wants to go to the left, one begins by going to the right, then suddenly stops and turns left. If one wants to crouch down, one first rises up on tip-toe and then crouches down. … At first I thought this was a scenic convention used by the Chinese performer [only …]. But I know now that this convention … is a rule which can be found throughout the Orient.
>
> (1991:176)

The principle of opposition exists at the pre-expressive level. In other words, opposition doesn't function only in terms of particular character types or genres. The principle of opposition is a key "secret" or "good piece of advice" shared by actors in many cultures. Nor does the principle of opposition apply only to movement. It is present in odissi's basic stance, the *tribhangi* or triple bend of the body – a stance seen also in Greek statuary, including the "Venus de Milo." According to Barba, this "dynamic undulation of the body around an axis, which is the reason why the figures seem so animated, was taken up by the Florentine sculptors in the fourteenth century" (Barba 1991:180). And from the Italian Renaissance it continued to appear and drive Western figurative sculpting and painting as well as ballet and modern dance. According to Barba, the principle of opposition exists not as an archetype or as a widely diffused "secret" but as the main way performers (and figurative visual artists) give "life" or "presence" to their works.

Beyond theory, at ISTA Barba is achieving something else. Over the more than dozen years of its existence, Barba has spun a network of particular individuals from Asia, Europe, and the Americas who gather together under the ISTA banner. Ostensibly they are investigating the pre-expressive, the principle of opposition, the various connections between Oriental and Occidental performance. But they are also part of an archipelago of artists, scholars, students, and travelers which Barba calls the "floating islands." As Barba has written:

> There are people who live in a nation, in a culture. And there are people who lie in their own bodies. They are the travelers who cross ... a space and time which have nothing to do with the landscape and the season of the place they happen to be traveling through. One can stay in the same place for months and years and still be a "traveler" ... journeying through regions and cultures thousands of years and thousands of kilometers distant, in unison with the thoughts and reactions of men far removed from oneself. ... The inhabitant of the great traditions and the traveler ... live together on the map of theatres and their histories, and it is difficult to tell them apart. The former lives inside a heredity which he passes on to successive generations. ... The latter, having arrived at a certain point on his path, looks at his hands, and discovers that with them he has built something very different from what he had in mind. ... The discovery of a common substratum which we share with masters far removed in time and space; the awareness that our action through theatre springs from an attitude towards existence and has its roots in one transnational and transcultural country. For a long time, I thought of this country as an archipelago. And its islands as floating islands. ... The floating island is that uncertain terrain which can disappear under your feet, but where personal limits can be overcome, and where a meeting is possible.
>
> (Barba 1986:10–11)

This romantic vision, driven by the insistent pragmatism of a theatre director (who knows that all "real work" takes place in the here and now of training, rehearsal, and performance) and carefully investigated by a core group of theatre artists, Asian and Western, is what ISTA is all about.

But is Barba an "anthropologist" in any generally accepted use of the term? And if not, which is to be revised, Barba's nomenclature or anthropological theory? In 1988, Barba and Phillip Zarrilli – a performance scholar and director with lots of experience in India – exchanged views regarding this question. Zarrilli, after attending the 1986 ISTA in Holstebro concerned with the "female role" wrote:

> Barba's vision of the "Oriental" actor is a composite devoid of sociocultural or historical contexts. There is little sense of the processual labors of a particular performer's movement toward specific acts of

embodiment. Nor does Barba acknowledge that even in those traditions where he finds his inspiration there are a great number of
performers who fail to achieve the high level of "presencing" with
which Barba is so fascinated. Nor is there any attempt to articulate
precisely what Barba receives as "presence." ... Barba defines theatre
anthropology as "the study of human behavior on a biological and
sociocultural level in a performance situation" (1986: 115). He draws
together an interdisciplinary group of collaborators in Europe including social and biological scientists. But he has yet to reconcile in writing
or practical work his particular definition of theatre anthropology with
the existing discipline of academic anthropology. Barba's voice remains single, essential, comprehensive, and authoritarian.

(Zarrilli 1988: 101–103)

Barba responded to Zarrilli:

The importance of studying the social and cultural contexts of a
specific theatre is obvious. But it is also obvious that it is not true that
one understands nothing of a theatre if one does not consider it in the
light of its sociocultural context. ... Each object, in fact, can belong to
innumerable, diverse contexts, all equally pertinent. A good method
is that in which the context is pertinent to the *questions* which have been
put to the object under examination.

(Barba 1988b: 12)

Barba says that his investigations concern the how theatre works

in a transcultural dimension. ISTA was created with this hypothesis in
mind insofar as it is based on a Eurasian vision of the theatre. ... I am
concerned neither with studying nor with interpreting the various
Asiatic theatres. ... I am concerned with something else: I collaborate
with certain professionals from different traditions researching certain
common principles of theatrical behavior.

(Barba 1988b: 13–14)

Barba emphasizes that theatre anthropology is not cultural or physical
anthropology. Theatre anthropology is a genre very different from what is
practiced by the inheritors of Tylor and Malinowski, one generation after
Turner and Geertz, the contemporaries of Clifford and Taussig. But, as
Barba asserts, "What is there to reconcile? Why should independent lines of
research become 'reconciled'?" (1988b: 14). The question cannot be put
easily to rest. Barba is, first of all, an artist who practices his own version of
the idiosyncratic tradition of the avantgarde.[4] Anyone who has attended
ISTA knows that it is not a forum modeled on an academic conference which
encourages the airing of contending viewpoints (in the "scientific tradition")
but, more or less, a platform from which Barba lectures on and demonstrates

his opinions regarding what constitutes theatrical excellence. In this he is joined by his longtime associates, Asian and Western. That Barba is influencing many in the West is obvious. What remains an open question is the two-way street. Sanjukta Panigrahi is working on her own experiments and productions in India, relating odissi to other kinds of classic Indian dance; and to modern theatre as well. Probably ISTA's influence will increasingly be felt in India (if not in other parts of Asia) through Panigrahi's work.

Concerning the question of Orientalism, Barba is no fool. He writes that

> In the meeting between East and West, seduction, imitation, and exchange are reciprocal. We in the West have often envied the Orientals their theatrical knowledge, which transmits the actor's living work of art from one generation to another; they have envied our theatre's capacity for confronting new themes, the way in which it keeps up with the times, and its flexibility that allows for personal interpretations of traditional texts which often have the energy of a formal and ideological conquest.
>
> (1988b:127–128)

The question remains, of course, precisely how balanced has the "reciprocity" between East and West been; and to what degree are theatre artists as implicated in the exchanges? That is, how do colonial and post-colonial history, practice, and theory affect theatre artists?

Barba's ISTA grew out of his Odin Teatret, a project he founded and continues to lead. The Odin was formed in Oslo in 1964 from performers nobody wanted – young actors who were rejected by the Norwegian national theatre school (the Odin later moved to its current center in Holstebro, Denmark). Barba, fresh from his own apprenticeship with Grotowski, wanted to make an off-center theatre, an organ of research that would be different from either the commercial or state theatres that dominated the European scene (and still do). Following Grotowski, Barba was determined that his theatre be intense in its dedication to training, careful in its preparations for production – rehearsals would last as long as necessary, up to two years in some cases, and indifferent to immediate public reaction. It was a "theatre laboratory" in the true sense: a place for research.

Over the years, Barba encouraged the formation of sub-groups, projects involving a few Odin members, off-shoots. These were often kept under the Odin umbrella – and individual members worked both with the whole Odin and on their own. Odin itself went on frequent tours where they performed their own works and "bartered" – exchanged theatrical techniques – with local theatre workers. Barba formed particular networks in Europe and Latin America especially. All the while, he continued to direct his own work with the Odin. Barba has never directed anywhere else. What Barba's leadership provided was critical yet supportive attention and criticism and an administrative structure underwriting the various experiments, trips, and productions. The Odin also published many important documents and articles, including the first edition of Grotowski's *Towards a Poor Theatre* (1968). The small city of Holstebro, in Jutland far from Copenhagen, generously supports the Odin although relatively few Holstebro citizens attend performances. Barba's work puts Holstebro on the map, and that apparently is enough for the town's pursers.

From the beginning Barba was deeply interested in training. The training at the Odin began under Barba's eye, but soon developed into "self-training." Each performer developed her or his own program of instruction. As Barba watched, and made his own suggestions, he began to see similarities between the work his actors were doing and work he had observed in his trips to India. From these similarities came the seed of what was to become ISTA.

What Ian Watson does in his book is to follow Barba's life and work from its beginnings in southern Italy. Before becoming a theatre director, Barba signed up in the Norwegian merchant marine, sailing the Oriental line where he first encountered Indian arts and religion. Wanderlust, and deeply imprinted rhythms of the sea – voyages, islands, journeys, ports of call – still course through his veins. Watson relates how the various strands of Barba's work weave into each other. And by dint of his research, his extensive interviewing, and his fieldwork – in Denmark, on the road in Europe and Latin America, and at several ISTAs – Watson unfolds a comprehensive account of how Barba's theories, practice, and projects developed. Watson takes a very close look at the Odin Teatret, its training, its collaborative structure, and its techniques of dramaturgy and theatrical production. He shows how ISTA is a logical outgrowth of Barba's work with the Odin. Through his study we understand the connections between Barba the artist, the actor trainer, the administrator, the theatre anthropologist, the evangelist, and the floating island. Unlike Grotowski, who ever increasingly isolates himself as he conducts his research into the "essence" of performance, Barba carries on much of his work in public. Whatever else they may be – art, entertainment – Barba's productions with the Odin Teatret and the meetings of ISTA are open rehearsals for an unfinishable theatre: an investigation, interrogation, and exploration of the performance process.

NOTES

1 See Brecht's famous essay, "Alienation Effects in Chinese Acting," 1964: 91–99.
2 *The Natyasastra* (Bharata 1967), a Sanskrit treatise on performance, dates from the period 2nd century BCE to 2nd century CE. Its putative author, the mythical sage Bharata, is probably not a single individual. The *NS* text is a compilation of "good advice" given in great detail concerning dramaturgy, acting, dancing, and music. It is still a very influential text in India and, by extension, throughout Asia. Along with his father, Kanami, Zeami Motokiyo (1363–1443) was the codifier of noh drama, a classic dance-theatre of Japan. In his nine treatises on performance

(see Zeami 1984), Zeami details a philosophy of noh – including many precise discussions of acting – closely related to Zen Buddhism.
3 See Barba 1988b.
4 Barba actually mediates several Western avant-garde traditions. He is not directly in the line that leads from Alfred Jarry through Dada and Surrealism, the Theatre of the Absurd, Happenings, and environmental theatre to postmodern dance and performance art. Nor is he directly in the line that leads from symbolism, expressionism, epic theatre, and performances with a deep social purpose to street and guerrilla theatre. Nor is he directly in the line of group theatres and theatres of alternative life styles and communities. Barba's Odin incorporates aspects from all these avant-garde and experimental tendencies. The result is what Barba terms the "third theatre."

REFERENCES

Barba, Eugenio
1986 *Beyond the Floating Islands.* New York, PAJ Publications.
1988a "Eurasian Theatre," *TDR* 32, 3: 126–130.
1988b "Eugenio Barba to Phillip Zarrilli," *TDR* 32, 3: 7–16.

Barba, Eugenio and Nicola Savarese
1991 *The Secret Art of the Performer.* London and New York, Routledge.

Bharata
1967 *The Natyasastra,* translated Manomohan Ghosh. Calcutta, Granthalaya.

Brecht, Bertolt
1964 *Brecht on Theatre.* New York, Hill and Wang.

Stanislavski, Konstantin
1993 *An Actor Prepares.* London and New York, Routledge.

Zarrilli, Phillip
1988 "For Whom Is the 'Invisible' Not Visible?" *TDR* 32, 1: 95–106.

Zeami, Motokiyo
1984 *On the Art of No Drama.* Princeton, Princeton University Press.

PREFACE

Eugenio Barba is one of Europe's leading theatre directors, theoreticians, and researchers and is considered, along with Bertolt Brecht and Jerzy Grotowski, one of the major influences on modern Latin American theatre (Peirano, 1987:10–13). Despite this prominence on two continents, there is no major study of Barba's work in English. In fact, even though there are several fine books on aspects of his work in Italian and Danish, there is no comprehensive study of his work in any language. This book is intended to address the oversight.

A major part of my research for this study was conducted "in the field." I followed Barba and his Odin colleagues closely from the latter part of rehearsals for *Oxyrhincus Evangeliet* in the summer of 1985 through until the group stopped performing the piece and took a six months' break prior to beginning rehearsals for their new production, *Talabot*, in early 1988. During that time I visited the Holstebro headquarters of the Nordisk Teaterlaboratorium twice, where I observed training and rehearsals, interviewed Barba and his actors, and spent time in the Odin archive, which contains reviews, programs, and articles about the group's work, as well as a comprehensive film and video library that has many films and tapes on the group's work and on the work of those who have influenced them.

I returned once more to Holstebro, in 1991, to complete the last part of my research.

Part of my initial field work involved touring with the company several times in Europe (in Denmark and Yugoslavia), and accompanying them on parts of two Latin American tours, the first to Uruguay and Argentina in 1987, the second to Peru in 1988.

Both of these Latin American tours included third theatre gatherings which I also attended, the 1987 gathering in Bahia Blanca, Argentina, and the 1988 Peruvian meeting in Chaclacayo. As well as these meetings, I have attended three of the International School of Theatre Anthropology sessions mounted by Barba since 1985, the Holstebro congress in 1986, the 1987 meeting in Salento, Italy, and the session in Bologna, Italy, in 1990.

Even though the studies of Barba's work by scholars such as Ferdinando

Taviani, Thomas Bredsdorff, and Eric Exe Christoffersen have proved an invaluable addition to my travels, my major source of written information has been Barba's own publications. He has written extensively on his approaches to training, his understanding of the connections between traditional Eastern performance and contemporary Western acting techniques, and the social function of theatre. These works, more than any others, have informed my field work, directed my line of enquiry in the many interviews I have done – not only with Barba and his immediate colleagues but also with those such as Taviani and Franco Ruffini who know Barba's work well, and, most importantly, they have provided a matrix for my own thoughts on Barba's history and contribution to theatre.

Of course, as with most major enterprises, there have been difficulties. Merely finding the time to sit in front of the computer with a family of four adorable children has been no easy task. But, family aside, my research and writing has been hindered most especially by linguistic and geographic considerations. Barba's group is based in Denmark and, as I have already mentioned, most of the scholarly studies of his work are in Danish or in his native Italian. I read Italian with difficulty, but do not speak the language, and my knowledge of Danish is limited to English cognates – hardly enough to conduct serious research. Luckily, most educated Danes speak excellent English, as do all the members of Barba's company, so I have had the services of countless translators, not to mention that I have been given the courtesy, more times than I can recall, of people conducting their conversations in English rather than in their native tongue so that I could understand what they were talking about.

Italian presented me with fewer difficulties, thanks to my wife, Susana, who is fluent in the language. My limited knowledge combined with her facility made reading simple, and I am indebted to her for her assistance during interviews I made in Italy in 1987 with the Italian scholars who have followed Barba's work for many years.

Geographical distance between myself in New York and Barba in any number of a dozen possible countries has been both positive and negative. Being so physically removed from what I am studying has allowed for a degree of objectivity, but it has also created problems similar to those of the anthropologist who, on returning to his/her office from field study in a distant land, has to piece together his/her understanding of the "tribe" s/he is studying from notes and memory. For all my field work, I could not see the group whenever I wanted. If I had a question, it had to wait till the next time I met Barba and his colleagues, or it was addressed in a telephone call or letter. This is not the ideal way to study a theatre company whose productions and rehearsal methodology are in a constant state of flux, or to have a thorough understanding of its director's ongoing research. Be that as it may, Barba and the Odin actress Julia Varley have been towers of strength, answering my every letter, keeping me abreast of the group's activities, and sending me copies of articles by Barba before they are even published. I very much appreciate their generosity.

Many people have assisted me in my research and writing. First, I should like to thank Richard Schechner, my teacher, who introduced me to Eugenio Barba's work and eventually to the man himself. I also owe Brooks McNamara, Richard's colleague at New York University, thanks for his moral support and constructive advice at crucial points in the planning and writing of the manuscript.

I must also thank the Odin actors and the staff of the Nordisk Teaterlaboratorium for their time, patience, and warm hospitality both in Holstebro and whenever I toured with the group. This is particularly addressed to Julia Varley, whom I mentioned earlier, without whose constant flow of letters I would know much less about the group.

A very special thanks to Eugenio Barba who, over the period of my research and writing, I have got to know. He has always been available for interviews and conversation despite a very busy schedule, he invited me to tour with his group as well as to attend international meetings he organized, and, even though he may not agree with everything I have written, he has read every word. In this reading, he took the time to correct factual errors in the manuscript and to discuss my various lines of argument. The book has benefited greatly from his input.

Last, but far from least, I want to thank my two families. Although they did not live to see this work even begun, my parents laid the foundations that made it possible. I will always be grateful to Susana, my wife, for her patience, translations, and proofreading of the manuscript; and to my son David as well as my step-children Violeta, Gaspar, and Carmen, all of whom continued to grow through the writing of this book.

Without their support, this work on Barba might well not have seen the light of day.

Note: I am following the current American trend, omitting all accents on words.

INTRODUCTION

No study of Eugenio Barba would be complete without at least a brief consideration of the Odin Teatret and its umbrella organization the Nordisk Teaterlaboratorium. This is because most of Barba's ideas stem from his close collaboration with his colleagues at the Odin, and because he has never directed a production outside of the company. Barba's professional history and the conceptual matrix of his ideas has been the theatre he founded in the early 1960s and the work he has done in it since with his actors. The actors' experiments in training and dramaturgy, as well as their achievements in performance have been shaped by Barba, but they have equally shaped his thinking and development.

Despite the importance of the Odin, its history would be an unnecessary addition to this consideration of Barba because two excellent histories already exist – both by Ferdinando Taviani, an Italian scholar who has followed Barba's work since the early 1970s and worked as the group's literary advisor for the past ten years (1979; 1986a). In these histories, he describes how the Odin evolved gradually from its humble beginnings in a borrowed room at Oslo University to the abandoned bomb shelter that became its home for a brief period, through its move to the small town of Holstebro in western Denmark, and its gradual emergence as one of Europe's leading independent theatre groups.

A brief description of the group's early years will be helpful to the reader unfamiliar with Barba or the Odin, however, since they were instrumental in establishing the character of the group, and saw the beginnings of the Nordisk Teaterlaboratorium. In addition to this brief history, I will also provide a short biography of each of the actors I talked with during my research because, even though this is Barba's story, they are more than Pirandello-like characters in search of an author. The actors deserve to share his credit as writers of the Odin's history in no small way.

Barba founded the Odin Teatret on October 1, 1964, shortly after his return from three years of working as Jerzy Grotowski's assistant at the Polish Laboratory Theatre. When he first returned to Oslo, Barba attempted to get a job in the theatre but he found it impossible to get employment because

1

he was a foreigner and because his apprenticeship with the Polish Laboratory meant little, since it would be several years before Grotowski's name became known in the West. Determined to make theatre one way or another, Barba obtained a list of the names of those rejected for the acting course that year at the National Theatre School. From these "rejects" he formed his own company and named it after the Nordic god of war, Odin – a name he came upon by chance when, in trying to think what to call the newly formed group, Barba happened to walk down a street called Odin.

The initial years in Oslo were difficult. Since the actors had few skills, the group began training immediately but, with no funds to pay teachers, the actors taught each other what they knew. Within a year of its formation the group was reduced to four actors but had mounted its first production, *Ornitofilene*, which was performed in Oslo and toured briefly in Sweden and Denmark.

Several performances were arranged at the University of Aarhus, Denmark's second largest city after Copenhagen. These performances were to have major repercussions for the group's future. A nurse from Holstebro, Inger Lansted, attended one of them. She was impressed with the production and, aware that Holstebro was instituting a new cultural policy, suggested to the town council that they invite the Odin to become the town's resident company. The council offered Barba and his colleagues an old farm on the outskirts of the town and a small yearly stipend. With no prospects of either a theatre or financial help in Oslo, Barba accepted the council's offer and the group moved to Holstebro in June 1966.

Only three of the four actors in *Ornitofilene* came to Holstebro, so the company could not perform the production. The actors continued training, however, and began to recruit new actors from within Scandinavia whom they taught and worked with to develop the company's second production, *Kaspariana*, which premiered in September 1967.

Kaspariana was the beginning of the Odin's gradual evolution into a major force in Europe's independent group theatre movement. Prior to *Kaspariana*, few theatre groups existed in Europe outside of the companies in residence at the subsidized theatres in major cities and towns. The Odin, Grotowski's Polish Laboratory Theatre, and groups like the Living Theatre (who began touring in Europe in 1961 and were based there from 1964 on) became role models for the gradually emerging independent theatre movement which saw the birth of many groups throughout the 1960s and 1970s.

Barba's next production, *Ferai*, established the Odin as one of Europe's leading companies when, in addition to being the hit of the 1969 Theatre of Nations Festival in Paris, the production was performed successfully in Scandinavia, Germany, Italy, Belgium, at the BITEF Festival in Belgrade, and at the Venice Biennale. With its subsequent productions, which are discussed at length in the following chapters, the group has become a fixture in European group theatre. Following its first performances in Latin America, at the Caracas Festival in Venezuela in 1976, it has also become important in Latin America, having toured extensively and conducted workshops in Argentina, Colombia, Cuba, Peru, Chile, and Mexico. As well as its tours in Europe and Latin America, the group has also performed in Japan (1979), New York (1984), Israel (1984), and India (1985).

The Odin's touring led to the gradual internationalization of the group. When the group was formed the actors were all Norwegian. With its move to Holstebro, performers were recruited from all over Scandinavia, the majority being Danish. As the group toured and became better known in Western Europe, actors from countries outside of Scandinavia joined, until today the nationalities of those who have worked at the Odin reads somewhat like a list of participants at an international conference. Since the early 1970s, when the first non-Scandinavians joined the group, it has included members from Italy, the United States, Britain, Canada, Germany, Spain, and Argentina.

This internationalization has led to several peculiarities in the group because the actors do not share a common mother tongue. Actors who join the Odin are required to learn Danish because all rehearsals are conducted in the language. The Danish is hardly that spoken by the average man in the street, however, since not only does it contain many foreign and specialist words developed by the group but it is a mixture of Norwegian, reflecting the group's roots, and Danish. Barba, for instance, who speaks many languages including his native Italian, French, Spanish, Polish, English, and enough German to get by, does not speak Danish. During rehearsals, as in his daily life in Holstebro, he speaks Norwegian, which, though it is understood by Danes, is recognized as a "foreign" language.

Another product of this linguistic mix has been the choice of languages in productions. The lack of a common tongue, combined with the group's tours in countries where different languages are spoken, has led to experiments with language, including doing productions in which different characters speak different languages, and developing pieces in fabricated tongues.

During the Odin's first year in Holstebro, when it had no production to perform, Barba introduced the name Nordisk Teaterlaboratorium for Skuespillerkunst (the Scandinavian laboratory for researching the art of the actor) usually shortened to Nordisk Teaterlaboratorium (NTL). The Odin was, and still is, the main production wing of the NTL, an organization that, in addition to studying the actor in performance, researches training and rehearsal methodologies, and also studies performance forms in various cultures. The latter culminated in Barba's founding of the International School of Theatre Anthropology (ISTA) in 1979, which is discussed in Chapter 6.

The NTL incorporates much more than research and ISTA. It is a major teaching center, it arranges performances for international companies in various parts of Scandinavia, it publishes and sells theatre books, it makes and rents films on the theatre, and it is the umbrella organization for several groups associated with the Odin.

When the company moved to Denmark, it initiated an ongoing series of what were called "Inter-Scandinavian Workshops" designed to introduce theatre workers from Scandinavia to a variety of theatre techniques. These workshops, which began in the late 1960s and continued on through into the late 1970s, included sessions on clowning, commedia dell'arte, mime, noh theatre, Balinese topeng and legong, as well as odissi dance from India, and were headed by teachers such as the Italian clowns Carlo and Romano Colombaioni, Dario Fo, Jean-Louis Barrault, Etienne Decroux, Jacques Lecoq, the noh masters Hisao and Hideo Kanze, I Made Djimat from Bali, and the odissi dancer, Sanjukta Panigrahi.

In addition to these workshops for Scandinavians, the company has mounted international training workshops from 1968 on, when Barba organized a workshop with Grotowski, his leading actor Richard Cieslak, and Stanislaw Brzozowski, from the Wroclaw Pantomime Theatre, which was open to participants from the United States and Belgium as well as Scandinavians.[1]

Following these Scandinavian and international workshops, Barba and his actors have taken over the role of teachers, conducting workshops and seminars on the methods they have developed at the Odin. These training sessions are often part of the company's touring schedule which, apart from performances, includes a number of workshops for local performers led by various members of the company. Since they were initiated in the early 1970s, these workshops have been held in most of Europe and all the countries the group has traveled to in Latin America. Similar workshops are also part of the "International Group Theatre Gatherings" organized by the NTL in collaboration with various groups from different countries.

The tours and performances arranged by the NTL in Scandinavia have often included workshops and/or seminars by senior members of the companies involved. Barba, for instance, was instrumental in arranging Grotowski's first tour outside of Poland in February and March 1966 which not only included performances of *The Constant Prince* in Oslo, Copenhagen, and Stockholm but also seminars in each city prior to the group's performances. Similarly, the NTL arranged performances by Dario Fo in 1968, Luca Ronconi's *Orlando Furioso* and the Renaud-Barrault Company in 1970, the National Theatre of the Deaf in 1971, The Living Theatre in 1975, and Libre Teatro Libre, Teatro Nucleo, and Cuatrotablas from Latin America in late 1976 and early 1977 – all of which included teaching sessions by principals from the groups in Holstebro. The company continues to organize performances of groups it has close ties with, though these are usually limited to Holstebro today and workshops or seminars have rarely been part of the program since the early 1980s.

4

The NTL's involvement in publishing began with a journal, *Teatrets Teori og Teknikk* (*TTT* – Theory and Technique of Theatre), edited by Barba. The first issue of *TTT* was published in 1964 in Oslo but, on the Odin's move to Holstebro, the journal became a regular part of the NTL's activities, twenty-three volumes being published between 1965 and 1974. Only one of the twenty-three issues dealt with the Odin (no. 22, which was devoted to the group's 1972 production *Min Fars Hus*), because Barba's primary aim in publishing *TTT* was to make the ideas that had influenced him readily available in Scandinavia. During its nine years of publication the journal covered topics such as Stanislavsky's theory and practice (no. 2), Jean Genet and Samuel Beckett (no. 5), commedia dell'arte (no. 6), the Russian avant-garde of the revolution (no. 12), as well as Asian theatre – Chinese and Japanese theatre (no. 15), and barong and kathakali (no. 21); and included articles by Antonin Artaud, Vsevolod Meyerhold, Yevgeny Vakhtangov, Giorgio Strehler, Michael Chekhov, Gordon Craig, Etienne Decroux, and Jean-Louis Barrault.

Several issues of *TTT* were published as books. These included one containing the writings of Erwin Piscator (no. 11), another the works of Zeami (no. 16), Sergei Eisenstein on theatre (no. 19), the major writings of Meyerhold (no. 23), and the famous Grotowski book, *Towards a Poor Theatre* (no. 7). The latter issue was published in English and became an international best seller. All other articles in *TTT* were published in either Danish, Swedish or Norwegian.[2]

The success of *Towards a Poor Theatre* and the other *TTT*s published as books prompted Barba to establish a publishing wing at the NTL, Odin Forlag, to handle books by Barba and/or on the activities of the NTL. Odin Forlag has published books entirely on its own, such as *Experiences* (Odin Teatret, 1973) and Barba's *Floating Islands* (1979), but generally speaking the books it sells are published by others in association with the NTL. The NTL handles some twenty titles published under this arrangement, including *Il libro dell'Odin* (The Odin Book – Taviani, 1977), *L'Odin Teatret et la naissance du tiers theatre* (Odin Teatret and the Birth of the Third Theatre – Daetwyler, 1980), *La Scuola degli Attori: Rapporti della prima sessione dell'ISTA* (The School of the Actors: Report on the First Session of ISTA – Ruffini, 1981), *The Dilated Body* (Barba, 1985a), *Beyond the Floating Islands* (Barba, 1986a), and *The Secret Art of the Performer* (Barba and Savarese, 1991).

The diversity of the NTL is not limited to Barba's initiatives. He has always encouraged other members of the company to pursue interests of their own that do not interfere with their commitment to the Odin. The most successful of these have become part of the NTL. Odin Teatret Film, for instance, is part of the NTL that produces, rents, and sells films and videos on theatre and owes its origins to the Odin actor Torgeir Wethal's interest in film-making and Barba's contacts in Italian television. In 1971 Barba approached Mario Raimondo, the head of the experimental department of Italian television, and suggested a co-production deal between his channel and the

Odin for a series of films on the work of the actor. Raimondo agreed to finance the films and to screen them on Italian television if the Odin provided the personnel and shot the films. Wethal made a series of six films between 1971 and 1972 under this arrangement, including two films on corporal mime, *Corporal Mime Parts I and II* (1971), *Physical Training at Grotowski's Laboratory* (1972), *Plastics Training at Grotowski's Laboratory* (1972), *Physical Training at Odin Teatret* (1972), and *Vocal Training at Odin Teatret* (1972). This was the beginning of Odin Film, which has continued, through various co-production deals and grants, to make and distribute films on the Odin's tours and productions. These films include other Wethal films such as *On The Two Banks of the River* (on the Odin's 1978 tour in Peru), *Ascent to the Sea* (a 1978 film about the Odin production *Anabasis*), and *Oxyrhincus Evangeliet* (a 1987 filmed version of the production) as well as films by other film makers, such as *In Search of Theatre* (a 1974 Italian television documentary on the Odin in southern Italy), *Theatre Meets Ritual* (an account of the Odin in Venezuela in 1976 made by Venezuelan television), and *Ferai* (a 1969 film version of the production by Marianne Ahrne).

The other major initiative by members of the Odin is the formation of off-shoot groups and one-person companies. The first time that the NTL included more than one group was between 1966 and 1969 when it was home to Studio II, the first professional mime troupe in Scandinavia, headed by Yves Lebreton and Ingemar Lindh. This model was repeated in the 1980s when several members of the Odin formed troupes of their own. The first of these, Farfa, was founded by Iben Nagel Rasmussen in 1980 and has continued producing works around her Odin commitments ever since – though the number of actors has varied from as many as seven to as few as two in its more recent works. The company Basho was founded by the actor Toni Cots in 1984 when he decided not to join rehearsals for the Odin production *Oxyrhincus Evangeliet*. Basho, of which Cots is the sole member, remained a part of the NTL only until 1985, however, when he left Denmark to settle in Italy. Another one-man company that was part of the NTL between 1984 and mid-1991 was the Canada Project, founded by the Canadian actor and director, Richard Fowler, who was Barba's assistant at ISTA. Roberta Carreri decided against joining rehearsals for *Talabot* and developed a one-woman piece, *Judith*, in 1987, which she tours under the name of Odin Teatret. Else Marie Laukvik also mounted an independent Odin production, *Memoria*, in 1989 which she performs with a musician, Frans Winther. And Julia Varley created a one-woman piece, *The Castle of Holstebro*, which premiered in 1990.

THE GROUP

The members of the Odin Teatret have played no small part in the evolution of Barba's theatrical ideas. Most, if not all, of his approaches to training, dramaturgy, and productions, as well as his views on the social role of theatre and his interest in research, owe a great deal to his years of work with the same core group of actors. When I began my research in 1985 the "youngest" member of the company had been working with Barba for almost ten years, while the "oldest" had been with him since the Odin was formed in 1964. Since these performers are referred to many times in the following pages, the reader may find it useful to know a little about each of them.

In 1985, and until rehearsals began for *Talabot* in 1988, the group consisted of seven actors: Torgeir Wethal, Else Marie Laukvik, Iben Nagel Rasmussen, Tage Larsen, Roberta Carreri, Francis Pardeilhan, and Julia Varley.

Torgeir Wethal is one of only two of the original Norwegian actors who formed the group with Barba in Oslo and who remained with him into the 1980s. When he joined the group in 1964 at seventeen, he was a very thin teenager unused to physical exercise. After several years of painful work and rigid discipline, however, he became the teacher of acrobatics and floor exercises for the group during the 1960s and 1970s when the company still recruited new actors. Wethal is the only performer who is a voting member on the Odin board (though all actors are welcome to attend board meetings few do). He is the group's resident film maker, and one of Barba's closest colleagues.

Else Marie Laukvik is the other original Norwegian member of the group who appeared in *Oxyrhincus Evangeliet*. She was the major teacher of composition exercises (discussed in Chapter 3) during the 1970s, and developed an interest in mask-making and design which led to the creation of several of the stock figures in the Odin's street theatre. Laukvik was the first member of the company to take a sabbatical rather than merely to leave the group (for most of 1974). During this time she forsook theatre to travel, an experience that she repeated in 1980, and which has led to other members of the group taking breaks from the heavy demands of constant touring and teaching – including Barba himself, who took a one-year sabbatical from October 1982 to October 1983.

In 1984, Laukvik was invited to direct a production for a newly formed Danish group, Theatre Marquez, and when the Odin stopped performing *Oxyrhincus Evangeliet* in 1987 she left to devote more time to Theatre Marquez.

Iben Nagel Rasmussen joined the Odin when Barba and his Norwegian colleagues first moved to Denmark in 1966. She had no theatrical experience when she came to the group, but has since become one of its central figures through constantly challenging the Odin's status quo and in doing so instigating changes that have had a major impact on its history. She was the first member of the group to develop her own training (1972) – a model which other actors have since adopted; she took on apprentice actors (1974) – highlighting the importance of teaching at the Odin when Barba had all but abandoned it; she formed her own group, Farfa, in 1980 – exposing yet more young actors to the Odin's methods when the group's doors were closed to new members; and her leading position at the Odin, combined with her powerful performances in productions such as *Come! And the Day Will be Ours* and *Anabasis* made her a role model for many women in the independent theatre movement during the 1970s.

Rasmussen was not in the cast of *Oxyrhincus Evangeliet*, choosing instead to devote herself full-time to Farfa. She returned to the Odin for *Talabot* in 1988.

Tage Larsen was a theatre student at Aarhus University in 1970 when the Odin gave a workshop in his department. After this workshop, he joined the group. He was initially taught by the older actors and, when he eventually developed his skills to the point at which he could initiate his own training, became an expert with hand props. He created training exercises with long poles, flags, and whips, much of which found their way into the group's street theatre. And, until he sustained a knee injury in the early 1980s, he was one of the group's leading stilt-walkers. Larsen left the Odin following *Oxyrhincus Evangeliet* to form Teatret Yorick with his wife Anna Lica.

Roberta Carreri, an Italian, became a member of the Odin in 1974. Prior to joining the group she was a student at the University of Milan, where she saw the Odin perform *Min Fars Hus* in 1973. Following this Bergamo season, she took part in a workshop with the company in Milan and was so impressed that she came to Holstebro to observe training and rehearsals for her graduating thesis. She abandoned the thesis, however, to become an actress with the company. Like Larsen, she was taught the basic Odin skills by the older actors before performing in her first production *Come! And the Day Will be Ours*. Carreri is especially interested in the Japanese dance forms nihon buyo and butoh which she has studied and used in developing her own training.

Carreri remains with the NTL but did not perform in *Talabot*. In order to spend more time with her school-age daughter, Alice, she developed a solo production, *Judith*, which she tours when it is convenient, and she conducts acting workshops in Holstebro and elsewhere.

Francis Pardeilhan, a Californian born of French parents, joined the group as Larsen's apprentice in 1976. Before coming to Holstebro, his only acting experience was a year's work in a small English touring company, known as The Ladies and the Gentlemen. He did most of his initial training with Larsen and performed a clown production, *Johan Sebastian Bach*, with other apprentices prior to being invited to perform with the Odin proper in the company's 1977 production *Anabasis*. Pardeilhan is particularly interested in vocal technique and was asked by Barba to develop the vocal and choral scores for *Oxyrhincus Evangeliet*, following which he led the Odin voice-training sessions for almost a year. Pardeilhan left the Odin when *Oxyrhincus Evangeliet* stopped touring and moved to a farm in Italy. He continues to do free-lance theatre work from time to time.

Julia Varley, who was born in Britain and raised in Milan from her early teens, joined the Odin in 1976 as Larsen's second apprentice. She had limited acting experience in agit-prop theatre before coming to the group and so followed in Pardeilhan's footsteps of training primarily with her mentor Larsen, performing in the clown production *Johan Sebastian Bach*, and joining her more experienced colleagues for the first time in *Anabasis*. Apart from her acting abilities, Varley is an excellent correspondent, administrator, and coordinator. She keeps in contact through letter with many groups and scholars in different parts of the world, and often works as Barba's assistant at festivals and international seminars. Varley is closely involved with the Magdalena Project, an ongoing series of workshops for women from independent group theatres instigated by Jill Greenhalgh from Wales. Not only has Varley attended all of the workshops (six between 1986 and 1989) but she has helped organize several of them in Scandinavia, two in Holstebro in 1987, and one in Norway in 1989.[3] Varley is the only one of the original apprentices who remained with the group after *Oxyrhincus Evangeliet*.

Apart from these actors, many other people are part of both Barba's and the Odin's story: actors who have been members of the Odin in the past, such as Toni Cots, one of Rasmussen's original apprentices who joined the company in 1974 and remained until 1984. He, probably more than any of the other actors, was responsible for the influence Asian performance has had on training at the Odin through his studies of Balinese dance-drama and his work with Barba at ISTA; Richard Fowler, the Canadian actor and director mentioned earlier who, in addition to being Barba's assistant at ISTA, is the official translator of his writings from Italian into English; Ferdinando Taviani, also mentioned earlier; Hans Martin Berg, one of Denmark's leading publishers who has been on the Odin board for fifteen years and who is the man primarily responsible for the business success of Odin Forlag; Leif Bech, the company tour director and manager who joined the company in 1970 and saw it through its rise from obscurity to one of the leading touring companies in Europe; the actor Jan Torp, who was so taken by the Colombaioni Brothers' clown workshops that he pushed to introduce clown material into the Odin's repertoire and in so doing influenced the company's approach to street theatre; and Tony d'Urso, the Italian who has been photographing the Odin's work since 1972, and without whom many of Barba's and other writers' books about the Odin would have been less successful.

But, with all due respect to these people and those who, for lack of space and time, I have not mentioned, this is Barba's story. Without him the Odin would not exist and it is his professional life that I will focus on in the following pages.

1

BARBA
The early years

The Odin Teatret has provided both a source for Barba's ideas and a laboratory where he can experiment. Those who work closest with Barba often say that he either lacks or suppresses his own originality, preferring instead to wait for his colleagues to instigate new ideas which he then uses as a point of departure for group investigation. Even though this may not be entirely true, it characterizes at least one of Barba's methodologies, the leader as catalyst. He promotes an atmosphere in which his actors feel free to experiment physically, vocally, and/or with their improvisations. Then, when he observes something that interests him, he suggests further avenues of research in the training, or ways in which what they are doing might be used to help shape the production they are preparing.

Nevertheless, Barba is not merely a vicarious artist or thinker. He is one of those rare theatre people who is both a practical man of the theatre and an intellectual. What his colleagues take to be passivity is, in fact, a capacity for observation and analysis. It is this capacity that has produced many articles and books which together include important writings on actor training, dramaturgy, performance, and theatre sociology. Barba has also lectured and taught on both the practical and theoretical aspects of his work in Europe, North and Latin America, as well as Asia.[1] He is on the International Committee of the Theatre of Nations and the advisory board of the International Association of Performing Arts Semiotics; he is a contributing editor of *The Drama Review* as well as an advisory editor of the *New Theatre Quarterly*. And, in 1988, his intellectual work was officially recognized when he was presented with an honorary doctorate from Denmark's Aarhus University.

But foremost, Barba is a practical man of the theatre. Since 1964, when he founded the Odin, he has created almost twenty original works, ranging from intimate theatre pieces to outdoor spectacles. He has established one of Western Europe's only government-funded theatre laboratories, the NTL – which incorporates all the activities described in the Introduction, and he formed ISTA to investigate the connections between traditional Eastern and contemporary Western performance.

10

HIS ROOTS

Who is this man, this southern Italian heading a group of international actors based in a small town in northern Europe who spend most of their time either closeted away in the studio working, or touring various parts of the world? He is an immigrant, a foreigner, a traveler, a man who was prompted to write, "My body is my country. The only place where I always *am*. No matter where I go, to Montreal or to Tokyo, to Holstebro, Bogota or New York, I am always at home, always in my country" (1988a:293). But, despite this rejection of nation and family, Barba describes his professional heritage in familial terms, seeing himself as a descendant of Stanislavksy, the "father" of modern Western theatre (1988a:292).

With all due respect, Barba's twentieth-century theatrical lineage appears to begin with Meyerhold rather than Stanislavsky. Granted, Stanislavsky conducted the major study of the actor's art in the early years of the century, and was followed in this by, among others, Barba's mentor, Grotowski, who no doubt influenced him to do the same. But Barba has rejected the very basis of Stanislavsky's system – psychological realism – embracing instead a theatre that explores a language of its own rather than one that simulates daily life on stage. He has developed a theatre in which the performance text takes precedence over a faithful interpretation of the author's words, in which causal connections between scenes have been rejected in favor of an episodic montage, and in which the actor–audience relationship and the performance space is adjusted for each production – all ideas more often associated with Meyerhold than Stanislavsky.

Whatever his professional lineage, Barba's childhood and youth were far removed from the theatre. He born in the southern Italian port city of Brindisi on October 29, 1936, the son of an Italian army officer. His father was a supporter of Mussolini who fought on the side of the fascists in Spain, Abyssinia (present-day Ethiopia), and in the Second World War. During the war, Barba and his family moved to Gallipoli, a small fishing and tourist village in the bootheel of southern Italy, where some of his father's relations lived.

When Barba was 10 years of age, in 1946, his father died of kidney failure which, combined with the financial devastation in Italy following the war, left Barba, his mother, and older brother, Ernesto, in poverty.

Because of the family's economic situation, and familial pressures to follow in his father's footsteps, Barba was sent to the Naples military college in 1951, at the age of 15. During his three years at the college, he had many problems with its harsh discipline, rebelling against it frequently – an ironic fact considering the legendary importance he has placed on discipline at the Odin.

It was during his freshman year at the college that Barba first went to the theatre. And, according to his own account, it made a major impact on the young man from the provinces:

I was fifteen years old when I went to the theatre for the first time. My mother took me to see *Cyrano de Bergerac*. The hero was played by Gino Cervi, a very popular Italian actor. But it was neither he nor the other actors who impressed me, nor the story which they were telling and which I followed with interest, but without amazement. It was a horse. A real horse. It appeared pulling a carriage, according to the most reasonable rules of scenic realism. But its presence suddenly exploded all the dimensions which until then had reigned on the stage. Because of this sudden interference from another world, the uniform veil of the stage seemed torn before my eyes.

In the theatres to which I went in the following years, I searched in vain for the disorientation that had made me feel alive, that sudden dilation of my senses. No more horses appeared. Until I arrived in Opole (Poland) and Cheruthuruthy (India).

(1985:27–28)[2]

NORWAY

During summer vacations from the military college Barba hitchhiked around Europe. These trips culminated in a journey that took him to the north of the continent in the summer of 1954, following his graduation from college. But, this was no ordinary trip. The 18-year-old adolescent wanted to be as far away from Italy and the discipline of military college as possible. Scandinavia, with its welfare state philosophy, its reputation as a haven for personal freedoms, and its austere Lutheranism, seemed the antithesis of everything Barba disliked in Italy. His shortage of money on his arrival in Oslo, Norway, therefore provided the ideal excuse to find a job and settle, at least temporarily. Rejecting his bourgeois background, in which manual work was shunned, he took a job as a welder.

Barba's wanderlust would not let him remain too long in one place, however, and in 1956, after a year as a welder, he joined the Norwegian merchant marine and became a sailor on ships plying the Oriental route. As with his move north, this was no casual choice. He had become intrigued with Indian religion and the merchant marine was one way for a relatively poor young man to visit the subcontinent. His travels extended beyond India, and during his two years at sea he traveled extensively in the Middle East, Africa, Lapland, and other parts of northern Scandinavia.

During the latter part of his first year in Norway, prior to going to sea, Barba enrolled at Oslo University. He continued his studies intermittently while on leave from the merchant marine, and in 1957, two years after becoming a seaman, he left the navy and, while continuing his work as a welder, devoted himself to his studies. He graduated in 1965 with a Master of Arts in French and Norwegian literature, and the history of religion.

Barba did not study theatre at university, save for several required courses in dramatic literature. Despite this lack of formal training, however, he had an interest in theatre which, combined with his developing political awareness, led him to the works of Bertolt Brecht. In Brecht he saw a model through which theatre could address politics.

POLAND

Barba decided to pursue his interest in theatre wholeheartedly. He applied for, and won, a UNESCO scholarship to study theatre in Poland. In the fall of 1960, at age of 24, he enrolled at the Warsaw theatre school.

Barba was not prepared for what he found in the Poland of the early 1960s. Certainly the theatre was rich and provocative, with world-class directors, like Konrad Swinarski and Bogdan Korzeniewski, creating works in a milieu that also included up-and-coming artists such as Andrzej Wajda and Tadeusz Kantor. Similarly, the school provided a stimulating atmosphere for learning since its staff included many of Poland's leading theatre people (Korzeniewski was Barba's directing teacher, for example). But the Poland Barba came to live in was not the Poland he had expected. It was a country that displayed the profound wounds of war. Much of Warsaw was still in ruins, with bulldozers clearing rubble and the skeletons of war dead being unearthed almost daily. Rebuilding was a slow process and there were chronic shortages of even the most basic food items. These harsh realities and their debilitating effect on the Polish people were not what Barba, with his leftist sympathies, had anticipated. There seemed to be an irreconcilable conflict between the quality of the theatre in Poland and the daily reality of most people's lives. This conflict led Barba to question the theatre's worth and his belief in its political value.

Barba's disillusionment prompted him to leave the theatre school after only six months of study and travel in northern Poland, where he even took a job as welder in a small sugar mill. The job was short-lived, however, and he returned to his studies.

Of course, nothing had changed in Warsaw. But, rather than leave Poland – which would seem to have been the logical solution for Barba's troubled spirit – the young theatre student traveled within the country whenever he had the opportunity. One of these trips took him to a tiny theatre in Opole, a town of 60,000 in southeast Poland some 80 miles from Wroclaw. There, in Teatr 13 Rzedow (Theatre of the Thirteen Rows) he saw the work of a then young and unknown Polish director that, though it did not capture his imagination at the time, was to have a profound influence on the rest of Barba's professional career. He saw Jerzy Grotowski's production of Adam Mickiewicz's *Forefather's Eve*.

Barba returned to Warsaw unimpressed by what he had seen, but several months later he met Grotowski casually in a bar in Cracow. During a lengthy conversation over drinks, the two young men discovered that they shared

13

many interests in Asian religions, ideas, and philosophies. Grotowski's knowledge of the East fascinated Barba, while Barba's travels equally intrigued Grotowski. During this chance meeting, Grotowski invited Barba to come and watch the work of his company and, even though Grotowski's ideas attracted Barba more than his theatre did at the time, he accepted the invitation.

After completing his first year at the theatre school, Barba left Warsaw and became an unofficial member of Grotowski's company. During his three years with what was eventually to become the world-famous Polish Laboratory Theatre, Barba observed rehearsals and the actors' performance research, was a source of ideas for the theatre, and helped promote Grotowski's work in Poland and abroad.

For the first few months in Opole Barba was merely an observer. He watched the company's rehearsals as well as their training experiments and discussed what he saw with Grotowski.[3] In fact, at no time during his years with the company did he direct the actors or run rehearsals. But his discussions with Grotowski and the company's literary advisor, Ludwik Flaszen, led to his working closely with them, both before and during rehearsals, on the changes made to Wyspianski's original script for the group's famous production of *Akropolis* (1962). In addition to working on the text, Barba also helped Grotowski design the sound montage – consisting of varying vocal rhythms, of scored scraping and drumming on the set's metal pipes, and of different rhythms of marching and stamping made by the actors' wooden-soled boots. In recognition of his contribution, Barba was credited as the assistant director of *Akropolis*, a role he fulfilled again on the group's next production, an adaptation of Christopher Marlowe's *The Tragical History of Doctor Faustus* (1963).

Another major contribution Barba made to Grotowski's creative work was his introduction of kathakali training exercises to the group. With all due respect to kathakali's eventual influence on Grotowski, there seemed little professional reason for traveling to India in 1963, since neither Grotowski nor Barba knew a great deal about Indian theatre at the time. According to Barba, he and his two companions – his future wife, Judy Jones, a cultural officer at UNESCO, whom he had met earlier in the year at the 10th International Theatre Institute (ITI) Congress in Warsaw, and a mutual friend unconnected with the theatre – went with the vague agenda of finding something of value for his colleagues in Opole, observing Indian religious rituals and sacred sites, and most of all, for the adventure of driving overland to the subcontinent (1986c). It was only when he had arrived in India that Barba heard of kathakali, through local theatre people he met in Bombay. He subsequently visited the major training academy in Kerala, the Kalamandalam at Cheruthuruthy, and was so impressed by what he saw that he wrote what was then one of the first technical descriptions of the form by a European.[4] This article was eventually published in many countries including France, Italy, Scandinavia, and the USA, and, along with the observations

Barba made while at the Kalamandalam, was the source of the kathakali exercises that Grotowski and his actors began experimenting with in the early through middle 1960s.

But this was not the end of kathakali for Barba. Not only were Grotowski's adaptations of the kathakali exercises going to be incorporated into the training of his own actors during the Odin's early years, but kathakali's dual ethics, of intense discipline and regarding theatre as a vocation rather than merely a profession, were to be a model for Barba for many years to come.

During Barba's first year in Opole, Grotowski worked in relative isolation with little recognition. His productions drew small houses and few people outside the group's immediate circle of acquaintances knew of the work. What small acknowledgment there had been by authorities was mostly negative, consisting of attacks on Grotowski for mounting incomprehensible productions and distorting the Polish classics.[5] Despite these attacks and lack of recognition, Barba felt strongly that what was happening in Opole had major implications for world theatre. The problems were how to reach a broader audience and how to encourage greater government support. In discussion with Grotowski, Barba devised a promotional strategy designed to attract international attention with the aim of embarrassing Polish authorities into providing greater logistical and financial assistance to the group. This plan owed much to the fact that Barba, as an Italian, was able to travel freely between Poland and Western Europe.

One of Barba's strategies was to publish material about Grotowski's work in the West. He and Flaszen wrote several articles which first appeared in French in 1962, following which they were translated and published in the United States by *The Tulane Drama Review* (Grotowski, 1964; Barba, 1965; Barba and Flaszen, 1965).[6] Barba conducted lengthy interviews with Grotowski and published them. His "Meetings with Grotowski" was published in the quarterly of the World Festival of Theatres in February 1966. And he published an entire book on the Laboratory's work in Italian, *Alla Ricerca del Teatro Perduto* (Padova: Marsilio, 1965), which remained the major work on Grotowski until 1968 when Raymonde Temkine's *Grotowski* and Grotowski's own *Towards a Poor Theatre*, edited by Barba, were published.

Another of Barba's strategies was to invite influential people from the West to see the company's work. During the 1963 ITI Congress held in Warsaw from 8–15 June several performances of the *Tragical History of Doctor Faustus* were given in Lodz, a town only some two hours by bus from Warsaw (compared with the seven-hour train trip to Opole). Prior to the official opening of the congress, Barba persuaded Jean Julien, the head of the Theatre of Nations Festival, and the president of ITI, Jean Darcante, to see the production. As Barba hoped, they were very enthusiastic and told other delegates about it. Barba then arranged a private bus to take all who were interested to see *Faustus*. Many of those who saw the production were as impressed as Julien and Darcante, which led to Grotowski's company being

15

officially invited to perform in Belgium, Holland, at the 1964 Theatre of Nations Festival, and in Paris the following year. Unfortunately, the group did not receive permission from the Polish government to travel to the West, but the seeds of international recognition were sown.

Another of Barba's ploys was to arrange lectures, demonstrations, and even eventually company tours in the West. This was where Barba's bus trip paid dividends. The ITI delegates who saw *Faustus* were influential people and, even if the Polish authorities would not allow the group to perform outside the country, they were persuaded to allow Grotowski and several of his actors to travel to the West in order to talk about their work.[7]

Even after leaving Poland and returning to Norway in 1964, Barba continued to promote Grotowski's work. He and his newly formed Odin Teatret were instrumental in organizing the Laboratory's first tour in the West from 6 February to 25 March 1966, in Scandinavia, for example. And he arranged a series of workshops in Holstebro, held each July beginning in 1966 and continuing through until 1969, to which he invited actors, directors, and scholars from around the world to study with Grotowski and Ryszard Cieslak. The alumni of these workshops include, among others, Margaret Croyden, an American critic who later wrote on Grotowski's work, and Joseph Chaikin, the founder of the Open Theatre.

POLAND'S LEGACY

It is hardly surprising that Barba refers to his time with Grotowski as his "period of apprenticeship" (1986a:239) since, despite the fact that he never undertook formal training at the Teatr 13 Rzedow, his three years in Opole laid the foundations for the rest of his career. In Grotowski's small theatre in a provincial town removed from the cutural centers of Poland Barba found both a model for his Odin Teatret when it was offered a home in Holstebro and a conceptual matrix for his writings on group theatre. Similarly, Grotowski's idea of a theatre laboratory, of a center focused on researching performance – which had its origins in Opole even though Grotowski's theatre was not officially recognized as a laboratory until 1966, after it moved to Wroclaw – inspired the creation of Barba's own NTL.

Despite the fact that there are differences between Grotowski's and Barba's dramaturgical methods, a major source of Barba's approach to creating theatre pieces also has its roots in his Polish experience of the early 1960s. Barba's rejection of realism and his preference for a presentational theatre, for instance, owe a great deal to his time with Grotowski. And, although there have been several changes in the Odin's approach to creating works, Barba continues to draw upon two of the dramaturgical tools he first encountered in Opole: collective creation and improvisation.

Likewise, Barba's political baptism in Poland continues to serve him well. The Odin's philosophy, that political didacticism is more important in the way the group lives and creates its works than in the content of the productions, echoes the way Grotowski molded his group.

Barba's promotion of Grotowski's work and his apprenticeship as a strategist have similarly played no small role in his subsequent career. He maintains that one of the most important lessons he learned in Poland was what he calls "collaboration with the circumstances" (1986b), by which he means exploiting a situation to induce change rather than attempting a change through revolution. It is this lesson that led to his writing about theatre (first to inform others of Grotowski, then later about his own work), and to the Odin's establishing a publishing house as well as a film rental and production company. Both strategies have not only helped promote the group, but have also provided an invaluable source of income for Barba and his colleagues.

Grotowski's most important legacy to Barba, however, is not a model which he has built upon or adapted. It is viewing performance as an intellectual enterprise as much as a practical, creative field. As Peter Brook says of Grotowski: " no-one else in the world, to my knowledge, no-one since Stanislavky, has investigated the nature of acting, its phenomenon, its meaning, the nature and science of its mental-physical-emotional processes as deeply and completely as Grotowski" (Grotowski, 1968:13). Barba has followed in his mentor's footsteps and his theatre in Holstebro has become a world-renowned center for performance research. It is this research that has led Barba to publish and lecture extensively on the theatre. Being familiar with the most important ideas contained in these writings and lectures is the ideal point of departure for a study of Barba's work.

2

THEATRE THEORY
Sociology and the actor's technique

Barba is essentially a creative artist, a poet both in the theatre and in his writings about it. This poetic quality calls for a careful reading of his ideas since he favors poetic metaphors over the more traditional intellectual approach of deductive logic to sustain his arguments. His two major books in English, *The Floating Islands*, and *Beyond the Floating Islands*, even contain a metaphor in their titles – the theatre group as an island – which he uses as the basis of discussion. Other metaphors abound in his theoretical writings, including describing the theatre as a body losing blood (1979:129), presence as body-in-life (1988a), and group theatre as pueblos (1986a:208).

Barba's theories are primarily concerned with two aspects of theatre: sociology and practice. His ideas on sociology draw mostly on his observations of the independent group theatre movement in Europe, Latin America, and the United States. The major concerns in these writings are the social dynamics of group theatre and the function of group theatre within the greater theatre community.

The theories underlying Barba's theatre practice draw heavily on his work with his own actors, his observations of Western performance, such as Grotowski's theatre and the corporal mime of Etienne Decroux, as well as on his studies of traditional Eastern performance both inside and outside ISTA.

THIRD THEATRE

Barba's ideas on the sociology of theatre are encapsulated in what he refers to as "third theatre," a concept which he defines in relation to institutionalized theatre and the avant-garde:

> A theatrical archipelago [third theatre] has been forming during the past few years in several countries. Almost unknown, it is rarely subject to reflection, it is not presented at festivals and critics do not write about it.
>
> It seems to constitute the anonymous extreme of the theatres

18

recognized by the world of culture: on the one hand, the institutionalized theatre, protected and subsidized because of the cultural values
that it seems to transmit, appearing as a living image of the creative
confrontation with the texts of the past and the present – or even as a
"noble" version of the entertainment business; on the other hand, the
avant-garde theatre, experimenting, researching, arduous or icon-
oclastic, a theatre of changes, in search of a new originality, defended
in the name of necessity to transcend tradition, and open to novelty in
the artistic field and within society.

(1986a:193)

Despite the fact that Barba's definition of third theatre has been adopted
by many groups because it both acknowledges their significance and defines
their character, the concept is not without its critics. Most of this criticism
stems from the definition's logic of negation, and from the connoted
relationship between third theatre and the Third World.

The third theatre is a concept arrived at through negation. A particular
type of theatre exists, it is not part of the institutional theatre, it is not part
of the avant-garde. If it is not the first or second theatre, what is it? It is the
third theatre. For some, this line of argument highlights the negative profile
of a theatre living a hand-to-mouth existence, lacking a sense of its own
identity, and barely surviving in the shadows of the first and second theatres
which it secretly wishes to be part of.

This criticism of third theatre is a misreading of Barba's definition. He
certainly derives the concept of third theatre through a process of elimina-
tion, but the concept itself is hardly negative. One only has to read the
paragraphs following his argument quoted above to appreciate the positive
nature of third theatre for Barba:

> The Third Theatre lives on the fringes, often outside or on the outskirts
> of the centers and capitals of culture. It is a theatre created by people
> who define themselves as actors, directors, theatre workers, although
> they have seldom undergone a traditional theatrical education and
> therefore are not recognized as professionals.
>
> But they are not amateurs. Their entire day is filled with theatrical
> experience, sometimes by what they call training, or by the preparation
> of performances for which they must fight to find an audience.
>
> (1986a:193)

In a 1977 interview, Barba stated that his concept of third theatre grew out
of his attempts to explain significant deviations from the theatrical mainstream, such as Spain's independent theatre movement (Teatro In-
dependiente) which consisted of over ninety groups at the time, a similar
movement in Italy which boasted hundreds of groups, the fledgling group
theatre movement in Denmark, and the explosion of group theatre in Latin

America (1977:1–2). That is, his argument begins with an implicit positive statement: "A" (the independent theatre movement) exists. He then reasons that it is neither "B" (the institutional theatre) nor "C" (the avant-garde), the two most common types of theatre, and concludes that it must therefore be a separate entity. Nowhere in his argument does he state that "A" is inferior to either "B" or "C," nor is there anything in his professional career, which has been devoted to the third theatre, that indicates he feels it is inferior.

In the same interview, Barba acknowledged the Third World connotations in his concept of third theatre. However, he argued that these connotations owe their origin to the discrimination found in both, rather than in equating third theatre with a Third World sense of inferiority, or its citizens' desire to become part of the First World (1977:2–3). In the late 1970s Barba even went so far as to identify discrimination as a defining characteristic of third theatre: "The groups that I call Third Theatre do not belong to a lineage, to a theatrical tendency. But they do all live in a situation of discrimination: personal or cultural, professional, economical or political" (1979:160–161).

In a recent article in which he reconsiders the third theatre in light of developments in the 1980s and the dawning of the 1990s, however, he denies that discrimination is any longer the defining characteristic (Barba, 1991:3). For Barba, the modern third theatre is one in which its members are concerned with meaning: "Today [1991] it is clear to me that the essential character of the Third Theatre is the autonomous construction of meaning which does not recognize the boundaries assigned to our craft by the surrounding culture" (1991:8). That is, the members of the third theatre are those concerned with exploring and cultivating a language of performance that gives "an autonomous meaning for the action of doing theatre" (Barba, 1991:4) rather than succumbing to commercial considerations or current trends in the avant-garde.

This change in Barba's thinking is not as far removed from his original understanding of third theatre as it may seem. In his first article on third theatre (originally published in French in 1976 and most recently in English in Barba, 1986a:193–194) he described ways in which members of the third theatre can survive. One is by entering the sphere of established theatre; the other could well be a definition of his later concept of autonomous meaning: " groups can ... survive by ... succeeding through continuous work to individualize their own area, seeking what for them is essential and trying to force others to respect this diversity" (Barba, 1986a:193–194).

The sociology of third theatre

The sociological dimension of theatre is more important than esthetics in the third theatre. Unlike either institutional theatre or the avant-garde, in which the emphasis is on producing, reflecting, and/or distributing culture, the focus in third theatre is on relationships: on the relationships between those in a particular group, on their relationship to other groups, and on their relationship with the audience. This focus on the network of relationships in third theatre has its foundation in the individual and his/her role in the collective.

In the third theatre there is no difference between a personal and professional life, since how theatre is made takes precedence over what is produced. For members of the third theatre, content and form are often less important than a group's socio-cultural philosophy and how that philosophy is realized in its daily work and reflected in its productions. The Odin Teatret, Barba's own group and the model for third theatre, has been criticized for lacking a political agenda in its productions. But these attacks fail to take into account the socio-political implications of group dynamics taking precedence over what is produced – the very foundation of Barba's approach to theatre. At the Odin he has encouraged a training process in which the actors both develop and are responsible for their own training. Similarly, the actors play a major part in creating mise-en-scenes during rehearsals, and they also help design and build the sets for each production, as well as design and make costumes, and assist with publicity.

In addition to this internal ethic of collective creation and responsibility, Barba's group also places great emphasis on its relationship with others who share its approach to theatre. Members of the Odin retain personal contact with many groups and theatre scholars in Europe, Latin America, and to a lesser extent, the United States, through mail, through commenting on the performances of young actors when they are asked for such feedback, and running workshops for those who request them.

In keeping with this concern for personal contact, Barba prefers to have tours arranged by theatre groups and individuals the Odin knows, rather than to use professional tour organizers. In this way, he is encouraging these groups to arrange residencies for his company so that he and his actors can run workshops, show films about their work, and establish a greater contact with the theatre community than if they were just another troupe passing through on tour.

Barba regards this networking not only as a means of establishing links but also as essential to the third theatre's survival. Many members of the third theatre are based in small towns, or are in big cities with little funding or support. It is from this sense of isolation that Barba coined his famous floating islands metaphor, comparing the groups of the third theatre to islands of the same archipelago separated by a huge expanse of sea (1979:145–164). From his own experience, Barba is well aware that it takes immense fortitude to continue working in isolation for long periods. Thus, the contacts between groups like the Odin and other members of the third theatre archipelago bring a sense of both psychological and concrete support. Groups arranging tours for each other, as well as exchanging ideas about training, rehearsal methods, and production techniques, forge links that transform the third theatre from isolated dots in the ocean to islands supported by a network of communication and travel links, like so many air routes on a map.

Despite the global nature of Barba's metaphor, the third theatre is not an official organization with headquarters in one place and members who pay dues. It is an unofficial, voluntary alliance based primarily on informal contacts. The nearest those involved come to establishing formal links is in the third theatre gatherings initiated by Barba in 1976. The first meeting – which took place in Belgrade, Yugoslavia – has been followed by seven subsequent gatherings to date (1991): in Bergamo, Italy (1977); Ayacucho, Peru (1978); Madrid and Lekeito, Spain (1979); Zacatecas, Mexico (1981); Bahia Blanca, Argentina (1987); Cuzco, Peru (1987); and Chaclacayo, Peru (1988). And though each of these encounters, as Barba prefers to call them, was subtly different, they all followed the same basic format. Organizers (who have usually been one or more theatre groups in conjunction with Barba) invited members of the third theatre from different parts of the world to come together in a closed workshop for up to two weeks at a time to share their ideas, work, and problems. The formal part of the program consisted of various training workshops led by master performers such as the Odin actors; lecture/demonstrations on training and dramaturgical methods led by Barba himself or by directors such as Mario Delgado who heads Peru's Cuatrotablas; seminars on various topics ranging from the role of violence in Peruvian society (by Juan Larco in Chaclacayo) to the use of Decroux's mime techniques as a source of training (Luis Octavio Burnier in Bahia Blanca); and performances by the groups. The most valuable aspect of these gatherings, however, has invariably been the informal encounters between members of the third theatre who rarely get to meet each other. From these discussions over coffee or a few drinks, friendships are formed, successes and difficulties shared, and professional contacts are made that often lead to tours or the ongoing exchange of ideas through mail or at subsequent meetings. In short, the "islands" are in touch with each other.

BARTER

Barter, a term Barba applied to the theatre in the early 1970s, is closely linked to the concept of "relationship" which underlies the third theatre. As in economic barter, the defining principle of theatrical barter is exchange, but in theatrical barter, the commodity of exchange is performance: "A" performs for "B" and, instead of paying "A" money, "B" performs for "A." A play is exchanged for songs and dances, a display of acrobatics for a demonstration of training exercises, a poem for a monologue, etc.

Barba's concept of barter is a clear example of theory originating from his own practical experience. One evening in 1974, toward the end of the first month of the Odin's residency in Carpignano, southern Italy, he and the actors were followed in the street on their way to visit friends. Prior to this outing, they had been training and rehearsing in isolation at a rented villa, and had never appeared together in public with their musical instruments or dressed in their colorful training costumes. The group eventually found itself in an open square surrounded by local people so, rather than offend, they did what the villagers asked – they performed for them. They played Scandinavian folk songs combined with vocal improvisations developed by the actors as part of their training. To their surprise when they finished, not only did the villagers applaud, but they asked them to listen to their songs. These songs were work-related pieces meant to accompany the harvesting of tobacco and olives, interspersed with occasional sentimental songs about love and death.

This experience reminded Barba of something that had happened some five months earlier in the mountains of Sardinia, following performances of *Min Fars Hus*. Odin's Sardinian audiences were primarily shepherds and peasants unused to the theatre who, after performances, often invited Barba and his colleagues to watch their local dances and hear their traditional songs.

The Sardinian and Carpignano experiences prompted Barba to see the intercultural potential in these meetings between performers from such different worlds. So, at the request of other villages near Carpignano, the Odin organized official exchanges and began developing material specifically for them. This material included fragments of training (which resembled dances), parades, and simple clown performances.

During a television interview at the time, Barba attempted to place these experiences in a theatrical and social context by explaining them in terms of cultures meeting, and of foreigners and "otherness." In doing so, he used the term "barter" for the first time:

> Foreign body is the best term for our presence in this southern Italian village [Carpignano]. Odin Teatret's actors and the population are poles apart .... But it is this difference, this "otherness" that has been our point of departure. We do not want to "teach" anything, nor inform the people here of their social or cultural situation. We do not believe we have a knowledge of something they lack. We are not here to entertain them ...
>
> Our stay here is built upon the idea of barter. Imagine two very different tribes, each on their own side of the river. Each tribe can live for itself, talk about the other, praise or slander it. But every time one of them rows over to the other shore it is to exchange something. One does not row over to carry on ethnographic research, to observe the other's way of life, but rather to give and take: a handful of salt for a scrap of cloth, a bow for a fistful of beads.
>
> The goods we trade are cultural.

(1986a:159)

Since this interview, barter has become common in the third theatre. Groups such as Potlach and Tascabile di Bergamo in Italy, Peru's Cuatrotablas and Yuyachkani, and Teatro Libre and Teatro Nucleo from Argentina, have all followed Barba's lead in using performance as a point of contact between cultures. Other theatre groups, though not directly influenced by Barba, have also used barter. The Polish group Gardzienice, for instance, mounts what its director, Wlodzimierz Staniewski, calls "gatherings," in which the group spends a week or more in a particular village, during which the actors present performances, are audience to the local people's traditional songs and dances, and often create original works in conjunction with the villagers (Staniewski, 1977). And Peter Brook's International Centre for Theatre Research (ICTR) employed barter-type techniques in meetings with various tribal groups during its famous trip through northern Africa.[1]

Barter continues to play an important role in Barba's work. He and his Odin colleagues have mounted barters in small rural communities in Wales (1980), Brittany (1977), among the Yanomami Indians in Amazonian Venezuela (1976), and as part of the 1987 ISTA Barba organized an entire program of barters over a one-week period in the villages of the Salento region in southern Italy which, in addition to the local people, included performers from India, Bali, and Japan, as well as his own Odin actors.

Barters have also been organized in urban settings. As early as 1977, the Odin mounted a barter in the working-class neighborhood of Paris' 20th arrondissement, and similar barters have taken place in the suburbs of Bahia Blanca in southern Argentina and Montevideo, Uruguay (both in 1987).

The basis of most of these adaptations is practical rather than esthetic. Performance spaces are often different in the urban environment from those in the country; town squares have to be replaced by parking lots, for example, and the volume of traffic often limits street theatre more in cities than in villages. Similarly, logistics are different in urban areas from those in the country, if for no other reason than the greater number of potential participants and spectators in a city. The barter in Bahia Blanca, for instance, was part of the third theatre gathering being held in the city, and included many of the groups from the meeting working together in the grounds of a large housing complex. These groups all began their performances at the same time in different parts of the grounds, and gradually moved toward a parking lot at one end of the complex. The various audiences followed the performers to the parking lot where volunteers from the local community had prepared dances, songs, and poetry recitals to entertain both the visitors and their neighbors.

The Montevideo exchange provided an even more sophisticated variation of the original barter format. While the Odin was on tour in Uruguay, a barter was arranged between Barba's actors and the local black community's candombe singers and drummers. It was decided that rather than the traditional barter format – having one group's performance followed by the other – the Odin actors and the candombe artists would perform together. This called for a brief rehearsal the day before the performance, in which the Odin actors and their candombe colleagues devised the rough outline of a scenario and mise-en-scene in a vacant lot in the run-down Ansina district of Montevideo where the barter was to take place. The local organizers knew there would be a large audience the following day so, in contrast to the usual barter, they arranged seating around the playing area both to define the stage and to ensure that as many spectators as possible could see the performance.

Barters can also involve solo performers. In 1975, during the second Odin residency in southern Italy, Rasmussen spent a week in the small village of Sarule meeting the local people through bartering. Each day she entered the village wearing her training costume, a white half-mask, and carrying a kettledrum with colorful ribbons attached. She walked and danced along the streets playing her drum or a flute she also carried, only entering houses and work places when she was invited. Once she felt a rapport with particular villagers she had met through her playing, Rasmussen discarded her performance persona and joined them in conversation, a drink, and even occasionally a meal. In this barter, the daily life of the performer was exchanged for the daily life of the villagers (Rasmussen, Barba, D'Urso, Taviani, 1979).

A somewhat similar series of barters was arranged by the Danish anthropologist Mette Bovin, in 1982, when she organized a field trip to Upper Volta (renamed Burkino Faso after the 1984 revolution) to study the non-Islamic elements of the region through performance. She asked the Odin actress Roberta Carreri to prepare a series of solo performances which Carreri then used when she entered various villages. Bovin and her small film crew followed Carreri at a discreet distance, recording both her meeting with the local people and the performances her unusual entry often provoked from the villagers (Bovin, 1988).

Yet another variation on the original concept of barter is its role at third-theatre gatherings. At these meetings, the underlying principle is exchange. Groups and individuals share their professional knowledge with each other through workshops, lecture/demonstrations, and performances. The exchange of performance and/or performance-related skills is thus the point of contact between groups of people, just as it is in the more conventional forms of barter.

Barter and cultural exchange

Barters are a point of contact between cultures. In any barter, the "micro-culture" of one group (or individual) meets the "micro-culture" of the other. This meeting is realized through the exchange of performances, that is, cultural products, but these products are not as important as the process of exchange itself. There is no question of an unequal exchange in barter since there is no pre-established value for what is to be exchanged. In the Bahia Blanca barter, for instance, European groups such as the Odin, Potlach, and Tascabile performed fragments of street works they have presented in many places around the world. These works – which consisted of skilled acrobatics, sophisticated mise-en-scenes with stilt figures, fire-eating, live music, and beautiful costumes – were exchanged in the barter for a number of different performances by the local residents which included a rudimentary tango done by two young people, and several songs by a guitar-playing singer who had seen better days. Comparing the work of the professional Europeans with amateurs from Bahia Blanca has no meaning in barter. As Taviani points out, it is the act of exchange which gives value to the transaction, not the quality of the items exchanged (1979:106).

The precedence of process over product in barter calls the conventional value of theatre into question. In the traditional paradigm, theatrical performance (cultural product) is exchanged for money. No matter what socio-political rationale these performances have, which can range from the multimillion-dollar Broadway spectacle through regional theatre to small-scale productions in the suburbs of many cities or towns, the aim is to produce a complete, finished work that will attract a paying audience. Performance is measured in terms of esthetic quality and dollar-value per seat.

This traditional paradigm is rejected in barter. Cultural product is exchanged for cultural product, rather than for money. Since the value of this exchange lies in the exchange itself, not in what is exchanged, esthetics and dollar worth are irrelevant. At the third-theatre meeting in Bahia Blanca, for example, Grupo Emanuel, consisting of peasants from a tiny village of some sixty inhabitants in southern Chile, with no training and little exposure to theatre, presented a performance, *Vivencias Campesinas*, for their colleagues. By most conventional standards the production was dreadful: the story, which was little more than a series of unrelated vignettes about life in their village interwoven with some of their local mythology, was uninteresting, the acting was terrible, while the sets and costumes lacked imagination and were a glaring advertisement for the group's poverty. By general consensus the production was an esthetic disaster, and most delegates agreed that they would not normally have paid to see it. But the exchange was a very moving event. The members of the third theatre in the audience saw the quintessence of all they stood for: a group struggling to make theatre against all odds, with a sincerity and conviction that many of the world's great theatre companies would envy. When the performance was over, the entire audience of some three hundred people gave the group a standing ovation. The value of the work lay in the exchange, in the communal solidarity it engendered, rather than in the "quality" of what was exchanged.

The emphasis on cultural exchange in barter does not mean that it cannot have an agenda beyond that of an intercultural meeting. At the request of various village leaders in southern Italy during 1975, for instance, the Odin used barters to help local communities in different ways. In addition to the exchange of performances in the village of Gavoi, the Odin asked people to provide information for a proposed publication on the region. Similarly, in Monteiasi the young people of the town wanted a library, so the Odin asked each villager to bring a book to the barter and these contributions formed the basis of what eventually became the local library. And, at the suggestion of local leaders in Ollalai, villagers were asked to bring old musical instruments, stories they could recall about the village's past, as well as examples of local legends and traditions, all so that they could establish a village archive.

As mentioned earlier, barter has also been used as an anthropological tool. Bovin, in writing about her trip to Burkina Faso with Carreri, refers to what she calls, "provocation anthropology," by which she means using barter to provoke responses in those she wants to observe. Her purpose in having Carreri enter villages performing was to elicit exchange performances from the local people which she could observe and record as part of her study of the non-Islamic elements in the culture. And, though she admits that the traditional anthropologist may find her methods overly intrusive, she maintains that "the presence of a catalyst in the fieldwork provoked the presentation of cultural products I would otherwise not have discovered, seen, or heard about" (Bovin, 1988:32).

Is barter theatre?

Taviani maintains that "barter ... is not theatre" (1986a:267). And, even though the differences between barter and theatre are not as clearcut as his statement might imply, what he says has more than an element of truth in it. The emphasis in barter is on its social agenda, on meeting and exchange, rather than on theatre's concerns with esthetics. Consequently, barters are rarely performed in conventional theatre spaces with structural divisions between actors and spectators or the assistance of stage technology. They invariably take place in streets, parks, plazas, and town squares, with the performance space defined by the inner perimeter of spectators.

The street-theatre quality and improvised nature of barters usually also means that there are no sets. Characters are identified by little more than costumes and a limited set of stock actions. And, excluding the few pieces specifically prepared for bartering by groups like the Odin, particular barters usually involve a minimum of rehearsal, and rarely have a repeatable mise-en-scene.

However, there is a connection between barter and theatre because performance is the commodity of exchange in barters. Barba's colleagues at the Odin, for instance, have created a collection of stock characters which they use in street theatre and barter situations. In addition, they have developed performance fragments which include parades, mock fights with musical instruments, and dances which they can arrange in various orders as part of an improvised narrative – much as the stock comic routines, called "lazzi," were used in commedia dell'arte. So that, despite the fact that few barter performances are the same, the prepared scenes and the characters who appear in them were developed through rehearsal in much the same way as in a more conventional theatre production.

In most barters, the preparations of the local people are less formal than those of the visitors. The villagers in southern Italy, where Barba's concept of barter has its origins, did not prepare specific dances and songs for their exchanges with the Odin. The songs and dances are part of their heritage, they have "rehearsed" them through first seeing and hearing them in the village as children, and since then they have sung and danced them with their fellow villagers at social gatherings and special events over many years.

But these folk traditions take on a new meaning in the context of a barter. In their traditional setting there is no audience in the sense of the conventional theatre, because the songs and dances are the celebratory or lamenting voice of entire communities, rather than professional performers' attempts to entertain an audience. In the barter, however, these same songs and dances become a "performance for spectators" insofar as they are presented to outsiders who are not part of the culture. Just as the villagers in Carpignano were spectators to the Odin's fragments of training and Scandinavian folk songs, the Odin actors became an audience to the villager's presentations.

Despite this similarity between the performer–audience paradigm in barter and theatre, there are differences between them. The conventional relationship between the actors and spectators in the theatre is passive. That is, the audience is presented with a prepared cultural product in which they rarely take an active part.

But, even though this is the dominant theatrical model, there have been many attempts, particularly in experimental theatre, to transform this traditional actor–audience relationship. Grotowski, Richard Schechner, and Barba himself, among others, have experimented with altering the playing space and audience seating arrangements from production to production in order to influence the contact between the performers and their audience. And The Living Theatre and Schechner's Performance Group experimented with audience participation in productions such as the Living Theatre's *Paradise Now* and Schechner's *Dionysus in 69*.[2]

These experiments tend to influence the qualitative rather than structural nature of the performer–audience relationship. Even in *Paradise Now* and *Dionysus in 69*, both of which had improvised sections in which the actors generated audience participation, those in the audience who did not take part were passive spectators to the action, much as in the traditional model,

28

while those who did join the actors shifted from being passive spectators to becoming part of the cultural product. The audience participation segments of these productions were less structured and more open to variation than the actors' scored sections of the mise-en-scenes which were prepared in rehearsals and repeated at each performance. The potential for variation in the participation sections of these productions, coupled with the fact that at least some of the spectators temporarily became performers, altered the nature of the contact between the actors and their audience. Certainly there were always those who chose to watch rather than participate, so that at least part of the audience–cultural product paradigm remained the same. However, those who chose to participate shifted back and forth from their conventional role to being part of the cultural product itself.

Barter tends more toward this participation model than to its conventional counterpart in which the audience is passive. This is because there are both those who remain audience members throughout the event and those who become part of a cultural product. In most barters, however, there is a shift between the audience and cultural product. "A" performs for "B," that is, "B" is audience to "A"'s cultural product, following which "B" performs for "A," so that "A" becomes the audience to "B"'s cultural product. Those who choose not to perform are audience to the entire exchange.

Barter introduces a degree of structural instability in the performer–spectator relationship. In the most common form of barter, a group performs for the local community and in return some members of the community perform their dances and songs for them. During one part of the barter, the actors are performers and the local people are their audience, following which roles are reversed and the actors are audience to the performers from the community. In the most successful barters, this temporary division of roles often dissolves during the latter part of the exchange as the actors are invited to join the local people in their dances and songs, or the local people join the actors in theirs. This invitation signals the dissolution of the "active" spectators as all the protagonists become performers simultaneously.

Regardless of the performer–spectator relationship in barter and its questionable connection to theatre, a knowledge of it is essential for anyone wishing to understand the role of theatre's social dynamic in Barba's theory and practice. Through the type of theatrical interchange embodied in barter, Barba underscores his concept of theatre as a means of realizing contact between different individuals, and different socio-cultural groups: "theatre can, in a way, destroy its artistic quality and become a sort of cultural instrument. By cultural I mean an instrument for creating relations, especially among persons who could never be able to create a dialogue between themselves" (Barba, 1985b:10).

It is worth noting that, despite the fact that this concept of theatre as "a cultural instrument" evolved almost as if by accident in southern Italy, it did not develop in a vacuum. Apart from the Brook and Gardzienice examples

29

cited earlier, the Brazilian theatre director and theorist Augusto Boal has created what he calls "forum theatre" in which he and his colleagues work with communities teaching them basic performance techniques which they then use to create productions about local problems. In this work, just as in barter, the spectator–performer paradigm is transformed as spectators become performers and social interaction rather than esthetics dominates the stage.

Even though there are major differences between forum theatre and barter, since the emphasis in the former is to have a community air social and political issues that affect it while the goal of the latter is to create a dialogue between different communities, the use of theatre as a cultural rather than esthetic tool is common to both. Yet, neither Barba nor Boal admits direct influence from the other. They are contemporaries working in a similar vein who have written about their ideas. Each is aware of the other's work and that they share a related vision of theatre.[3]

THE SOCIO-CULTURAL DYNAMIC OF GROUP THEATRE

Barba defines theatre as a form of social action:

> What is theatre? If I try to reduce this word to something tangible, what I discover are men and women, human beings who have joined together. Theatre is a particular relationship in an elected context. First between people who gather together in order to create something, and then, later, between the creation made by this group and their public.
> (1988a:292)

This definition identifies what Barba regards as the dual bases of group theatre, the social dynamic inside the group, and the group's relationship to those outside the group through its work.

Inside the group

For Barba, the internal dynamic is the most important aspect of group theatre. He maintains that since performance is temporally limited, both through each production being retained in the repertoire for a limited period and performance generally taking up no more than a few hours each day, and because it is the end product of a much longer process within the group, the process itself – that is, how the group creates its productions, the members' attitudes to the work, to each other, to the collective, and to their professional life – is what is important (1986a:175). He further argues that it is this process which determines the group's place and influence in society because it provides the foundation for the group's survival strategies, its professional ethics, and its esthetics (1986a:198–199).

The Odin, for example, has always been based on the premise underlying third theatre, that theatre is a way of life rather than a mere profession. The actor is at the center of Barba's ethic so the performers' research, training, and creative work are the dynamics upon which he has shaped his role as the Odin's director. Actors are chosen for their attitude to the work rather than for their innate talent (Barba, 1986a:44). Self-discipline is all-important since they work long hours training, preparing productions, designing and building sets, making costumes, helping with public relations for upcoming tours, maintaining contact with other groups through mail, and running workshops, in addition to which they have a rotating roster for cleaning the Holstebro theatre complex – all without any supervision. The Odin Teatret is not a company they work for, they are the Odin, so what they do defines both it and them. According to Barba, this definition is based on balancing the needs of the individuals that make up the group with those of the collective to which they belong (1985c).

The group and its public

Despite his socio-political bent, Barba acknowledges that theatre cannot change society as a whole. Nevertheless, he maintains that it has the potential to change both those who do it, through making theatre a way of life rather than just a profession, and those who come in contact with people who have made theatre the focus of their lives:

> We've [the Odin] been building something autonomous, but it's changing all the time, and changing the view of theatre. In Europe and in many other countries, we are a factor which has changed many things. Theatre can change only theatre; it cannot change society. But if you change the theatre, you change a small but very important part of society. In the end, what did Stanislavsky influence? The spectators or the age or the history of theatre which came after him? When you change theatre, you change for its audience a certain way of seeing, a change in perception, a special kind of perceptivity.
>
> (1985b:17)

The social value of theatre for Barba is in the way those who make it go about their work, rather than in the socio-political content of productions. Even though several of the Odin's pieces have had their origins in political themes, the major socio-political thrust in the group's work comes from the contact made between its members and those who host them on tour.

The key to understanding Barba's approach to theatre is his emphasis on process. Even though he acknowledges the value of socio-political commentary and esthetics, these are less important for him in the long term than the process through which a group arrives at them. Barter, with its emphasis on the meeting of cultures, is, in many ways, the quintessence of Barba's

31

theatrical ideas. Sociologically speaking, he views theatre as a point of contact between cultures in which the exchange is as important as the quality or content of the product. It would be fair to say that one of Barba's major contributions to theatre history is his attempt to understand the social value of those who *make* theatre.

ESTHETICS

Barba's esthetics have always been concerned with concrete questions of how theatre is done rather than meditations on its philosophical implications. These esthetics cover the spectrum of theatre practice, ranging from performance to rehearsal methodology through dramaturgy and dramatic structure to the connections between the performer and audience. But, despite the scope of these concerns, his major focus has always been on the actor: how the actor can shape the training–rehearsal–performance process, and how s/he can become an autonomous entity, independent of teachers, writers, and directors.

The importance of the actor in Barba's esthetics stems from both his apprenticeship with Grotowski and from his own interest in presence: "I am interested in a very elementary question. Why, when I see two actors doing the same thing, I get fascinated by one and not by the other" (Barba, 1985b:12). Barba's analysis of presence, for which he prefers to use the more descriptive terms "body-in-life" or bios (life, from the Greek), and how to control it technically, are the essence of his acting theory.

Daily and extra-daily behavior

Barba's initial analytic work on body-in-life focused on the distinction between what he calls daily and extra-daily behavior. Daily behavior refers to the largely unconscious process through which our bodies and voices absorb and reflect the culture in which we live. We slowly learn how to stand, walk, talk, and behave through parental guidance, role models, and by mirroring those around us. Through this process we gradually acquire a body technique that reflects both the society we come from and our role in it.

Extra-daily behavior, on the other hand, refers to a body technique that is other than daily. Performance forms such as ballet, corporal mime, kathakali, or noh require actors to master movements, ways of holding the body, and/or vocal techniques which are very different from daily behavior.

The pre-expressive

The source of presence in extra-daily behavior lies in what Barba calls the "pre-expressive," which he defines as: "The level [of performance] which deals with how to render the actor's energy scenically alive, that is with how the actor can become a presence which immediately attracts the spectator's attention" (Barba and Savarese, 1991:188).

Most codified performance body techniques –particularly those from the East like noh, kabuki, kathakali, and Balinese dance-drama, establish a pre-expressive mode that engages the actor's energies in a particular way. The basic grammar of these forms alters the performer's center of gravity, his/her distribution of body weight, as well as the way s/he walks and/or moves, all prior to expressing character, situation or plot. In noh, for example, the performers are required to stand with the knees bent, the legs locked together, and to move with the entire sole of the foot gently touching the stage. Similarly, in many forms of Balinese dance-drama the dancer widens his/her gait and bends his/her knees, which alters the center of gravity and normal position of the spine. These codes define their form since no matter what play or dance is being presented, the performers in noh or Balinese dance-drama must engage their bodies in this way. And, even though this engagement is a form of personal expression, since each individual engages his/her body in a slightly different way, the codes that govern the engagement are so precise that variations between individual performers are minimal. The major components of expression are character, situation, and plot, all of which are laid on top of these codes.

The pre-expressive level of performance is governed by three principles: alterations in balance, the law of opposition, and what Barba calls coherent incoherence. The first two principles require the performer to engage his/her energies in an other than ordinary (i.e., daily) way, while the latter refers to the consistent logic of a particular form's performance codes, no matter how removed the logic may be from the daily body technique.

Altering the performer's center of gravity and normal balance transforms weight into energy. Most daily body techniques tend to a point of inertia which demands a minimum expenditure of energy for standing, sitting, and walking. Codified forms, on the other hand, distort this normal equilibrium, calling on the performer to engage additional energy in order to move, remain still, or even merely to retain balance. As noted above in noh, for instance, the hips are locked, the knees bent, and the actor walks by sliding his/her feet across the stage without lifting them. This changes the normal position of the spine, alters the center of balance, and engages the trunk as a single unit – all of which creates opposing tensions in the upper and lower parts of the body that force the performer to find a new point of equilibrium. In odissi dance, the tribangi, which is a major component of the form, requires the dancer to manipulate his/her body as if the letter "S" were passing through the hips, trunk, and neck. This position, which distorts the line of the spinal column, affects the performer's balance and thereby alters the normal relationship between body weight, center of gravity, and the feet. Similarly, in many forms of Balinese dance-drama the performer pushes down on the soles of the feet while at the same time lifting the toes, thus reducing contact with the ground. To compensate, the dancer widens his/her stance and bends his/her knees, which alters the center of gravity and the normal position of the spine. These adjustments increase the level of muscular activity, which, as in similar distortions in odissi dance and noh, produces a dynamic, rather than static, physical state.

Barba's law of opposition engages the performer's energies in a way somewhat similar to that of altering balance insofar as it also calls for distortions of daily behavior. In daily life we attempt to minimize the amount of energy needed to counter the force of gravity, for instance, but maximizing the opposition between body weight and gravity plays an important part in the pre-expressive codes of most dance forms. The leap in ballet is one of the West's most common uses of this law of opposition as dancers "free" themselves from the earth's downward pull through soaring feats of lightness and grace. This principle of countering gravity through opposition is also used in traditional Japanese performance forms. Unlike ballet, however, this opposition involves pushing against gravity rather than trying to leap away from it. In noh and nihon buyo the performer pushes his/her weight into the floor in opposition to the force of gravity. This resistance through opposition engages the energies of the performer in an other than ordinary way and, as in ballet, brings a quality of lightness and grace to the movement.

This law of opposition is not limited to how gravity influences movement. If performers intend to indicate an object, point someone out, or move across the stage in Beijing opera, they will invariably begin their action in the opposite direction to the one in which it will eventually proceed in order to make the action more dynamic and dramatic (Wichman, 1983:190). And the way in which Decroux infuses movement with a dynamic quality in his corporal mime technique is through establishing opposing tensions in different parts of the body (Sklar, 1985:67–68).

Extra-daily techniques are both incoherent and coherent. They are incoherent insofar as they involve an excessive use of energy. Daily behavior is invariably based on conserving energy through minimum energy expenditure for maximum results. Extra-daily techniques, on the other hand, are not concerned with the most efficient use of energy but rather with maximizing the energy produced, in order to induce the actor's body-in-life (i.e., presence). As Barba puts it:

> It is totally inconsistent, from the point of view of an action, its goal, and economy, for the Oriental actor or the European classical dancer to assume positions which seem to hamper his freedom of movement, and to remove himself from daily body techniques in order to use a technique which is characterized by strenuous artificiality and waste of energy. But it is just this extra-daily technique which permits him to discover a different quality of energy.

> (1986:119)

The distortions of balance described above – the locked-hip walking position in noh, the odissi tribangi, and the basic bent knees position in many forms of Balinese dance-drama, are all examples of body positions which are "strenuous" and far removed from "daily body techniques." They all call for a greater expenditure of energy than merely standing or walking, and it is this surplus energy which induces a dynamic state in the performer. So that, even though their call for excessive energy expenditure is "incoherent" (i.e., makes no sense from a practical, daily life, point of view), it is also "coherent" (i.e., understandable) insofar as it is a major source of the dynamic in each of the genres.

The pre-expressive East and West

The pre-expressive functions across cultures. In traditional Eastern performance, as well as in the few codified Western performance forms such as ballet and corporal mime, the pre-expressive principles are embedded in the codes themselves. This is not to say that the pre-expressive has no application outside of traditionally codified performance. In his writing, research at ISTA, and in his directing, Barba has spent many years working on the relevance of the pre-expressive for Western actors, always maintaining that, instead of learning a codified form in which the pre-expressive principles are already embedded, performers should identify the principles underlying the pre-expressive and make these the basis of their training and performances.

In traditional Eastern theatre, there is a more direct connection between training and performance than there is in mainstream Western theatre. In most Asian forms, performers do not learn a grammar of performance which they apply to each new play they rehearse, as in the Stanislavsky tradition. Students learn the forms by imitating their teachers, who pass on the repertory of plays and characters they were taught by their masters and have played for many years. Unlike the West, in which new plays and mise-en-scenes are all important, traditional Eastern performance generally consists of a set repertory of plays which both the actors and their audiences know. Since young performers begin learning this repertoire from the very beginning of their training, they develop body techniques – that is, the codes that define the genre – through learning roles and plays. Performers may have to master particular physical and vocal techniques – such as the open gait, mudras, and facial muscle control required in kathakali, or the stylistic declamation, stance, and way of moving in noh – but these are taught as an integral part of the repertoire. They are not techniques that the traditional Asian actor separates from the plays in order to apply them to new works.[4]

This connection between training and performance in traditional Eastern performance highlights an important aspect of the pre-expressive. The prefix "pre" implies that the pre-expressive precedes the expressive chronologically. This is only part of the story, however. The distribution of body weight, the center of gravity, and the opposition of muscular tensions in kathakali, noh, and other similar forms is based on the extra-daily techniques that define the forms. But, by virtue of the connection between training and performance, these techniques are inseparable from the roles played by the performers. The pre-expressive thus not only precedes the expressive chronologically, it also underlies expression (Barba and Savarese, 1991:188). In noh, for example, the locked-hip walk is used for each charac-ter, and much of the choreography for every role is made up of the same set patterns of movements that incorporate the pre-expressive, called *kata*, which range from realistic actions, like scooping up salt water or reading a book, to symbolic actions, such as drooping and raising one or both hands to the face to indicate weeping or turning the face left and then right to indicate searching or the blowing wind, and abstract movement patterns that include various forms of stamping and a zigzag pattern that indicate the beginning or end of many dances. As one of the leading scholars of noh, Kunio Komparu, points out, "In Noh, the same basic movement patterns are used for every role. Only by donning a mask and robes to perform the full play can an actor acquire the spirit (chi), creating on stage a being with a mind" (1983:221).

Despite this dual role of the pre-expressive, it carries no signification other than that of characterizing a genre. The pre-expressive is not the open gait of kathakali that alters the performer's center of gravity, the position of his spine, and forces him to bend his knees, nor is it the equally unnatural stance of noh theatre described above. It is the principles of precarious balance and muscular opposition underlying both techniques. The codes of a particular genre are based on pre-expressive principles, but they are not the principles themselves.

Sats

In attempting to explain how the pre-expressive underlies signification, Barba adopted a Norwegian word "sats," which he identifies as the moment just prior to an action in which a performer's energies and focus of attention are concentrated on proceeding with the action (1982a:23). The analogy he makes between a bow and sats may make the term clearer. In this analogy he compares sats to an archer with his arrow in a fully drawn bowstring: all is poised with a maximum of tension and attention in order for the arrow to hurtle through space and claim its target (1982a:23).

Every action has a point of sats. These points are invariably part of the codes in traditional Eastern and codified Western performance forms. But for the performer who wishes to develop his/her own technique and explore the body-in-life for him/herself, as Barba has encouraged at the Odin, s/he must first find the point of sats in each action. This point is a precise moment in the flow of one action when the next action is poised to begin. As, for example, when a trapeze artist is swinging backward and forward on the trapeze preparing to catch his/her partner. His/her initial action is the moving back and forth but during his/her swinging there is a point at which s/he is "poised with a maximum of tension and attention" for the following action, to catch his/her partner.

Once the performer has discovered each sats point s/he must then establish a flow in the actions which moves, not from the beginning of one action to the end of another, but rather from the point of sats in one action to the corresponding point in the following action. It is through this flow from one point of sats to another that the pre-expressive underlies expression. As Barba puts it, "The essential thing for the actor is not merely to carry out an exercise, but – in response to the demands made by each exercise – to find the moment of *sats*, the basic opposition which from action to action characterizes the dialectic of *bios*, of the living organism" (1982a:23).

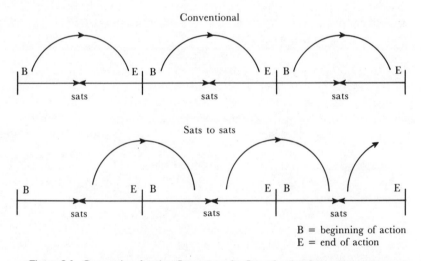

Figure 2.1 Conventional action flow versus the flow of action from sats to sats

Incultured and accultured behavior

As a complement to his explanation of the pre-expressive, Barba has introduced a cultural dimension to his concepts of the daily and extra-daily, through a distinction he makes between what he terms incultured and accultured behavior. Incultured behavior is essentially what he previously called daily behavior, but with an emphasis on what he perceives as the broader parameter of cultural rather than social roots. Acknowledging his debt to anthropology, Barba defines inculturation as the "process of passive sensory-motor absorption of the daily behavior of a given culture. A child's organic adaptation to the conduct and life norms of his culture" (Barba and Savarese, 1991:189).

Accultured behavior, on the other hand, equates more closely with the extra-daily since it is based on the premise that, just as inculturation produces an ordinary culture of the body, performance body techniques produce an other than ordinary body culture:

> In all cultures, it is possible to observe another path for the performer [i.e., other than incultured]: the utilisation of specific body techniques which are separate from those used in daily life. Modern and classical ballet dancers, mimes, and performers from traditional Oriental theatres have denied their "naturalness" and have adopted another means of scenic behaviour. They have undergone a process of "inculturation" imposed from the outside, with ways of standing, walking, stopping, looking, and sitting which are different from the daily.
>
> (Barba and Savarese, 1991:190)

In keeping with this cultural dimension in his thinking, Barba refers to both the incultured and accultured as colonizations of the body (1982a:21). Incultured behavior is a colonization which is generally perceived as "natural" since it is the norm in any given culture, but accultured behavior involves what could be termed a deconstruction/reconstruction colonization. During training the performer is required to deconstruct his normal way of moving, standing, and/or talking in order to replace it gradually with a newly acquired (reconstructed) technique, specifically designed for performance.[5] This is a "second naturalness" (Barba, 1988b:8), another form of body colonization.

In making the distinction between these different forms of colonization, however, Barba points out that the extra-daily is not limited to this "second naturalness." In codified performance forms, such as corporal mime and kathakali, extra-daily techniques are obvious since actors utilize learned body techniques in performance which are far removed from the way in which they walk, move, sit or stand in daily life. But Stanislavsky developed an extra-daily technique based entirely on inculturalization, on the concept of producing a stage fiction which mirrors daily life. A Stanislavsky trained performer learns vocal and physical techniques, as well as ways of simulating emotions, all of which are extra-daily, in order to reproduce, among other things, a convincing imitation of daily life on stage (Barba and Savarese, 1991:189).

The performer and the role

The dichotomous relationship between the role and the actor during performance is an important one for Barba. The representational world of the first, in which the fictional narrative of the play and the characters in it dominate the stage, is the primary domain of conventional theatre. The latter, on the other hand, which recognizes the actor's experience during the production as an integral part of the theatrical event, has become associated with the experimental theatre of the 1960s and 1970s – primarily through the theories and work of directors such as Grotowski and Schechner, who not only acknowledged the experience of the actor during performance, but made it a part of their esthetics.[6]

Barba's esthetics have much in common with these other experimentalists. He maintains that performance is neither entirely the fictional world of the play, nor the actor's experience in portraying it. It is the dialectic between these two, what Barba calls the anatomical theatre: a theatre in which the relationship between the "external surface of the actions and their internal parts" (1982a:37) is the central core of any production.

In Barba's theatre, an actor not only portrays the fictional score (i.e., the physical actions and vocal delivery decided upon in rehearsal and repeated in each performance), but also his/her meeting with it. Ryszard Cieslak, Grotowski's leading actor, in talking about this process in an interview with Schechner, used the metaphor of a candle contained within a glass to explain the difference between the score and his meeting with it during performances of *Akropolis*: "The score is like the glass inside which a candle is burning. The glass is solid, it is there, you can depend on it. It contains and guides the flame. But it is not the flame. The flame is my inner process each night. The flame is what illuminates the score, what the spectators see through the score" (in Schechner, 1977:19). Cieslak goes on to describe how the score remains the same but that the flame varies from performance to performance.

Variations in the flame, in the meeting with the score, are based on several factors in Barba's approach to performance: the audience's reaction to the piece, the actor's psycho-emotional responses to events on stage as well as in the theatre, and the actor's personal associations with particular actions and/or situations in a work s/he has developed with his/her colleagues over a period of some eighteen months to two years.

The tensions between these variables (i.e., the flame) and the score provide the means of realizing the anatomical theatre since the score provides a structured resistance ("the external surface of the actions") against which the actor struggles in order to display his/her inner processes:

The play is a tightly woven net, which we must break through in order to liberate, in an unforeseen moment, fragments of our past and our experiences.

Every evening the actors struggle with this net. Every evening they try to dissolve, to annul the rigid iron structure through which they reveal themselves and which makes them into actors and those who surround them into an audience.

39

The resistance that the performance opposes to testimony makes the play into an organism which changes form and turns the rehearsed gesture of the actor into a gesture which appears to have the force of an improvised reaction.

It is through the convergence of these opposite forces, that our personal experiences can reach others, and be transformed into a social experience: through theatre.

(Barba, 1979:134)

Unlike his mentor, Grotowski, for whom this convergence was the means by which the actor instigated a process of self-revelation that affected the spectator, Barba uses the convergence to enrich the relationship between the performer and his audience directly. This is because the emphasis in Barba's esthetics is on the interaction between the performer, his/her role, and the audience, rather than on the performer's catharsis that in turn induces a similar response in the audience.[7]

Sophisticated though this and other esthetic and sociological theories of his may be, Barba is essentially a practical man of the theatre. His theories are an attempt to understand his and his actors' work in the theatre, an attempt to come to terms with his own history. This history is intimately connected with the Odin Teatret, the NTL, and ISTA. Their history is his, and his history is theirs. The following chapters explore this history.

3

TRAINING

Barba's approach to training at the Odin Teatret is much closer in spirit to the biomechanics of Meyerhold than it is to the psychological realism of Stanislavsky. His work is in the vein of Europe's physical theatre tradition, created by people like Vsevolod Meyerhold, Julius Osterwa, and Jacques Copeau, in which physicalization and paralinguistic interpretation of the text take precedence over naturalism.

In these physically oriented theatres, training has always played a major role because of the physical and vocal demands made on the actor. This is equally true at the Odin, where training is the foundation of the group's entire esthetic: it is training that provided the basis for the company's unique dramaturgical and rehearsal processes; it is training which established both of the Odin's major production styles – the studio/theatre performances and the open-air street spectacles; and the research orientation of today's training continues to inform the creation of new theatre pieces.

Training has been a major factor in the Odin's approach to theatre since the company was formed in 1964. The initial working sessions were devoted entirely to training and the actors have continued to train ever since. This training usually consists of separate physical and vocal sessions because Barba believes it is necessary to explore physical and vocal rhythms independently to ensure that neither dominates the other. These sessions, which usually follow directly on from each other with little break between, have varied in length from the extreme of twelve hours per day to periods when there is little training at all. These variations reflect both the Odin's concept of training as a means of exploring the acting process and the evolution of Barba's ideas about training.

The major influences on the Odin's early training were, according to Barba, the experiments of the "Great Reform" – especially the work of Meyerhold, Stanislavsky, and Copeau; Oriental theatre – particularly kathakali and Beijing opera; and the work of Grotowski (Barba, 1979:76). The most important of these influences was Grotowski, since Barba had been his assistant immediately prior to forming the Odin. During Barba's years in Poland, Grotowski initiated his now famous "poor theatre" performer training program. Barba's exposure to it, combined with his knowledge of kathakali training, gained on his visit to the Kalamandalam training school in Kerala, India, in 1963, led him to establish an intensive training regimen when he formed his new company. This regimen focused on the acquisition of skills and later evolved into using training as a research tool.

The focus on skills in the Odin's early years was born of necessity because the young actors Barba recruited had little or no training. The fledgling company not only lacked experienced actors but also the funds to pay teachers. This disadvantage, like so many in the group's history, proved to be instrumental in establishing its unique approach to theatre. Because the actors could not afford teachers, they taught themselves. Members of the company with skills, no matter how rudimentary, taught them to the others. Gradually, in this way, the original members of the group developed a body of skills that formed the basis of their future training and that they were able to teach new actors as they joined the company.

The group's training was not as hermetic as this description may seem to imply, however, since several external factors contributed to its development. The Scandinavian workshops Barba organized when the group first moved to Holstebro, described in the Introduction, exposed the Odin actors to the techniques of major Western performers and directors as well as Oriental masters. In addition to these contacts, the actors attended workshops conducted by Asian performers of kathakali, noh, and topeng at the third theatre gatherings in Belgrade and Bergamo; and at these same gatherings other groups similar to the Odin demonstrated and discussed their approaches to training. Except for a few obvious examples, such as the influence of Grotowski, it is difficult to establish a direct connection between external factors and developments in the Odin's training. But, given the correlation between the group's present training and Oriental theatre, it is clear that this early exposure to Eastern masters has at least influenced the evolution of the group's training considerably.

The most important feature of this evolution has been the gradual shift in emphasis from skill-oriented training to the use of training as a research tool. As the company stabilized and ceased to take in new actors, the need to teach and learn basic skills became less necessary. In the best tradition of the autodidact, the actors turned their attention to developing their own individual training programs. The performers no longer concerned themselves with accumulating skills but rather with testing and exploring their own individual potentials and limitations. And, despite the fact that this focus on researching one's own potentialities as a performer has undergone many subtle changes over the years, it continues to form the basis of the Odin's training even today.

Needless to say, in a company that has been together for over twenty years there have been many changes, none more evident than in training. The present training, for instance, is different from the training ten years ago, which in turn is different from the training in the early 1960s. These changes may appear dramatic when viewed over such long intervals, but they have been more of a gradual evolution than a series of revolutionary developments.

PHYSICAL TRAINING

Beginnings (1964–1968)

When Barba formed the Odin he had little or no experience of working with actors. He had no formal theatre training other than his years as Grotowski's assistant, during which time his work with the performers consisted mainly of observing rehearsals and training sessions. Unsure of how to proceed with young, untrained performers, he asked each actor who joined the group for a detailed biography, including a list of any relevant skills. In this way two of the actors, one of whom had studied jazz ballet and gymnastics, and another who was familiar with pantomime, became the Odin's first teachers.

The group met and trained three nights per week. In these three-hour sessions Barba sat and observed while the actors learned the basics of jazz ballet, gymnastics, and pantomime. From time to time he passed comment on the work or helped the actors by assisting them with particularly difficult gymnastic exercises, but he never taught any practical skills.

After the first few weeks, Barba divided the classes. During the first one-and-a-half hours the group continued to study jazz ballet and pantomime while the second half of the class was devoted to acrobatics and exercises designed to develop physical precision. Building on the actors' early exposure to gymnastics, Barba introduced some of the acrobatic exercises – such as forward and backward rolls, body flips, head stands, shoulder stands, and handstands – he had observed at Grotowski's Laboratory.

Given the fact that the Polish Laboratory Theatre had been Barba's only practical theatre experience, it is understandable that other Grotowski exercises also became part of his group's training. These exercises included, among others, work with the facial and eye muscles as well as the famous cat exercise adapted from kathakali training.[1]

In addition to these "borrowed" exercises, Barba and his actors developed several martial art-type exercises of their own invention, including ones with short sticks in which two actors worked together in mock combat, and body contact exercises which called for the actors to face each other some 2 to 3 feet apart while each tried to touch the chest of the other with the sole of one foot as they moved around the room, much like sparring boxers.

Barba did not explain the cause-and-effect links between these exercises

43

and performance to the actors, no doubt largely due to the fact that he himself did not fully understand the connections at the time. He did, however, have specific reasons for introducing the exercises. His reason for placing so much emphasis on acrobatics, for example, was not so much to improve the performance skills of the actors but rather for the psychological benefit of setting them a difficult task which they could master reasonably quickly (Barba, 1982a:24). Similarly, he borrowed and adapted many kathakali exercises because of his fascination with its superb actors. He reasoned that, if he could adapt the Kalamandalam's models of discipline and of a way of life centered around rigorous training which gives actors precise control over their bodies, he would eventually produce equally skilled actors (Fowler, 1985b:2–3).

During these first months, when he began working with acrobatics and muscle control exercises, Barba also introduced improvisation into the training. The first improvisation exercises were very simple and relatively naturalistic. One of the exercises, for instance, involved miming the baking of a cake (Laukvik; 1985). Despite these modest beginnings, improvisation has proven to be the most important legacy from this period because it has since become not only the basis of the Odin's training but also the major source of its productions.

At the end of the first month, the training sessions were extended to four hours, and Barba began teaching the voice exercises he had observed at Grotowski's Laboratory. Part of each session was set aside for voice work, establishing the pattern of separate voice and physical training sessions which the company has maintained, with a few minor exceptions, to the present day.

During this same period the actor who had been teaching jazz ballet and gymnastics left the group, which gave Barba the latitude to introduce more new ideas into the training. He encouraged the actors to read the works of Meyerhold and Stanislavsky, and to look at Oriental theatre, particularly noh and kabuki (Barba, 1979:49; Wethal, 1985). Since there were no Japanese companies performing in Oslo at the time, most of the research into Oriental theatre consisted of reading and looking at photographs. The photographs of Asian actors performing proved especially useful, because they gave their Odin counterparts models to imitate in order to discover what physical adjustments were needed either to maintain certain poses or to facilitate movement in and out of these frozen tableaus.

This work, combined with the group's studies of Meyerhold's biomechanics, led to a major innovation in training. Barba and his actors developed a series of etudes which consisted of short movement sequences that were, in the words of one actor, "brief silent scenes made up entirely of physical actions" (Wethal, 1985). Even though these "silent scenes" owed much to Meyerhold, they were not reproductions of his biomechanics. The Odin's etudes were entirely original, developed by the actors through improvisation and, unlike Meyerhold's exercises, usually involved only one performer and were in a constant state of flux.[2]

At first the Odin's etudes consisted of set movement patterns which all the actors learned together. There were several of these original etudes, none of which has been documented because they were primarily sources of improvisation and remained fixed for only a short period of time. From what members of the company recall, however, they were basically a synthesis of their Eastern theatre studies and their earlier acrobatic work in which the actors used simple images – such as walking over a bed of damp leaves in a thick forest to reach out and touch a particular tree – as the basis of pantomime-like sequences of action (Wethal, 1985).

Despite the fact that Barba abandoned the etudes after only two years, they remain historically significant because they contained the seeds of what has dominated the company's training philosophy ever since: that training is a process of exploration, of constant evolution, rather than only a means of acquiring skills.

Barba changed the group's schedule radically in January 1965 when he began rehearsals for the Odin's first production, *Ornitofilene.* The actors now met from 9:00 a.m. to 5:00 p.m. five days a week, with each day divided into two sessions, the first for training from 9:00 a.m. to noon, and the second, from 1:00 p.m. to 5:00 p.m., devoted to rehearsals. From the beginning of these rehearsals, the group's creative energies were understandably focused on its first production. This is not to say that the actors or Barba dismissed the importance of training, but rather that there were no significant changes in it while the company was so preoccupied. The next major developments in training had to wait until the Odin moved to Holstebro, Denmark, in June 1966.

Only three of the original actors moved from Oslo to Holstebro, which meant that the group could no longer perform *Ornitofilene,* and that Barba had to recruit new actors. These new actors, like the original members of the Odin when they first joined the company, had little or no theatre experience. Faithful to the tradition established in Oslo, the more experienced actors became the teachers of the new recruits. Wethal, Laukvik, and Anne Trine Grimnes taught the new actors their system of training. Wethal, who had become an expert in the group's physical work, taught most of the acrobatic and muscle control exercises, while Laukvik and Grimnes taught the etudes.

With the emphasis on teaching there were no major innovations in the training during these initial months in Holstebro, but it was an important period in the group's history, nevertheless, because it was the first time that a "true" teacher–pupil relationship was established among the actors. In Oslo the actors had taught each other what they knew, but this was little more than the blind leading the blind, whereas almost two years later the more experienced actors had a significant body of knowledge to impart. As Wethal put it when I interviewed him:

When we moved to Denmark in '66 the company had changed. Only three of the original actors moved to Holstebro, so we met new people. This meant confronting yourself for the first time with pupils, being put in a situation where you had to explain yourself. These times of the first teaching are always important, they are when you realize your own experience. You start to understand what you are doing. That first time for me in Denmark was hard, you must understand that when I started with the Odin I had a body like a stick and no experience of physical theatre. Learning to do headstands and somersaults was so difficult ... and then to be teaching these things. It was not easy but it was all-important for me. I learned more than I taught. We all did.

(Wethal, 1985)

The teaching established a reflexivity among the actors which has played an important part in the development of the Odin's training over the years. So much so, in fact, that even today most actors at the Odin spend as much time thinking about possible avenues of exploration in their training as they do working physically and vocally in the studio.

No member of the group has devoted more time to the consideration of training than Barba. Most recently this consideration has been based on the comparative studies he has made between the training evolved by the Odin actors and his observations of various traditional Eastern forms. In these early years, however, he was preoccupied with adapting the kathakali approach to training for his company. The training he encouraged focused on developing technique, on building body strength, on increasing physical flexibility, and, above all, on mastering specific skills (Barba, 1979:76; 1985c). But a change was in the wind.

Composition exercises and individual rhythm in training (1968–1972)

During the development of the etudes, the actor's research included studying illustrated woodprints of kabuki actors. Barba and his colleagues observed that these prints conveyed a distinctive mood or character through emphasizing a part of the figure's body, such as the position of the feet and hands or the angle of the spinal column. Several of the actors began to work with the concept illustrated in the prints of accentuating particular parts of the body to capture what the artist viewed as the essence of the person who was being depicted. They explored stationary positions, movements through space such as twists and turns, as well as simple tasks like walking and running, at the same time accentuating a specific body part.

Eventually the actors extended this physical work to include not only the human body but also natural phenomena. They began exploring ways of using the hands, arms, and chest to physicalize elements like the wind, rain, and sunshine.

At the same time as the actors were developing their work with the kabuki prints, Grotowski and his leading actor Cieslak were invited to Holstebro to conduct the first in the series of Scandinavian workshops organized by Barba (1–15 July 1966). During these workshops, Grotowski and Cieslak explained two aspects of their recent research which had important implications for the development of training at the Odin: psycho-physicalization, and making a single exercise out of several different exercises strung together.

The actors at Grotowski's Laboratory had begun to explore the connections between physical action and the performer's inner processes. These experiments were based on the premise that an actor's physical actions can be colored by his/her inner reactions to an external stimulus (Grotowski, 1968:133–146). Grotowski's theory helped the Odin actors to a better understanding of their experiments with the kabuki prints and natural phenomena because it established a causal connection linking stimulus, inner processes, and physicalization. This clarification encouraged the group to experiment with a broader range of stimuli, including sounds, proximic variations, and interpersonal interaction, in order to appreciate how these influence physical actions (Laukvik, 1985).

Meanwhile, several of the Odin actors also began experimenting with Grotowski's idea of linking several exercises together to form a single unit. These actors were intrigued by the possibilities offered in the longer exercises, possibilities that allowed them to explore a greater range of physical movement than in the past, and that forced them to consider rhythm in training for the first time – as they attempted to discover the precise rhythm(s) that eliminated the points at which each individual exercise began and ended. The actors did not merely copy the Laboratory's exercises. They developed their own montages based on the skills, such as acrobatics and physicalization, that they were already working with (Laukvik, 1985). Gradually the entire company began experimenting with these montage exercises which, combined with their psycho-physical work, led to the next major innovation in the Odin's training, composition exercises.[3]

Barba defines composition as "the actor's ability to create signs, to mould his body consciously into a deformation which [is] rich in suggestiveness and power of association" (Barba and Savarese, 1991:244). Unlike the Odin's skill-oriented gymnastic and acrobatic work, Barba's composition exercises did not consist of specific tasks like body rolls or headstands. In fact, they incorporated virtually any series of movements, since the focus was not on the movements themselves but on the physical ideograms realized during the movements. These ideograms were made up of a combination of psycho-physical association and precise body control. A typical composition exercise, for instance, was using the image of a snake to influence one's movements through space. This use of the snake image did not mean that the actor imitated or illustrated the movements of a snake, but that s/he explored various actions – such as twisting, turning, walking, dancing, moving in and out of a seated position, tumbles, and cartwheels, as well as variations in speed and rhythm – while retaining the mental image of a snake. That is, the psychological image influenced how the movements were done, rather than initiated them.

There were no pre-established composition exercises that actors had to learn. Each performer was free to choose his/her images and to interpret them in whatever way s/he wished. Once an actor had developed a sequence of actions, however, s/he continued to work with it until s/he had exhausted all the psycho-physical connections between the actions and the image they were based on, and until s/he could repeat every movement precisely.

As the actors slowly mastered composition exercises and began to integrate them into their training, Barba noticed several changes. He realized that there was a subtle rebellion in the group against heavy, physical work, and that equally subtle changes in speed and spatial dimension were developing in the actors' montage exercises.

At the same time as he observed these changes Barba became aware that when the actors strung a chain of exercises together the results varied from actor to actor. Part of this variation was understandable, since each actor was free to develop his/her own composition exercise. But what struck Barba was that, even though all the actors had basically the same repertory of skills, each had his/her own way of stringing these skills together. On reflection he realized that these variations were not so much dependent on the different ways in which each actor executed a cartwheel or body roll as to individual differences in rhythm.

This realization, coupled with the actors' tendency to avoid extreme physical work, led the company to begin investigations of individual rhythms. The more experienced actors developed chains of exercises which included gymnastic floor exercises like forward and backward rolls with and without the use of hands, headstands, shoulder stands, and cartwheels, and they continued the mock combat work in pairs, described earlier. But there was a shift in focus in these exercises, from using them to develop skills to using them as a means of exploring one's own, individual rhythm.

Regardless of these new developments in training, the tradition of older actors teaching new arrivals continued. Everyone who came to the company was taught a basic repertory of skills. When Larsen joined the group in 1970, for example, he was taught acrobatics by Wethal, gymnastic floor exercises by Rasmussen, and composition by Laukvik (Larsen, 1985). Once the new actors had mastered these skills they linked three or four exercises together as their more experienced colleagues did, and began searching for their own rhythms within the montage by repeating the sequence of exercises at different speeds, in different directions, and with different degrees of intensity. For both the new and the old, training became a process of personalizing the work through a regimen of daily self-discipline.

Despite Barba's awareness of the actors' subtle protests against heavy physical work, the training sessions were often very long and arduous during this period, which lasted for some two to two-and-a-half years in the late 1960s and early 1970s. The group frequently trained eight to twelve hours per day, six days a week, with half of the day devoted to teaching the new actors and the other half to working individually. For the new actors many of the gymnastic exercises were particularly difficult to master, and the long hours, combined with the intensity of the work, were exhausting for even the most experienced performers.

These long hours of work were primarily due to a shift in Barba's thinking. In addition to viewing training as a means of acquiring skills, he now realized that it could also be used to build endurance. He further realized that endurance introduced a mental component into the training since long, tiring hours of intense work not only developed the actors' physical stamina but also helped build what Barba called a "muscular psyche." That is, he induced a somatic state in the actors by pushing them to their physical limits for extended periods, in which they achieved break-throughs in their physical work that they would otherwise have been unable to realize (Barba, 1985c). Rasmussen, for instance, joined the company when it first moved to Holstebro in 1966 and was involved in all the training and in every performance from then until rehearsals for *Min Fars Hus* in 1970–71. During this period her voice, which has since become one of her most important tools, was, according to both herself and Barba, thin and lacking in projection (Rasmussen, 1985; 1986; Barba, 1985c). Immediately prior to and during rehearsals for *Min Fars Hus*, the Odin's training was at its most intense, with the actors working twelve hours per day. Rasmussen, like everyone else, was tired and constantly being pushed to her physical and psychological limits. During one of the seemingly endless vocal training sessions, according to Barba who was present at the time, Rasmussen "suddenly, and without warning, found her voice which changed from its normal thin texture to a rich, sonorous instrument that she was able to manipulate freely for the first time" (1985a). Rasmussen recalls the break-through as being a more gradual process:

> Everything in the training prior to *Min Fars Hus* was as if I was a pupil, I was still uncertain and I had not found what was my own. I never doubted what I was doing but I also knew that I had not found what I could do or say. Just before and during *Min Fars Hus* doors began to open. We were working very long hours training and rehearsing. It was during this intense work that I found my own voice, I found what was my own way out of exhaustion or through pushing past what blocked me. From here I had a beginning, a place to discover who I am as an actress.

(1985)

49

Regardless of whether the breakthrough was immediate or more gradual, it was no magical event; Rasmussen had worked toward it for five years, and she has continued to build on it ever since. But she dates the realization of her vocal potential to this period in mid-1970 in which, out of exhaustion and the confrontation with her own limitations, she extended herself beyond what she thought she was capable of achieving.

Individual training and Barba's exit from the studio (1972–1974)

Rasmussen's realization of her vocal potential made her aware of other possibilities in the training. Prior to 1970, the group's training essentially consisted of all the actors doing variations on a given set of exercises. Everyone learned the same basic skills, which they linked together in a sequence of three or four exercises to form a single montage exercise, so that, even though each actor's montage was different, its component elements were identical. Rasmussen's vocal discovery made her aware that these exercises were not extending her as fully as they might, so she began to use her montage exercises as the basis for further physical and vocal improvisations. These experiments proved so successful that gradually, over a period of several months, she developed a sequence of exercises which she felt best served and challenged her own potentials and limitations.

Even though collective training continued during this period, Rasmussen's experiments did not go unnoticed, and there was a great deal of discussion between her, Barba, and her fellow actors. Gradually everyone began to develop their own training, and eventually, between 1972 and 1973, collective training was abandoned altogether. Each actor now explored what s/he felt was important for him/her, but within the supportive environment of a single room where others were engaged in similar research.

This research varied from performer to performer, but everyone followed the same basic steps: each actor used improvisation to explore a particular area s/he wanted to work on, gradually built a training exercise out of his/her discoveries which s/he worked with until s/he felt s/he had exhausted its potential, then abandoned it and began the cycle over again. Larsen, for example, developed a series of improvisations based on the physical impulse exercises he was introduced to by Cieslak while they were working together in 1972 on a film about Grotowski's performer training methods. He chose sections from these improvisations as separate exercises, which he then linked together into a single montage. He worked with this montage exercise, repeating it many times, learning to control it both backward and forward, experimenting with varying speeds of execution in different segments of the exercise, and moving in different directions through space while doing it. This constant process of exploration and repetition helped him to discover his own rhythm within the exercise, as well as to gain precise control over his body, balance, and center of gravity. These discoveries were then incorporated into the exercise as he attempted to gain complete mastery over it by reproducing it precisely in his own organic rhythm. Once he felt he had gained mastery over the exercise, he abandoned it, and began the procedure over again, because Barba and his actors thought that continuing to work with an exercise you were no longer exploring meant that you were merely reproducing a learned skill, rather than using the exercise as a tool for personal research.

The development of individual work confirmed a gradual shift of focus in the Odin's training that had begun during the experiments with composition and individual rhythm: a shift from training concerned with accumulating skills (or "product") to one focused on process. Barba's preoccupation with kathakali in the group's formative years, combined with the inexperience of his actors, prompted him to center the group's training on learning and developing techniques. As their research gradually led to the emergence of composition exercises and they began to explore personal rhythm, however, they became less concerned with acquiring new skills. In composition exercises, for example, the actor's focus was on exploring his/her own rhythm and the balance of opposing tensions in his/her body, rather than on learning a skill such as how to execute a perfect backward somersault.

The shift from product-oriented training to a training concerned with process was taken a step further with the development of individual training. Despite the fact that each actor could now choose what s/he would work on, the focus in the training was always on exploring rhythmical patterns, physical precision, the balance of body tensions, and on the relationship between relaxation, momentum, and acceleration, that is, on *doing* the exercise. This focus meant that the actors had to have mastery over a skill they chose to work with, otherwise they would be preoccupied with learning the skill rather than being able to use it as a training tool. Thus, if an actor chose to work with a skill s/he did not have, s/he first learned the skill – in what might be termed a "pre-training" period – before using it in his/her training proper.

The distinction between learning and using skills in training was particularly evident with new actors. When Pardeilhan and Varley joined the company in the mid-1970s, for instance, they were taught a variety of skills, such as acrobatics, and the gymnastic-oriented floor exercises, by the more experienced actors. During this learning period, they were gradually introduced into the group training sessions in which the older actors were developing their individual work. But, according to Varley, it was only after a considerable period of time that these sessions were productive for the new recruits because their entire energies were devoted to learning what for them were new and difficult techniques:

When you start doing this work it is difficult. You can start by saying find me five different ways of walking. And Tage [Larsen, her teacher] will be watching and he will say, "Yes, keep that one, fix it." So you remember it ... things like, before you put your foot down make the step a bit longer, change the rhythm. And at the end, after years these things become part of you without even thinking about it.

(1985)

The personalization of training was a natural development, stemming from the Odin's early autodidactic tradition in which the actors taught each other. Despite their initial inexperience, the members of the group developed an impressive array of skills during these formative years. Rather than continuing to accumulate skills, however, they began to use those they had mastered to explore the processual nature of training. Each performer developed his/her own set of exercises, the inevitable result of which was a highly individualized form of training, as is obvious from Taviani's brief description of a training session he observed in the late 1970s:[4]

Some actors begin with gymnastics, while others run or do acrobatic exercises. Then slowly, everything is transformed. The room becomes animated by images, costumes and props appear and disappear: two actors twist and turn on unicycles, like circus acrobats; Kathakali scenes appear as sudden flashes, and funny or tragical characters, a chanteuse and a witch, a clown on skates, a waltz; a man in tails dances, as if an electric current is running through him; a swordsman duels with his shadow, the colors of Bali burst forth, followed immediately by the bright presence of the mute Kathrine from Mother Courage.

(1979:56)

The ascendancy of the individual led to Barba's exit from training. For almost the entire first decade of the group's existence Barba was present at every training session. During its formative years, he was primarily a guide and disciplinarian who suggested areas of work, but rarely taught. He was the constant observer, often intervening to assist an actor in a particular exercise or to offer advice. With the shift in focus from skill acquisition to process, and then the emergence of individuality, Barba gradually ceased to function as the leader of the training sessions. He now allowed the actors to explore whatever they chose out of discussion with him and/or their colleagues.

As individuality began to dominate training, Barba also became involved with various commitments outside of the Odin. He was invited to teach workshops in different parts of Europe, he was on the board of the Theatre of Nations Festival, and he was busy with initial planning for the first third theatre gathering. The fact that these commitments frequently took him away from Holstebro, combined with a philosophy in which the individual actor is responsible for his/her own training, led Barba to remove himself from training. So much so, in fact, that today it is rare for him to attend training at all. In the Odin of the 1990s training is entirely the domain of the actor.

Requisites in the training (1974–1975)

Barba's departure from the training studio was a gradual process taking several years, but, prior to his final exit, he organized two lengthy residencies in southern Italy that were to have a major impact on the Odin's future training. During these residencies – the first in Carpignano from May to October in 1974, the second divided between Carpignano and Sardinia between August and October the following year – the company began rehearsals for its new production, *Come! And the Day Will be Ours*, and continued its regimen of daily training. Most of the rehearsals and training sessions were now held either in the courtyard of the villas they lived in or in the fields surrounding the villages. This move, from the confined studios in Holstebro into the open air of southern Italy, inevitably affected the group's training, and eventually produced an entirely new relationship between training and performance.

The roots of this changed relationship lay in the group's exploration of requisites (i.e., hand props) as training tools. A short time after their arrival in southern Italy, two of the actors, Rasmussen and Jens Christensen, began training with sticks which had long colorful ribbons attached, flags, spear-like poles, and various types of drum. Barba saw their work and, considering its use of large areas of space to be a direct response to training in the open air, suggested that the other actors might also use these and other props in their training, as well as musical instruments such as piano accordions, flutes, and cymbals.

Despite the innovative nature of this work with requisites, the training model changed little. Each actor continued to develop his/her own training, using improvisation to build up a chain of movements that s/he strung together as a single exercise. The focus in the training continued to be on personalizing the exercise, but the personalization was now expanded to include how one worked with the requisite. By examining how to work with the requisite as a partner, how to use it as an extension of the body, and playing with the differences between its daily use and how it could be used theatrically, each actor explored the creative possibilities of the prop. As Rasmussen put it, "we were searching for the life in the requisite" (ISTA, 1980).

Through a combination of circumstances, including the climate, the lack of a prepared performance, and the demands of the local population to see the work of the actors, the company began developing open air-performances and street-theatre pieces during their 1974 stay in southern

Italy. The first of these productions, *Johan Sebastian Bach* (1974), was a simple clown performance based on workshops done in Holstebro with the Italian clown duo, the Colombaioni Brothers. When several different groups of villagers asked to see more of the work, however, other performances were also prepared which were basically nothing more than demonstrations of the company's training exercises. These demonstrations were so effective that Barba and his actors eventually developed an entire production based on the training, *The Book of Dances* (1974), the success of which led to the creation of *Anabasis* (1977) and *The Million* (1979).

Most of these street-theatre pieces required the actors to learn new skills. In order to be seen above the heads of the crowds, for example, the company began to work with stilts, which the actors had never used before. Similarly, several members learned how to rappel down the side of village buildings. And company members began to develop their musical skills because most of the street pieces called for dances, fanfares, and parades done to live musical accompaniment. The majority of these skills were practiced away from the formal training sessions, which were usually held from early morning until midday. But once a particular skill had been developed to a reasonable degree of proficiency, it invariably found its way into the training.

Apprentices (1974–1977)

The next development in the Odin's training did not so much produce a fundamental change in the group's approach as reassert the teacher–student relationship. Prior to its residencies in Italy, the group invariably disbanded at the end of one production and re-formed after a short break to rehearse its next work. These rehearsals generally lasted anywhere from twelve to eighteen months, then the new production was performed and toured for about three years. During this touring period, Barba usually recruited new actors whom he and the more experienced actors trained between tours. These new actors, along with those from the previous production who were invited or wished to remain, formed the company which then began rehearsals for the next piece.

While in residence in southern Italy in 1974, Barba realized that he had a group of committed actors who wanted to continue working together. He therefore no longer felt the need to replace anyone and decided to close the company to new recruits. This is not to say that he denied access to the Odin's experience, but rather that he made it available in a very different way.

In 1974, following their stay in southern Italy, and again in 1975, Barba organized two eight-month training sessions in Holstebro for members of what he called the International Brigade. As the name implies, this brigade was made up of people from several countries who had expressed an interest in learning more about the Odin's approach to theatre. Members of the brigade – which consisted mainly of Italians, but also included theatre workers from Spain, France, and Germany – studied primarily with the Odin actors and occasionally under Barba himself, with the understanding that they would take back what they had learned to their own countries and teach others. Following the 1974 session, two members of the brigade – Toni Cots from Spain and Sylvia Ricciardelli from Italy – wanted to remain at the Odin and continue their training. Consistent with his decision to retain the status quo, Barba refused to allow them to join the group.

Rasmussen did not entirely endorse Barba's decision. She agreed with him on the stability of the company, but she felt that it was also important to pass on her knowledge and experience. As she herself put it, "Once, everyone at the Odin thought that there were enough actors, and that new ones weren't necessary. For me, the problem was to transmit, to feel that what we had acquired did not stop with us. I had no choice but to show in practice that Eugenio and those who thought with him were wrong" (1979:11). Late in 1974, therefore, inspired by seventeenth- and eighteenth-century actor training methods, she decided to "adopt" Cots and Ricciardelli as apprentices, taking full responsibility not only for their training, but also for housing and feeding them.

Early in 1976, Larsen followed Rasmussen's lead and "adopted" an apprentice of his own, Francis Pardeilhan, who had been following the group's work off and on for twelve months. Later the same year, he took a second apprentice, Julia Varley, who joined Pardeilhan and Larsen in Holstebro.

On arriving in Holstebro, the apprentices either lived with their teachers or rent-free in the Odin theatre complex. They paid a share of the food and were entirely responsible for personal expenses such as clothing. Barba, meanwhile, said nothing but ignored their existence.

All of the apprentices were initially taught the skills that formed the basis of the Odin's training – that is, the gymnastic-oriented floor exercises, composition, acrobatics, and voice. The adoptive leaders were primarily responsible for this training. However, they recruited other members of the company, as well as outside teachers from time to time. Wethal, for instance, was the major acrobatics instructor, and both Pardeilhan and Varley studied mime with Ingmar Lindh.

Most of the apprentice's training was mimetic, much as in traditional Asian performer training. The teacher demonstrated the exercise and the pupil attempted to copy it. Eventually the apprentice was able to reproduce a rough outline of the exercise. S/he then used the same methods the more experienced actors employed to control and explore the exercise: repetition, moving the exercise backward and forward, variations in speed, and expanding and contracting the exercise spatially.

In addition to this general training, both groups of apprentices worked extensively on areas of specific interest to their adoptive leaders. These areas included an exploration of various folk and social dances instigated by

Rasmussen with Cots and Ricciardelli, and Larsen's work with Pardeilhan and Varley using large props such as flags and spear-like poles.

After the apprentices had learned some of the basic skills, they were invited to join the collective training sessions in which each actor was developing and working with his/her own set of exercises. This was both a difficult and rewarding time for the new recruits. Their lack of many of the basic Odin skills meant that much of the training was difficult and, as Varley described earlier, the focus of their energies was on merely being able to do many of the exercises rather than on using them to develop their own training.

Despite these difficulties, the collective training sessions were an important part of the apprentices' gradual integration into the Odin. As trainees, the apprentices did not perform with the company, and, since the two groups of apprentices had different master teachers with different interests, they did not generally train together. The collective training sessions were therefore the only time in which the apprentices were together, and when they worked as equals with their more experienced colleagues. This was also one of the few occasions when they had direct access to Barba, who at this stage still attended many of the training sessions. Pardeilhan describes the experience:

> I was alone, really. Julia was with Tage mostly, so I was alone with Sylvia and Toni, but we didn't have much contact because they were Iben's.... but in the beginning training was the only situation in which I could meet others. At first it was Tage, then later, because the training was collective, Eugenio. It was the only situation in which I could confront others as some kind of equal. I could meet the resistances of my body and the others. In those days, Eugenio was still sitting in the corner observing training. Not that he would say anything, especially to me or the other apprentices. But many times he would walk up to one or other of the Odin actors and whisper suggestions in a low voice. Sometimes he would stop and we would all watch while one person worked on the floor with Eugenio. We were there together.
>
> (1985)

Eventually the two groups of apprentices began working together on the clown piece *Johan Sebastian Bach*, which had been developed by their colleagues in 1974 in southern Italy. They then toured the production in Denmark under the name of Hogin (one of the birds that flies around the god Odin as he rides his horse) during late 1976 and into 1977, which provided them with their first income as fledgling members of the company. Barba, having worked briefly with the apprentices for the first time when he insisted on tidying the production prior to its going on tour, followed their success with *Johan Sebastian Bach* and their development in the training studio. He was so impressed that he invited them to join their more

56

experienced colleagues in creating the street theatre production, *Anabasis*. By mid-1977 the apprentices were full members of the Odin.

A pause in the training (1976–1977)

During the early apprenticeship period, from roughly 1974 to 1977, there was a general movement away from the intense training of the Odin's formative years. Prior to 1974, everyone had to train and the training schedule was rigidly adhered to. These rules began to change in response to various developments, however, the most important of which was the evolution of individual training. This development, combined with Barba's exit from the studio, meant that the actors were not only responsible for their own training, but that they had also lost the director who was previously following and encouraging their work.

While these changes were taking place, several of the company's leading actors developed interests outside of their immediate training and performance commitments. Rasmussen's and Larsen's teaching took up much of their day, for example, and Wethal devoted a great deal of his time to film-making.

Despite these changes, the Odin continued to perform, but company members trained only when and if they wanted. In fact, according to Taviani, regular scheduled training was abandoned altogether during this period (1979:53). But this break in the training regimen was short-lived, as the more experienced actors gradually returned to the studio revitalized from their sabbatical, and as the apprentices eventually became full members of the company.

The fishtank (1977–1981)

The renewed interest in the studio led to yet another important development in training. When the actors returned to their regular daily schedule, they continued to base their work on psycho-physically oriented improvisations. But, within a year, their focus of attention had shifted from the psycho-physical to what the group regarded as the root source of all physical and vocal expression, energy. This shift in focus meant that the actors were now more concerned with the technical problems of how to control their physical and vocal instruments, in order to engage and give expression to their energy, than with the quasi-psychological connections between an imagined stimulus and the response it elicits.[5]

Not only was this work more technically oriented, but it eliminated part of the previous training model, as well as altering the relationship between the exercise and the source it was drawn from. The psycho-physical work began with an image that colored the actor's responses. S/he then selected segments of these improvised responses and developed a single montage exercise from them, thus retaining the original connection to the psycho-logical image that inspired them. In the energy-oriented work, however, the actors used technical tasks – such as balancing opposing tensions in the body, or being able to repeat an action precisely – rather than imagery to structure improvisations. Unlike the preceding exercise, in which the original stimulus is at the core of the exercise, in this approach the exercise is structured by the task at hand.

The shift in emphasis, from a response-based training to one concerned with structuring and articulating one's energy, owed its origins to the Odin's earlier composition work, and a renewed interest in performances from other cultures, especially Asian. Several of the actors had incorporated elements of their earlier composition work into their individual training. Composition consists of two basic components, the psycho-physical use of imagery to influence one's movement, and the composition of different parts of the body through a balance of oppositions and tensions. Consistent with the Odin's tendency toward physical disciplines, the composition work gradually moved away from its psycho-physical concerns, and the actors began to focus their attention exclusively on body composition. This shift in emphasis meant that the actors were no longer as interested in developing exercises influenced by images, like the snake image exercise described earlier, as they were in developing exercises that explored different align-ments of the spine, different centers of gravity, or different ways of moving through space (Laukvik, 1985). It was only a small step from these composi-tion exercises, based entirely on technical control of the body, to a training concerned with how the actor engages and structures his/her energies.

At the same time as these changes were taking place in composition exercises, there was a revival of interest at the Odin in performances from outside the mainstream of the Euro-American theatre tradition. This resur-gence owed much to the preliminary work on what eventually became *The Million.* From the end of January to the end of April, 1978, Barba called a three-month break in the rehearsals for *Brecht's Ashes 2,* during which most of the actors chose to research and study a performance form they were unfamiliar with. Two of the actors, Varley and Larsen, remained in Denmark to study ballroom dancing, Laukvik went to Haiti where she studied mask making and voodoo, Pardeilhan and Carreri went to Brazil to learn the capoeira (a dance based on an ancient form of street fighting), Tom Fjordefalk studied kathakali in India, and Rasmussen and her apprentices, Cots and Ricciardelli, went to Bali to learn baris and legong.

Despite the fact that many of the Odin's actors had been exposed to traditional Eastern performance during their years with Barba, the experi-ences in Bali and India had a major impact on the group's subsequent training. This influence was initially most obvious in the training of those who went to the East. The actors who learned kathakali, baris, and legong all studied with teachers in their native villages. Their training, though much shorter than that undertaken by the local people, was done in the traditional way – that is, learning a set repertoire of dances by attempting to imitate their masters, with a minimal amount of discussion or explanation. Since their training was relatively short, they spent a great part of it learning the technical aspects of the particular form they were studying – such as choreographed steps, hand positions, and body movements – rather than the myths or theories underlying the work.

On their return to Holstebro, parts of what they learned found their way into *The Million*. But, in addition to this immediate application, the actors began to adapt their training to their Eastern experiences. Since these experiences had been primarily technical, it was these technical elements that they adapted most readily. Following his studies in Bali, for instance, Cots explored the use of opposing tensions in the body, controlling different parts of the hand, and alterations in the spinal column and center of gravity in his training (Gough, 1979:3–4). After his exposure to kathakali, Fjordefalk began to work with different movements based on the circle, with lowering his center of gravity, and with using the hands as a means of expression (Pearson, 1979:6–7).

The influence of traditional Asian performance on the training of those company members who did not study in the East was less direct than on those who went to Bali and India. This is not to say, however, that it was less important. Actors such as Pardeilhan, Varley, and Carreri did not use Asian forms as a source of training research, but they discovered an empathy with the codification of the forms that their colleagues shared with them. They, and others at the Odin, recognized codification in their own work which paralleled that of the East. But, unlike the codes of baris or kathakali which are traditional and passed on from master to pupil, the Odin actors' performance codes are individual. These codes are developed over a period of years from a combination of training, rehearsals and daily life, and they vary from performer to performer. Nevertheless, the performance knowledge embedded in these traditional codes struck a responsive note in Barba and his actors. They recognized that many of the ways in which these codes helped project presence on stage – through structuring the actors' movements in precise patterns, counterbalancing tensions in the body, and requiring alterations in balance – shared much in common with similar ideas underlying their own, individual codes.

These concerns with codification, physical precision, and energy led to a training session being referred to as a "fishtank." As in the earlier individual training period, each actor continued to create his/her own exercises while working in the same studio as his/her fellow actors. It is likely, despite the emphasis on individuality in the past, that the actors had influenced each other while they were working. This influence was not acknowledged, however, until the shift in emphasis to energy, at which time it was realized that one actor could affect the work of another, without either of them consciously attempting to interact. In the late 1970s and early 1980s the group used a fishtank metaphor to describe the phenomenon. The actors were like fish in a pool, each swimming and exploring his/her own territory alone. But, despite this apparent isolation, each movement and change in direction reverberated through the "water" and influenced everyone.

As in the past, repetition played a large part in the exploration of these fishtank exercises, but, with the new awareness of how each actor was influencing his/her colleagues, it took on an added dimension. No longer were performers focusing entirely on themselves; they now had to contend with the added variable of their response to others. The actors' solution to exploring these dual influences on their improvisations and the exercises they developed from them was to repeat material many times, initially focusing on each variable separately and then in combination. Repetition became such an important part of the work during this phase that they introduced a new word into their training lexicon, fastlegge (to fix), which Barba used when he wanted an actor to repeat and improve a particular sequence of actions.

During this fastlegge/fishtank period, Barba's realization of the connections between traditional Asian performance and the work of the Odin actors prompted him to begin a systematic study of various Eastern forms such as odissi dance from India, Balinese legong and topeng, as well as Japan's noh and kabuki. These studies eventually led to the next, and present stage of development in the Odin's training.

Principles East and West (1981–1991)

An Odin training session today is not what one might expect of training. The following description is from notes I made while observing a training session in the summer of 1985:

Barba is not present. There are five actors in the room, three women and two men, all working separately. Following a brief warm-up, consisting of simple stretch exercises, the actors begin to work on their individual activities. Actress 1 is sitting in a deck chair. She moves her right arm across her body, then her left arm. She moves her head from right to left, then up and down. All actions are slow, precise, and punctuated with a brief pause. She sits up in the deck chair, she sits back, she sits up again, then repeats this up and down action several more times. During these actions her trunk appears to move as one unit, with no curve in the spine or separation between chest and waist.

Meanwhile, Actor 1 moves to the back of the room and begins to do a tap dance type shuffle. He raises his arms in the classical ballet position and spins around several times. He lowers his arms and begins what appears to be a simple dance. The top half of his body does not seem to be engaged in the dance. He stops suddenly and does several shoulder stands, returning to the upright position each time. He lunges into the shoulder stands, but has great control and executes them precisely. He returns once more to a simple dance and moves around the room, occasionally breaking into the tap dance shuffle he began with.[6]

This brief description of one session typifies most of today's training. It is obvious from this and other sessions that the actors possess various skills, such as gymnastic and pantomimic techniques. It is evident that they have supple, flexible bodies, and that they are able to reproduce actions precisely. The work is also clearly different from most of the previous training since the performers are no longer repeating and exploring the same exercise continually. But, despite the actors' skills and these changes, there seems to be little or no connection with traditional Eastern performance, which Barba maintains that there is. Further analysis reveals that such a connection does exist, however, but that this connection is based on a set of underlying principles common to both, rather than on the Odin mimicking the East.

The importance of acting principles in the group's training can be traced directly to Barba's studies of Eastern performance. According to Barba, he first became interested in Asian performers because he was fascinated by their ability to project a powerful presence on stage. This fascination prompted him to begin researching Oriental theatre with the express aims of discovering the source of the presence:

> I couldn't understand how Oriental actors, even during a cold, techni-
> cal demonstration, always retained a very striking presence which
> inevitably captures one's attention. In such a situation the actor is not
> interpreting or expressing anything. Yet he seems to have a kernel of
> radiating energy, evocative, knowledgeable, and yet unpremeditated,
> capturing our attention and magnetizing our senses. For years I
> thought it was a question of technique, understood as skill. But in trying
> to go beyond this habitual definition, I realized that what we call
> technique is in fact a particular use of the body.
>
> (Barba, 1986:115)

Barba's research was directed toward discovering the relevance of what he saw in Asian performance for Western actors. But he rejected the idea of Western actors merely reproducing Eastern forms. He reasoned that Westerners could study forms such as kathakali or noh but since they, like most other traditional genres, involve a lifetime of study begun at a young age, the results would be poor imitations of the original. He further reasoned that the greatest value for those training in the West is to use Eastern ideas to explore their own training (1985a).

Barba's interest in cross-culturalism found an echo in the 1977–1980 Theatre of Sources Project of his mentor, Grotowski. The intercultural nature of the project, in which Grotowski explored the connections between ritual and ceremonial practices in different cultures, inspired Barba to draw direct parallels between Eastern forms and the Odin actors' training (Barba, 1986a:156).[7] Through this comparative study Barba was able to conceptualize two of the fundamental elements of Oriental forms that contribute to the actor's commanding stage presence: the use of learned body techniques designed to break the performer's automatic daily responses, and the codification of principles which dictate the use of energy during performance.

In daily life, much of our physical action is automatic because of constant repetition. Our body "knows" how to accomplish relatively complex tasks, like walking and climbing stairs, without our having to think through the various muscular adjustments involved, because we have done them so often. In Eastern traditional forms such as kathakali and noh, on the other hand, the body is intentionally distorted, constituting what Barba refers to as extra-daily technique. As was discussed in Chapter 2, this extra-daily technique is a major source of actor presence during performance, according to Barba, since it establishes a pre-expressive mode in which the actor's energies are engaged prior to personal expression.

Personal expression in traditional Eastern performance is rigidly codified, and can vary greatly from one form to another. Barba's studies revealed that, despite these differences, the codes incorporate similar principles which dictate the body's use of energy.[8] Through his knowledge of the similarly codified Western forms of mime and ballet, Barba realized that many of these same principles are part of the Western tradition. The principle of opposing body tensions, for example, is a major component of mime, and the alteration of normal equilibrium is a fundamental element of ballet. He further realized, in observing the individual training of his Odin actors, that they were employing similar principles without being aware of them.

These discoveries led to a re-evaluation of training which produced a gradual shift in emphasis at the Odin: from concerns with energy to a training based on the principles underlying performative action.

The actors continue to use improvisation in training, but its role has changed greatly. Instead of developing a chain of exercises which they repeat, they select principles they wish to explore, and use them as the basis of different improvisations in each training session. The physical form of the exercises, that is, the movement and action patterns, changes from session to session. The principles underlying the exercises remain the same, however. As the Odin's Carreri described it, "training is improvisation structured by the application of principles" (1985). A simple example, cited by her colleague Wethal, clarifies what she meant:

> To stand on one's head involves mastering particular technical skills such as placement of the hands, legs, and head, and the adjustment of body weight and balance. It also involves the principle of shifting the body's weight quickly so that one is off-balance, finding a point of

equilibrium which is held for a period, and returning to the normal body position. Standing on one's head is a skill that has to be learned, the principle underlying it, meanwhile, can be applied to many situations including walking, sitting, and working with a requisite.

(Wethal,1985)

Physical training at the Odin today focuses on exploring this and similar principles. In the training session quoted from my diary above, for example, the actress working with the deck chair told me after the session that during her training that day she had worked with several principles at different times, including moving with one part of the body at a time, leading all movement with the eyes, and segmenting various sections of the body. What appeared to be haphazard movements were, in fact, strictly monitored by adherence to consciously chosen principles.

There is nothing mystical about the Odin's principles. Most experienced Western actors and dancers use them, either consciously or unconsciously, when performing. One commonly sees principles such as alternating one's balance to create a dynamic stage presence, shifting the center of gravity to engage certain muscles for the same effect, the use of counter impulse in which a movement begins in the opposite direction to that in which it will finally proceed, working with different resistances and opposing tensions in the body, continual changes in rhythm, and the importance of the eyes and eye contact in aiding concentration on stage. The difference between the Odin's use of these principles and that of most other Western performers is that the Odin actors use them as training tools, while the majority of actors use them as devices that aid a particular performance.

The use of performance principles as a source of training is an endless process. Actors work with one or several related principles for extended periods, applying them to a broad range of different activities from walking to running to dancing, and even gymnastic exercises such as somersaults and shoulder stands. Once an actor feels s/he has mastered the particular principles s/he is working on, however, it is time to move on to another cycle of exploring new principles because there is a danger that mastered principles will produce mechanical actions. As Carreri put it, "training is a constant process of becoming" (1985). It is this "constant process" which has led to so many changes in the company's training over the years, changes which no doubt will continue to feed even further developments in the future.

VOCAL TRAINING

Despite the fact that the Odin's vocal and physical training have invariably been separate, the group's investigations of the voice have evolved in much the same way as its physical work. In the early years, members of the company focused on learning and developing vocal techniques, and, as they acquired these, the emphasis shifted from skill acquisition to a process-oriented training. This move from product to process has not involved as many changes, nor has it produced as many developments as in the group's physical research. But the history of the Odin's vocal training is a rich and important one nevertheless.

Beginnings (1964–1972)

When the group was initially formed in 1964, voice was not part of the training program. It was only after the first month of working together, when training sessions were extended to four hours, that Barba himself began teaching voice. Following what he observed at the Polish Laboratory, Barba avoided the traditional theatre school approach to voice with its emphasis on projection and clarifying linguistic meaning through skills like diaphragm control, rib reserve breathing, and enunciation. He preferred, instead, to teach Grotowski's resonator exercises, and explore the paralinguistic potential of the voice.

The early voice work focused on five resonators: the back and top of the head, the mouth, the chest, and the stomach. None of the original exercises have been documented, but they involved a combination of imagery and placement of the voice. Using vocables rather than words, the actors imagined the sound as coming from the particular resonator they were working on, so that the sound, which originated with the breath and vocal cords, was placed in, and amplified by, one or other of the particular resonators. Once they were able to control these resonators at will, the actors repeated the process with spoken texts, and explored the resonation quality of other parts of the body, such as the hands, shoulders, and knees (Wethal, 1972; ISTA, 1980; Rasmussen, 1986).[9]

As they gradually mastered the use of resonators, the members of the group broadened their interest in voice to an examination of what Barba termed "vocal scores." This research included studies of the voice in Oriental theatre, jazz, and even musical hybrids such as the Peruvian singer Yma Sumac whose four-octave voice draws on her American Indian heritage. Through records and tapes, the actors explored vocal tones, timbres, pitch, and the intonations of artists such as Sumac and Louis Armstrong, while at the same time doing similar research into traditional Eastern performance forms such as Beijing opera, kabuki, and noh. The group developed voice exercises from this research that were essentially vocal scores consisting of vocables (i.e., vocal sounds rather than words). These scores were then learned and practiced daily, along with the resonator work.

When the company moved to Holstebro in 1966, language became a major concern. All of those who came from Oslo spoke Norwegian and, even though Norwegians, Danes, and Swedes can communicate with each other, there are differences between the languages, especially in pronunciation.

Those who joined the group in its first years in Denmark were from all over Scandinavia. Eventually, as the Odin became better known, performers from other parts of Europe came to work with the group. This trans-European component, combined with the fact that most of the Odin's performances were given in different parts of Europe where no one language was sufficient for their work to be understood by everyone, led to a re-evaluation of language – both in productions and in training.

Following on from the vocal work done in Oslo, the actors began to explore the sonorous and tonal quality of speech. They developed exercises in which they learned texts by rote, without considering grammar, linguistic logic, or meaning. They then used these learned texts to explore paralinguistic elements – such as rhythm, timbre, silence, tone, volume, and intonation – of the spoken words. Barba describes this process, and the rationale behind it, in the film *Vocal Training at the Odin*:

> I ought to mention the spoken text. In our daily life when we talk we don't concentrate on the words, we don't coldly interpret the words. Our speech is carried on a wave, the respiratory wave, which may be long or it may be short. If the process is spontaneous, we do not think about the words. Nothing impedes us or restrains us if we have a sense of security; in other words if we are not afraid, if we are not embarrassed, if we do not have to be careful of what we say or are not speaking in a foreign language that we are not altogether at home with. This sense of security must be recreated within the artificial situation that is the theatrical situation. We must therefore eliminate the objective blocking of the text which can occur if one is continuously to force oneself to remember it. The text must be learned by heart so perfectly that it flows out without the least difficulty as if it were a spontaneous process allowing the actor, through his action, to reach out in space, oblivious of the words he has learnt ... these words assume life and presence through my whole being as personal reactions.
>
> (Barba, 1979:69–70)

The rejection of linguistic logic and meaning was taken a step further when some members of the company began working with invented languages. This development owed its origins to several workshops conducted by Dario Fo at the Odin in the late 1960s and early 1970s. In these workshops Fo demonstrated his use of fabricated languages which later formed the basis of one part of his famous production *Mistero Buffo*.

Rasmussen was particularly interested in Fo's linguistic inventions and began developing a language of her own based on a combination of sounds from Danish, Norwegian, and Swedish. Others soon followed her lead and invented languages derived from Nordic, Portuguese and Greek sources. These experiments carried the rejection of text as linguistic information to its logical extreme and, to paraphrase Rasmussen herself, attempted to explore the relationship between expression and reception by focusing on the emotional and musical potential of the voice, rather than on words as signifiers which limits them to their need to specify meaning (in ISTA, 1980).

Vocal action (1969–1972)

As members of the Odin continued their exploration of resonators and the sonorous potential of the voice, they became increasingly aware of vocal differences in the group. Each voice not only sounded slightly different but, paralleling their discoveries in physical training, they realized that each actor's voice had its own rhythm, its own distinctive qualities, and its own center within the body (Barba, 1979:77). The group began to explore this vocal individuality in training, through the use of improvisation. Once an actor had developed his/her resonator and paralinguistic skills, s/he began to improvise with the same techniques s/he had used in his/her initial training, that is, with vocables, rote learned texts, invented languages, and resonators. But the focus in training was now on discovering the individual nature of the voice, rather than developing technique.

The shift in vocal training from learning techniques to exploring individuality was only one of several instances in which the vocal work mirrored developments in physical training. The use of stimuli to induce responses, for instance, was another technique common to both the physical and vocal training. Just as the actors had experimented with psycho-physical techniques in which actions are colored by the use of imagined stimuli, so the actors developed psycho-vocal exercises that used imagery to influence vocal expression. In the Odin Teatret film *Vocal Training at Odin Teatret* Barba and a former member of the company, Jens Christiansen, demonstrate one such psycho-vocal exercise:

> *Barba:* Here is a demonstration of how the voice reacts to stimuli. I am going to ask Jens to hold my hand with his voice and let his speech emerge from that part of his body nearest to my hand. Just that, hold my hand with his voice and answer the movements of my hand; in other words, react to its actions.

> *Demonstration:* Barba slowly moves his hand to different parts of the actor's body: from his chest to the top of his head into the shoulder region and to the center of his back. Christiansen, meanwhile, attempts to "place" the voice as near to the hand as possible and also to make his voice responsive to the different degrees of pressure Barba exerts against his body with his hand.

> (Wethal, 1972)

Another common psycho-vocal exercise developed during this period involved a combination of imagery and improvisation. William Farrimond, a researcher familiar with Barba's work, describes one of these exercises he observed in 1981:

> Barba asks the actor to work with vocal improvisation using her training text. Her text is in Italian. He gives her an associative point of departure:
>
> B [Barba]: Imagine the inside of the earth.
>
> There is evident a concentration on the vowel-sounds, the consonants taking a secondary relationship. During her improvisation, it is also clear that her various physical postures are the result of natural inclination. She is not consciously assuming these positions.
>
> In asking her to listen to the external echo of her expression, Barba encourages the removal of noticeable blockages. He employs further associative images to draw her away from involvement with the physical process, with self-analysis.
>
> (1981:75–76)

Another example of the way in which developments in vocal training paralleled those in the physical work was the gradual use of the voice as a spatial entity. This use of the voice owes its origins to Barba's realization of what he calls vocal action, that is, considering the voice as an invisible extension of the body, which, like its physical counterpart, has spatial dimension (Barba, 1979:78). Using this concept of the voice, the actors no longer focused their improvisations entirely on the resonators and the sonority of vocal expression but also on placing the voice accurately: reaching a particular point in the room with the voice, for instance, filling the entire space with it, or using the voice delicately to "touch" a fellow performer.

These training exercises employed similar psycho-vocal techniques to those used for placing the voice in different parts of the body: the actors worked with an image of where they wished to place the voice, and with vocal action based on the manipulation of resonators and the sonority of the text. Since these exercises were improvised they have not been documented, but a hypothetical example will serve to illustrate them: If a performer wished to bounce his/her voice off a distant wall and fill the entire studio with its echo, s/he could work with the image of his/her voice as a single rushing stream pouring from his/her mouth, hitting the wall, and splashing back to fill the room while at the same time exploring how the image affects his/her choice of resonators and his/her use of the various timbres, tones, rhythms, vowels, and consonants in the text.

Individualized vocal training (1972–1991)

Just as psycho-vocal exercises and vocal action reflected a connection between the company's voice and movement work, the development of individualized vocal training mirrored the same development in the actor's physical research. During the group's formative years in Oslo and Holstebro, the focus was on mastering techniques, on being able to manipulate the resonators at will, and on controlling tone, pitch, and the timbre of the voice.

Barba continued to teach voice for ten years. Carreri, who became a member of the company in 1974, was his last pupil. After that time, as Barba gradually extracted himself from the training studio, new actors who joined the company were taught voice by their more experienced colleagues. This autodidactic model followed much the same pattern as the physical training. Those who studied with Barba taught the new arrivals basic vocal skills, and then each worked with these skills to develop his/her own training. Since the training drew so heavily on improvisation and experimentation, it led to the same research orientation that was so important in the group's physical work. This research eventually centered on two areas, both of which still dominate the Odin's vocal training: continued study of the voice as an invisible physiological force (i.e., the voice as action), and exploring the individual nature of each performer's voice.

Several of the Odin actors are particularly interested in the voice and have pursued individual research that has influenced other members of the company. Rasmussen was the first to develop an invented language, for instance, a technique which the company continues to use both in training and in productions. She has also studied how the peasant women in southern Spain are able to project their voices when they sing in street parades, and her adaptation of these techniques to her own work with resonators and the group's street performances has led to others in the company experimenting with them.

Pardeilhan has also had a major impact on vocal training at the Odin. He is particularly interested in singing, and developed the choral score and vocal techniques used in the Odin's production, *Oxyrhincus Evangeliet*. In fact, his work on *Oxyrhincus Evangeliet* formed the basis of an entire cycle of vocal training in which he taught his fellow actors singing and breathing techniques that he had adapted from their earlier experiments with resonators and vocal action.

WHY CONTINUE TO TRAIN?

Why is it that, after over twenty-five years of work, training continues to be so important to Barba and his Odin colleagues? In the early years, it was clearly a means of learning basic skills, but by the late 1960s the group had abandoned skill-oriented work and shifted its attention to the processual nature of training.

This process orientation goes a long way to explaining why training remains so important. Much as physical exercise, like aerobics or jogging, is an on-going process which maintains fitness without new skills continually having to be learned, training at the Odin is a daily workout that exercises each actor's body and voice.

But this is a long way short of the entire story, because the daily regimen of training has ramifications beyond merely tuning the actors' physical and vocal instruments. Despite the rejection of training as a means of learning techniques, it continues to be an indirect way of developing new skills. It plays an important part in maintaining the actors' physical and mental disciplines, as well as providing a means of honing the skills they have already learned. It also prepares them for the Odin's somewhat unusual approach to dramaturgy, and is a source of personal development as well as social cohesion within the group.

The secondary role of skill acquisition in today's training stems from the emphasis on acting principles. The performers may no longer be concerned with learning new gymnastic exercises or perfecting the high-pitch singing technique of Beijing opera, but they are continually exploring ways of mastering the principles of acting. These explorations include devising solutions for physical and vocal problems – such as how to control a particular fall, or how best to use one's voice in street performances – while remaining faithful to the principles they are working with. This problem-solving expands their skills by demanding an ever-increasing repertoire of physical and vocal techniques, even if this expansion is not the primary focus of their research.

Discipline has always been an important factor in training. In the group's early years this discipline was imposed by Barba. But, as individual training gained ascendancy, the onus of discipline shifted to the actors, and they continue to be responsible for the schedule and content of daily training. The most obvious aim of this daily discipline is to prepare the actors for performance. Just as an athlete trains daily for competition, the Odin actor's physical and vocal training prepares him/her for performance. Barba maintains that this preparation is not directed only toward expression, however, since continual training also helps the actor tap the pre-expressive, the source of presence:

> Using the training exercises, the performer tests his or her ability to achieve a condition of total presence, a condition which he or she will have to find again in the creative moment of improvisation and performance

> (Barba and Savarese, 1991:246)

As well as developing pre-expressive and expressive skills, training prepares the actors for rehearsal. New productions rarely begin with little more than a theme and/or fragments of texts that are explored in rehearsals. These explorations begin with improvisations which are directly related to the way in which improvisation is used in training. In training, improvisation is an integral part of the daily work. In dramaturgy, on the other hand, even though the final production montage is set and repeated in each performance, improvisation provides the raw material for the production. The actors rarely develop this material during training, but their studio research builds a lexicon and grammar of improvisation which they draw on during rehearsals to create new pieces. As Carreri put it, "I keep training in order to be ready to respond, to be able to meet the demands of the new performance" (1985).

Barba regards training as a form of mental conditioning as much as a way of exercising and investigating the means of expression (1985a:15; 1985c). The on-going process of developing one's own training – of self-discipline, research, and concrete physical and vocal tasks – develops an attitude towards the work and the work process. In this way, the actors are exploring their physical and vocal potentials not only through exercise but also through a process of mental discipline. Every day at a prescribed time, the actor enters the training studio and works for at least two hours. During this time his/her mind and body are directly concerned with exploring the principles s/he is working on, and indirectly on developing his/her improvisational skills. His/her mind is thus daily focused on the work at hand, and on its potential implications for the next production. Barba maintains that this mental focus is as much part of the training process as the physical and vocal exercises because, just as these exercises build a physiological routine, the daily mental engagement builds an intellectual discipline. The body and the mind are equally engaged.

Barba's concern with the mental component of training has taken on a new dimension in recent years. In his book *The Dilated Body* (1985a) Barba discusses what he sees as the connections between physical and mental training:

> If there is physical training, there must also be mental training.
>
> It is necessary to work on the bridge which joins the physical and mental banks of the creative process …
>
> The "dilated body" [a body empty of expression but actively prepared for it] evokes its opposite and complementary image: the "dilated mind" …
>
> There is a physical aspect to thought: its way of moving, of changing direction, of leaping, its "behaviour", in fact. There is also in this area a pre-expressive level which can be considered analogous to the actor's pre-expressive work, that work which concerns his "presence" (his energy) and which precedes – logically if not chronologically – real and actual artistic composition.
>
> (1985a:15)

For Barba, there is a dual dilation at the pre-expressive level of performance. Just as the trained body is engaged prior to expression – or, as Barba now puts it, dilated – the trained mind is dilated, i.e., it is in a constant state of mental pre-expression. As the body is both engaged in expression and also shapes the performer's energy at the pre-expressive level simultaneously, the actor's mind is likewise synchronically focused on the act of expressing and on how the expression is conceived and composed.

Barba goes on to argue that this link between the dilated body and mind can begin from either a physical or a mental dimension, that physical dilation can lead to mental dilation or vice versa. He does not discuss the relationship between mental and physical pre-expression that originates in the psycho-emotional. Presumably he is referring to the Method school and other approaches to Stanislavky's technique, however, in which the psychological components of character, situation, and action are the source of physical expression.

Understandably, since it is the basis of his approach to theatre, Barba focuses his discussion on dilation that originates from the physical. He argues that the Odin actors' focus on physical work for so many years has developed a particular way of conceiving and creating dramatic action, which is analogous with their structuring of physical energy. Just as the focus on performance principles in training both prepares an actor for expression and taps the pre-expressive, the way of thinking this generates shapes how the actors both originate and construct improvisations.

In addition to the psychological and physical components of training at the Odin, there are important personal and social ramifications. The Odin's training is, in essence, a process of professional self-definition. Each actor develops his/her own training, based on what s/he perceives as his/her potential and the limitations s/he wishes to challenge. A major aim of this approach is to make the actor autonomous, to allow him/her to create his/her own training without relying on specific techniques or particular teachers. Through this process, the actor is attempting to discover what Barba refers to as his/her own "personal temperature," that is, his/her own rhythm, boundaries, abilities, and what is unique about him/her as a performer (Barba, 1988a:298). When s/he begins work on a new production s/he does not therefore merely apply a set of learned techniques to interpret a text or the director's vision, as, say, a Stanislavsky actor might, but rather s/he uses improvisation to explore the relationship between themes suggested by Barba and his/her own "personal temperature." Thus, the actor's development of a personal training forms the basis of both rehearsals and productions.

Training has always been a major source of social cohesion at the Odin, despite its emphasis on individuality. This is because it is an activity that involves all the actors and has been part of the company's daily routine since it was formed. The group has stopped performing from time to time; it has disbanded for periods; teaching and other concerns like film-making have occupied the interests of some members, but training has always remained. Even during the mid-1970s when most of the company abandoned training, the new recruits and their teachers continued to train.

Training is a time when the actors meet and work together in the same room. Their interests are focused on the one concern: developing and exploring their potential as performers. All are equal in this research, and, no matter what form it takes, each has the respect of his fellow actors in it. Training is the one time in a busy schedule of performing, rehearsing, or other duties when the group is together, separated from the outside world, with its entire energies focused on a single concern. Training is the group's time together: even Barba has largely removed himself from this "special" time when the actors must work together for tomorrow.

The concern with tomorrow, on using training as a research tool that feeds into the next production, is embodied in the process orientation of the Odin's training. Training is not so much concerned with mastering skills as it is with "doing the exercise," and personal discovery. This focus on process, with its roots in individualized training that draws its inspiration from various cultures as well as different teachers, has inevitably produced a diversity of skills and techniques within the company. As Farrimond notes, "It is only in the principles and not in the techniques ... that one can trace an element common to the whole group" (1981:92).

Regardless of this diversity, the training developed by different actors at the Odin has some basic common features. The focus is on physical and vocal techniques rather than psychological elements, as in Strasberg's training, for example. Likewise, the psycho-physical and psycho-vocal exercises that dominated the 1960s and 1970s continue to play an important part in some aspects of training, while the manipulation of resonators and the view of the voice as a physiological extension of the body also remain important in voice work. The emphasis on research in training, with the aim of applying discoveries to rehearsals and productions, has always been a significant feature of the group's methodology.

Training is the foundation of the Odin's creative work; as Taviani puts it, "Odin culture is incarnate in its training" (1986a:256). The research and process orientation of training engenders a continual cycle of growth and renewal. This cycle is a constant source of inspiration for rehearsals, productions, and the Odin's unusual dramaturgy.

4

REHEARSALS AND
DRAMATURGY

Barba's years in Poland gave him a great deal to take back to Norway. Apart
from Grotowski's research into actor training, he had been exposed to a
theatre which rejected realism and had much in common with the presentational style of traditional Eastern performance genres such as noh and
kathakali. Unlike its Asian counterparts, however, this presentational style
was not based on conventions handed down over generations, so rehearsals
played a large part in establishing the form and content of each performance. In Grotowski's rehearsals, the Stanislavskian convention of interpreting the playwright's intentions was abandoned in favor of exploring the
group's reaction to the scripts. The two Grotowski pieces that Barba worked
on as assistant director, *Akropolis* and *The Tragical History of Doctor Faustus*,
were, for example, based on classic texts, but the productions were far
removed from their original sources. They consisted primarily of improvisations, adaptations of the original scripts, and, in the case of *Akropolis*,
even fragments of texts from other sources.[1]

Barba's original intention had always been to work in the legitimate
theatre when he returned to Norway. But when he was rejected on all fronts
and formed his own company, Grotowski's pursuit of his artistic goals, with
a small group of actors in the relative isolation of Opole, proved an invaluable
model. This was nowhere more evident than in his rehearsals and dramaturgy where, from his first production, *Ornitofilene*, he established a method
of workshop/rehearsals in which improvisation played a major role. These
initial workshop/rehearsals were all based on adaptations of literary texts.
Eventually, however, Barba, like Grotowski, abandoned working with play-
wrights, and has for some twenty years now created his productions entirely
from improvisations. Although this method of developing productions has
undergone several changes during that time, the lengthy workshop/
rehearsal period and improvisation have remained mainstays of Barba's
dramaturgy.

ADAPTING LITERARY TEXTS FOR
PERFORMANCE (1965–1969)

Unlike Grotowski, who invariably began rehearsals with European classics, Barba's first three productions, *Ornitofilene* (1965–66), *Kaspariana* (1967–68), and *Ferai* (1969–70), were based on original material written by living authors. *Ornitofilene* was a new play written by Jens Bjorneboe, a leading Norwegian writer, while *Kaspariana* was based on the scenario of the Kaspar Hauser story by the Danish writer Ole Sarvig. This scenario called for four roles but there were seven actors in the group at the time so, as they did when they were faced with a similar problem in *Ornitofilene,* Barba and his performers created entire scenes and new roles from improvisations explored during the workshop/rehearsals. *Ferai,* the final production in the cycle of works based on literary sources, was written by a Danish novelist, Peter Seeberg. As with their previous productions, Barba and his company did not adhere rigidly to the script during rehearsals, preferring instead to use it as a point of departure for their mise-en-scene.

Despite differences between these three productions, the rehearsal process was essentially the same each time. Barba and his actors began with a literary text, a completed draft of a play in *Ornitofilene,* a scenario for *Kaspariana,* and a script inspired by mythology in *Ferai.* In each case, the text was only a beginning point for rehearsals. Barba and his actors used the scripts as the basis of improvisations from which they developed a final production rather than as the blueprint for a staged version of the writer's vision.

Neither Barba nor the Odin actors documented their work at the time, so it is impossible to cite specific examples of the process. However, members of the Odin have all described it to me in essentially the same way. After choosing a scene to work on, Barba would discuss the possible themes he felt were contained in it, and ask his actors to explore these themes through physical improvisation. These explorations were initially collective, but eventually the group abandoned this approach in favor of individual improvisations. Some of these improvisations were discarded, though many were either used to "flesh out" the scenes provided by the writers, or adjusted and incorporated into the gradually evolving production.

As the physical score of the performance text gradually took shape, the actors also began to work with spoken text, but separately from their physical work. The early stages of this work on *Ornitofilene* used the dialogue provided by Bjorneboe but, as these original scenes were elaborated in rehearsals and a few scenes developed which were not in the original script, improvisation became more important. Initially, these improvisations were concerned with discovering realistic dialogue but eventually, no doubt influenced by Grotowski and the vocal training initiated by Barba, they focused more on the musicality of vocal sound than on the semantic aspect of language. *Kaspari-*

ana provided further scope for this interest in the musicality of language since Sarvig wrote a scenario containing no dialogue. And Seeberg's *Ferai* script, which owed much to lyrical poetry, was even more conducive to exploring the musicality of the voice.

Since the physical and vocal improvisations were developed separately, the next step in the process was to combine them. In those scenes written by Bjorneboe and Seeberg which were retained in the final productions, this was relatively easy because the physical and vocal improvisations had a common origin, the dramatic text. But in the scenes created entirely from improvisation this was not so simple, since the physical and vocal material was often derived from different sources, and lacked the structural framework of a dramatic text. This lack of a common underlying structure forced Barba and his actors to make many adjustments to the vocal and physical improvisations in their attempts to find the best way to combine them. According to those who are still with the group from these early years, this was a very difficult process initially. However, Barba's separation of the physical and vocal in both training and the early stages of rehearsals, in order to explore the rhythms of each without one or the other dominating, is something the group has continued to do ever since. And it was this difficult early period, of discovering how best to separate and combine physical and vocal improvisation in creating the performance text, which laid the foundation for the unusual dramaturgy which Barba has evolved in his mature years as a director.

Regardless of the differences between physical and vocal improvisations during these formative years, both types of improvisation were either directly or indirectly based on a dramatic text. Each production was a combination of the original written script or scenario, improvisations developed from scenes in the text, and original material created by Barba and his actors that grew out of associations drawn from their work on the dramatic text.

Richard Schechner, who used a somewhat similar approach in creating many of his works with the Performance Group (1967–1980), describes this method of developing a performance text as a "deconstructive/reconstructive workshop process" (1985:287–293). This process begins with a lengthy workshop period, during which the actors and director "deconstruct" the original dramatic text through their explorations of the associations it has for them. That is, rather than attempting only to discover the writer's intention in the dramatic text, they examine their personal and collective responses to it through improvisation. As Schechner puts it: "The deconstruction of a text involves not only the analysis of what the author has written – that's just the first step – but an analysis-through-action" (1985:278). During this active analysis, the actors and the director accumulate a stock of material which can include staged versions of the playwright's original scenes, alterations in other scenes, and new scenes created entirely from improvisation, as well as the addition and deletion of characters. In his production of Genet's *The Balcony* developed in this way, Schechner changed the gender of several characters, altered the order of scenes, began the play with a scene that does not exist in the original, and added a singer-pianist in the bordello who played and sang songs of her own composition during and between many of the scenes (Schechner, 1985:261–293).

As material is being accumulated, the director and his actors begin to implement the reconstruction process in which they explore ways of putting the material they have developed into a cohesive whole. This process accelerates as the production nears opening night and as it gradually incorporates many of the more conventional aspects of rehearsals, including design considerations, the quality of actors' performances, and lighting.

In this deconstrucion/reconstruction approach to dramaturgy, the script is a mere catalyst for the performance text rather than a detailed map it must follow. The writer's words only provide a point of departure and a framework for the final production. The performance text is thus neither a staged version of the original dramatic text nor a piece created entirely from improvisation without regard to the writer's original script. It is a product of the meeting between the dramatic text, the director, and the actors.

This notion of a meeting characterizes Barba's dramaturgy during his formative years as a director since, despite their individual differences, his productions of *Ornitofilene*, *Kaspariana*, and *Ferai* all owed their dramaturgical content and structure to the interaction between the dramatic text and the group. In each instance, the script was a catalyst for the actors, which also provided a basic thematic and dramatic framework for the final production. But not one of the productions was entirely an interpretation of the writer's ideas, or a work solely derived from improvisation. All of them were the product of improvisations based on the actors' and Barba's responses to what the writer had written. The performance texts were the end result of an active meeting process: the meeting between the written word and those in the rehearsal studio.

PERFORMANCE TEXTS BASED ON THEMES SUGGESTED BY BARBA (1971 to the present)

The Odin's next production, *Min Fars Hus*, saw a major change in rehearsals when Barba and his actors developed the performance text entirely from improvisation, without relying on a previously written script. This change was a natural progression because Barba and his colleagues had been gradually increasing the role of improvisation in rehearsals, and because it was during this time that the group began developing individual training based on improvisation.

With minor variations, this is the method Barba has used to create all his studio productions since the 1971–72 rehearsals for *Min Fars Hus*. Besides *Min Fars Hus*, productions developed entirely in this way include *Come! And*

Eugenio Barba with Mei Bao-Jiu, the son of Mei Lan-Fang who, like his father, specializes in dan (female) roles in the Beijing Opera, 1986 (Photographer: Nicola Savarese.)

Else Marie Laukvik, Torgeir Wethal and Tor Sannum in *Ornitofilene*.

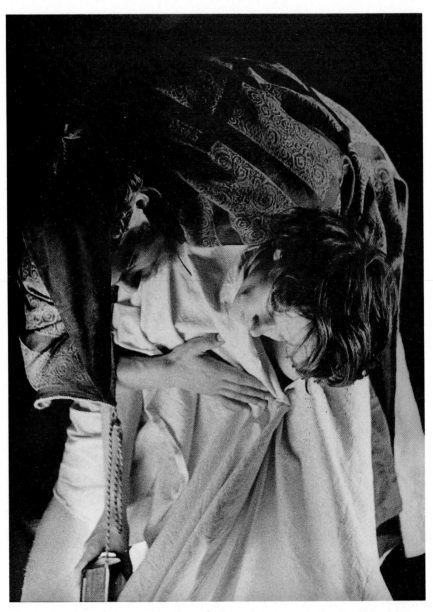

Dan Nielsen and Torgeir Wethal in *Kaspariana*. (Photographer: Roald Pay.)

Torgeir Wethal in *Ferai*.

Tage Larsen, Torgeir Wethal, Iben Nagel Rasmussen and Ragner L. Christiansen in *Min Fars Hus*. (Photographer: Roald Pay.)

Iben Nagel Rasmussen and Torgeir Wethal in *The Book of Dances*.
(Photographer: Tony D'Urso.)

Tage Larsen and Else Marie Laukvik in *Come! And the Day Will be Ours*.
(Photographer: Tony D'Urso.)

The company of actors in *Anabasis.*

The company of actors in *The Million.* (Photographer: Reinhard Goldmann.)

Richard Fowler and Julia Varley in *Talabot*. (Photographer: Tony D'Urso.)

Tage Larsen, Torgeir Wethal, Francis Pardeilhan and Roberta Carreri in *Oxyrhincus Evangeliet*. (Photographer: Jan Rusz.)

Roberta Carreri and Francis Pardeilhan in *Brecht's Ashes 2.* (Photographer: Tony D'Urso.)

the Day Will be Ours (1976), *Brecht's Ashes 2* (1982), *Oxyrhincus Evangeliet* (1985), and *Talabot* (1988).

Individual improvisation[2]

At the beginning of a new project, Barba suggests a basic theme or cluster of themes that he wants to explore in rehearsals. In *Min Fars Hus* these themes were drawn from Dostoyevsky's biography and novels. Rehearsals for *Come! And the Day Will be Ours* were based on the meeting between European immigrants and the indigenous population of the Americas. *Brecht's Ashes 2* started as an exploration of Brecht's writings, but, when his estate denied copyright to the Odin, Barba turned to Brecht's life, the influences on his work, and the writings of his contemporaries as a point of departure for the piece. The initial work on *Oxyrhincus Evangeliet* began by developing material based on the Jorge Luis Borges story *The Dead Man*. This material was later augmented with themes drawn from original scenarios developed by the actors based on their characters, as well as books and films on Brazilian outlaws, the story of the ancient Egyptian city of Oxyrhincus, and parts of Vargas Llosa's novel *The War of the End of the World*. And *Talabot* had its origins in the writings of a Danish anthropologist, Kirstin Hastrup, as well as the lives of historical figures such as Antonin Artaud, Ernesto (Che) Guevara, and Knud Rasmussen.

Prior to rehearsals, Barba compiles material on the themes he wants to use as the basis of the production. He collects poems, stories, newspaper clippings, photographs, illustrations, anything that he intuitively feels is relevant to the themes. Some of this material he shares with the actors, to give them a better sense of the direction of his thought, but most of it he does not show to anyone. This is his own private resource for ideas and associations that he will draw on as he observes his actors' work.

Unlike Barba's meditative/cognitive understanding of themes, the actors explore these themes actively, through improvisation. As rehearsals begin, Barba explains his thematic interests and discusses them with the actors. He then suggests particular aspects of a theme which he asks his actors to use as the basis of a purely physical improvisation. Farrimond describes an example of this approach in a workshop session he observed in early 1981:

> Barba tells an actor the story of Tristan and Isolde. This technnique of "telling" a story as an introduction and background to an actor's improvisation exercises (most often a story with which the actor is familiar) is often employed by Barba. He discusses the action and the reasoning of these stories, the moral message if any, and the possible contemporary interpretations of these elements. In discussion he employs the form of the hypothetical question. After telling the story

of Tristan and Isolde, he discusses what the sword which is kept between them implies.

B [Barba]: What is the significance of the sword? Are there parallels in this story which are not so alien to us? (to the actor) Make an improvisation about the sword.

(1981:34)[3]

These initial physical improvisations are invariably solo affairs, each actor exploring by himself/herself the theme suggested by Barba. Sometimes the improvisations are done by individual actors while the others watch; at other times several or all the actors work at the same time – but with no conscious effort to relate to each other.

This is not to say that Barba never uses collective improvisation at this stage of rehearsals. One of the first improvisations done for *Min Fars Hus*, for instance, involved all the actors playing peasants who sneak into their master's mansion in the dead of night in a futile attempt to kill him. And, in an initial series of improvisations explored in preparation for what eventually became *Oxyrhincus Evangeliet*, the actors, Barba's assistant at the time, Christolph Falke, and his long-time collaborator Taviani each wrote and directed the scenario of a different character's story which involved all of the actors. These collective improvisations are the exception, however, and, according to Barba, in neither of these two notable instances did any of the original material become part of the final work (Barba, 1985a:32; Barba, 1986c).

Barba's preference for individual improvisation as the basis for his dramaturgy stems from his concept of collective creation. For him, the root source of collective creation lies in the connections between an actor's mental associations drawn from the theme and his/her responses to them. Unlike North American directors – such as Joseph Chaikin, Andre Gregory, and Schechner – who have worked extensively with collective improvisation, Barba feels that the individual psycho-physical connections between the theme and the expression it generates precede interaction. He maintains that, in improvisations involving more than one performer, the actors tend to focus on the interactive process rather than the theme of the work. That is, they are more concerned with "reading" the other person and responding appropriately than with exploring their own physical dialogue with the theme. Barba is not opposed to others using collective improvisation. He merely says that he finds it inadequate because it combines two steps which he separates in his dramaturgy: the individual actor's psycho-physical response to the theme, and the actors' various responses to each other. For Barba, the individual's reactions come first and are the source of everything else.

Once an actor begins an individual improvisation, Barba never interrupts him/her, since he believes it is essential that the actor explore the

78

psycho-physical potential of a theme freely. Yet he remains an active observer, and once the actor has completed the improvisation, he invariably poses technical questions and makes suggestions – about the uses of rhythm, variations in energy (physical intensity), and *sats* points in the action – aimed at clarifying the actor's physical expression. Barba rarely asks the actor about the psycho-physical connections between the theme and his/her improvisation because he is only interested in the physical responses he sees, not the thematic associations underlying them.

As with other forms of improvisation, the actor must remain open to all possibilities in this initial phase of the work. S/he must not edit his/her reactions or pre-plan his/her responses to the theme before s/he begins. Consider the comparison Rasmussen makes between doing an unannounced solo street performance in a small southern Italian village and beginning a new improvisation:

> I am not afraid to be alone – as an actress, in a country I don't know. I have no physical fear that people will laugh at me or hit me ... It is a different type of fear, like the one I have during an improvisation. In that situation I never feel at ease, and I am frightened I won't succeed in making things seem real and alive. Today I was frightened I wouldn't be able to do that. To begin with, I thought it was the first time I had done something like this, alone, but afterwards I decided that it was similar to an improvisation. It involved the same way of facing a situation, with no idea of a beginning, but remaining open only to what happens. It is not that one thinks of being open, it is simply a matter of being so. In both instances it is like a journey which has only a certain point of departure and whose destination I don't know. It is a matter of being ready.
>
> (Rasmussen, Barba, D'Urso, and Taviani, 1979:14–15)

Composition improvisation

Following Barba's suggestions, an actor reworks his/her original improvisation while others observe and take notes or videotape the work in progress. Through a combination of the working actor's memory, his/her colleagues' notes, and/or the tape of his/her improvisation, the actor establishes a pattern of physical actions which s/he can repeat. During this process, Barba continues to ask questions at the completion of each run through, which the actor attempts to answer physically when s/he next repeats the improvisation. Gradually, through a synthesis of the actor's free-flowing psycho-physical associations based on the theme and Barba's "reading" of what he observes, he and the actor attempt to find the ideal physical expression of the mental image they began with.

This expression is rarely pantomimic. Using the Odin lexicon, it could be termed a "composition improvisation," that is, an improvisation which focuses on the actor's physical response to the theme rather than on illustrating it. Several actors often use the same theme as the basis for their improvisations, but inevitably produce entirely different results. These improvisations do, however, share at least two things: the same thematic source, and a reliance on the acting principles (such as counterbalancing body tensions, and alterations in one's center of gravity or distribution of body weight) that underlie all the Odin's physical work.

Barba's commitment to improvisation as the basis of his dramaturgy frequently leads to the original themes being abandoned in favor of others that emerge during rehearsals. He may begin rehearsals with particular thematic ideas in mind, but, during the actors' improvised explorations of them, other material may emerge that suggests a richer performance text which he and the actors decide to pursue. As mentioned earlier, for instance, the initial work on *Oxyrhincus Evangeliet* was based on Borges' *The Dead Man*. During rehearsals, this work led to an exploration of Brazilian cowboy-like outlaws, and eventually to a collection of characters including, among others, Joan of Arc, Antigone, and the Grand Inquisitor from Dostoyevsky's *The Brothers Karamazov*. The end product of this process was a piece which included fabricated versions of Coptic and Yiddish, as well as a leading character drawn from the European Hasidic tradition – most of which had little to do with Barba's first thematic inspirations.

Registering

Once an actor and Barba are both happy with a composition improvisation, the actor begins what is referred to as "registering" – learning the improvisation so that s/he can repeat it at will. This process is a continuation of the composition work in which the actor learns to repeat sections of his/her initial improvisation through a combination of memory, notes made by fellow actors, and videotape.[4] During this registering phase, the actor concentrates on rote learning the improvisation so that s/he can repeat it precisely. The focus is entirely upon building a physical score, without regard to the theme or psycho-physical connections which prompted it. Once the actor is able to repeat the improvisation, s/he is ready to complete the final stage in the registering process: reconnecting the improvisation to the psycho-physical source which inspired it.

In much the same way as a classical dancer learns the choreography for a particular ballet or a mime artist learns his/her physical routine, the Odin actor transforms his/her composition improvisation into a memorized physical score. Just as the ballet dancer and mime artist no longer have to think about which movement follows which in a piece they have prepared, so Barba's actors learn their composition improvisations so that they can repeat them without having to consider the sequence of actions. The body "remembers" the patterns of movements, freeing the mind to concentrate on the associations which inspired it. That is, once the physical score of the improvisation is committed to memory, the actors turn their attention to recapturing its initial emotional potency. Barba and his actors characterize this as a three-part process: creating the initial composition improvisation, with its "warm" response to the theme; rote learning the improvisation "coldly," which entails repeating the improvisation many times and committing it to memory without regard to the thematic associations which gave rise to it; and repeating the composition improvisation precisely while focusing mentally on the associations that produced the improvisation in the first place in order to *reactivate* the original "warmth."

When the actor has learned the improvisation and is able to repeat it with the "warmth" of the original, Barba is ready to begin the next stage in developing his performance text, refining the composition elements of the improvisation in detail. Working one-to-one with the actor, Barba makes various adjustments to the original physical score. He may alter its dimensions, by asking the performer to reduce the size of the actions in one section by 50 percent, 75 percent, etc. He may simply alter part of an action, such as the position of the fingers as the hand sweeps across the body, or the angle of the elbow in relation to the shoulder as the actor turns. He may take one fragment of the action and place it elsewhere in the improvisation, he may drop sections altogether, and he may even ask the actor to develop new material from time to time. Notes from my diary made during a lecture/demonstration presented by Barba and Rasmussen, at the 1987 ISTA conference in Salento, Italy, may clarify this stage of the work:

> Eugenio begins to work on Gretchen's mad scene from *Faust*. He asks Iben [Rasmussen] to sing Gretchen's song and develop a physical improvisation based on it. He then asks her to improvise fragments of action based on several words he chooses from the song. She does this. Several images are repeated: lifting and flapping her skirt, crouching to the ground then slowly rising almost to her full height before returning to her "normal" slouched shoulder stance, and taking several short steps, first forward then backward. Using a combination of the initial improvisation and these images, she selects segments of action and, with the help of Cesar [another Odin actor], who has been taking notes, fixes elements of the improvisation. Once she has fixed these elements, she strings them together into a single improvisation about two minutes long, which she repeats many times in order to learn.
>
> It is clear that Iben is having difficulty with the work because, as she herself points out, she only has thirty minutes to complete a task that normally takes many days. Nevertheless she presses on.
>
> Once she can repeat the improvisation, both physically and with something approaching the same emotional intensity of the original,

Eugenio begins to work with her. He first marks out a square metre on the floor and asks her to limit her improvisation within the square. Iben repeats the improvisation many times, reducing her steps and the distance she walks. She shortens her strides without limiting the movements of her head, arms or torso.

When Iben seems to be comfortable with this reduction, Eugenio asks her to rearrange the order of several sequences. He first asks her to run through the improvisation and explore possible sections to be rearranged, which she does. He then specifies several changes: he asks her to take a fragment of action with her hands and arms near the beginning of the piece and place it toward the end of the improvisation, and he takes a short sequence of movements done with her elbows from near the middle of the piece and asks her to place it near the beginning. He then asks her to fix these changes so she can repeat the improvisation with these changes intact.

Some ten minutes or so later, when Iben seems to have command of these changes, Eugenio asks her to alter the speed of her improvisation. He asks her to do the entire piece at half the speed she has been working with. All the variations remain intact, but everything is now done at half the previous speed.

Eugenio begins to work in great detail with Iben. He asks her to drop two short action sections. She re-works the improvisation without these. He then introduces several "freezes," that is, he asks her to break the flow of the action by pausing for a moment then continuing. He asks her to reduce some sections of action by half; he alters the direction she is moving through space; and even suggests images what she can use to color parts of the action – example: he asks her to do one fragment of the sequence as if she were moving through a fog.

During all these changes, Cesar makes notes and helps Iben reconstruct the final improvisation. Iben then repeats it many times, until she can do it without faltering.[5]

Following Rasmussen's demonstration, Barba pointed out several things he was attempting to do in his work with her. Firstly, he was ensuring that each section of the improvisation was relevant to the theme of madness they were exploring. Secondly, he was working to exclude any general or personal cliches such as madness being portrayed by flapping the arms about and distorting the face, or a particular mannerism that an actor has a habit of repeating. And thirdly, he was measuring the improvisation against the principles of acting he and his colleagues use to ensure the dynamic quality of physical actions.

The concern with the dynamic quality of an action was also being addressed in Barba's fragmentation of the original improvisation. This fragmenting was aimed at redirecting Rasmussen's natural flow by forcing her to replace her own process of initiating an action with one imposed from outside. Doing this, Barba pointed out, helps the actor retain the spontaneous quality of the original work by focusing attention on the effort needed to initiate and complete an action. The "freezes" he introduced into Rasmussen's original improvisation, for instance, broke the flow of her action. Rather than repeating what had come naturally, she had to consider how to end the action prior to the freeze and then how to begin what was now a second action, after the freeze.

Another consideration of Barba's at this stage in rehearsals is based on the distinction he makes between an "action" and a "movement." For Barba, an action requires a change in energy, rhythm, and the impulse underlying the action, whereas a movement is a physical gesture that involves no such change. In order to retain its dynamic quality, every component part of an improvisation should be an action rather than a movement, according to Barba. So, a major concern for him is therefore to eliminate all "movements" and replace them with "actions."

Refining a composition improvisation for a new piece can take anything from a few hours to several days or even months as the actors work alone and with Barba exploring ideas of their own, integrating his suggested changes, and fine-tuning the results. In the meantime, they continue to work on new material, which in turn is refined through the same process. In this way, over a period of many months, the actors gradually accumulate a stock of composition improvisations.

At this and, in fact, every stage in rehearsals, discussion between Barba and his actors influences the material being developed. These discussions, some of which are formal meetings in rehearsals while others are informal exchanges outside the rehearsal studio, provide much of the psychological framework for the group's dramaturgical work. An excerpt from a letter by Richard Fowler to Barba during rehearsals for *Talabot* gives an insight into the importance of these discussions in Barba's dramaturgy:

Some thoughts about me and *Talabot* which may help us.

I very much liked Kirsten's text [a text by the Danish anthropologist Kirsten Hastrup whose biography was a major source of the production]. I found it moving, open-ended, subjective, stimulating and ambiguous. Reading it immediately made me interested in doing something with it, i.e., using it to make living work from. And reading this text was the first time I found anything in the "Kirsten story" as it relates to our performance that grabbed me in more than an intellectual way.

Certain aspects of her text made a particular impression on me. Among these are the importance of her father in her life [Fowler played her father in the production]; the fact of her describing herself to her father as his son, not his daughter. I felt that the conflict in her story resides within Kirsten herself, in the relationship between her evolving identity/knowledge of self/experience and society/people around her. This is the essential conflict that the story contains and is in part what makes reading the text so interesting – one follows her groping through life, dealing with her various relationships, crises, and experiences and one waits as one reads to see how she is going to come out of it all.

What is therefore dramatically necessary, as we said yesterday in the meeting, is to find a concrete, theatrical form for this conflict. Some kind of alter ego, devil's advocate, other-aspect-of-self (Kirsten as the son of Dr. Hastrup and not the daughter??). In some way which is not yet clear to me, I think this is something I could do/be. This also ties in, in some way, to the relationship between Julia [Varley who played Hastrup in the production] and I – not that in reality I am in any sense her alter ego or whatever – but that she and I are close, more than friends and less than lovers.

(1988a)

During the lengthy process of building a stock of composition improvisations the group also explores three other areas: character, music, and vocal material.

Character

Barba's concern with the actor's psycho-physical relation to a theme or cluster of themes, rather than a more conventional plot-oriented narrative with identifiable roles, does not mean that he rejects the notion of actors portraying characters. His focus on the actor is only one step in the complex mosaic of his emerging production. Consistent with his emphasis on active analysis and his rejection of realism, however, character is generally explored physically and vocally through improvisation instead of through psychological examination.

Since rehearsals involve neither a script which includes characters, nor realistically oriented improvisations, the characters in a Barba production either evolve from the group's thematic explorations, or they are suggested by Barba as one of the initial themes to be explored. During the later stages of developing composition improvisations for *Brecht's Ashes 2*, for example, Rasmussen became fascinated by Kattrin, the deaf daughter in Brecht's *Mother Courage*. Part of her fascination was with how Kattrin's handicap (i.e., being mute) might be physicalized. She began to explore different ways of walking: pigeon-toed, walking on the inner sides of the feet, walking on the heels, on the toes, etc. She became so absorbed in this physical exploration of the character that not only did she work on it in rehearsals, but she also began to develop exercises based on her rehearsal research during training.

84

was little concerned with Kattrin's emotional or psychological life, either in Brecht's play or in the improvised scenes outside it. Her work primarily consisted of her own rehearsal and training research, as well as with other material she accumulated outside of the studio. She studied sign language at night school, for instance, and added what she was learning to both her rehearsal and training work. She also began to build a tactile, visual sense of the character by choosing elements of Kattrin's costume. She found a red military jacket in the costume shop at the main theatre in Aarhus which she began to work with in both rehearsals and training. She bought a pair of Danish clogs. And while on tour during breaks from rehearsals she bought a hat in Peru and a pair of woollen gloves in Japan, both of which she added to her work on returning home. All of these elements eventually became part of Rasmussen's Kattrin in performance (Rasmussen, 1986).

The gradual emergence of character during rehearsals is the most common way in which roles develop in Barba's dramaturgy. Most of these are not as well documented as Rasmussen's work on Kattrin but her shaman character in *Come! And the Day Will be Ours* was developed in much the same way as Kattrin, as were most of the characters in *Brecht's Ashes 2*, and *Min Fars Hus*.

This is not the only approach to developing roles in Barba's work. In *Oxyrhincus Evangeliet* character was one of the major points of departure for rehearsals rather than something that emerged during them. After an eighteen-month break following the initial Borges workshops, the group began rehearsals in earnest with an exploration of various characters. In the early stages of these rehearsals, Barba asked each of his actors to choose a character from different stories he suggested. The characters included, among others, the Grand Inquisitor from Fyodor Dostoyevsky's *The Brothers Karamazov*, Herman Melville's Moby Dick, and the seventeenth-century false messiah, Sabbatai Zevi. From a combination of readings about the characters and improvisations, six of them were finally chosen: Antigone, Joan of Arc, a nameless Brazilian outlaw, an Hasidic Jew, the Grand Inquisitor of Seville, and Sabbatai Zevi. The actors then used these characters as the basis of their composition improvisations. Varley, who played Joan of Arc, for example, worked with the image of a horse, basing her exploration of the character on the rhythm, energy, and idea of a foal in the stable. In addition to this initial physical work, she read that Joan always wore men's clothing and that she was fascinated by her sword and banner. She carefully chose parts of her costume, such as her belt and leather hat, from stock material at the Odin, and eventually made an entire costume consisting of a simple yellow cotton dress with a decorative cape. She also made a special banner from a tree branch, and decorated it with spurs. She incorporated all of these things into her work on the horse image (Barba, 1985h:11; Klein, 1988:177).

Music

Most of the Odin actors play one or more instruments, and music is invariably an important part of productions. Initially, this music is usually developed separately from the physical and vocal rehearsals. For most productions, Barba and his actors collect musical material – songs, instrumental pieces, musical phrases, or particular rhythms – that they feel is either appropriate to the orginal themes they began with, or related to developments in the rehearsal room. Despite their musical skills, none of the permanent members of the company are specialists and, even though several of the actors have studied music, none of them sight-reads well. Tunes that seem to hold some value for a forthcoming production are therefore usually learned by those who suggest them or by actors Barba selects.

Occasionally, a musical director works on productions. A Danish musician and actor, Jan Ferslev, for instance, worked on Carreri's one-woman performance, *Judith*, and on *Talabot*, in which he also performed. But this is the exception rather than the rule. The actors usually prepare a rough version of the material alone and then play it for their colleagues who collectively decide its appropriateness.

If a particular piece holds promise, the actors who have learned the basic tune begin to work on it in detail. They first learn the melody so that they can play it reasonably well. Once they have mastered the piece, they explore possible variations in tone, pitch, and rhythm, as well as how to use the instrument as a hand prop. Thus the music gradually moves from the privacy needed to master the tune into the public forum of rehearsals, where both it and the instrument become yet other tools to improvise with. Slowly, in addition to the initial composition improvisations, the group accumulates a body of music and a stock of composition improvisations developed out of their explorations of the instruments as props. During the early rehearsals for *Min Fars Hus*, for instance, Ulrik Skeel learned to play the piano accordion. He then explored its music as an alternative to words, and developed composition improvisations with the instrument in an attempt to make it part of the physical nature of the servant character he was playing. The music eventually found its way into the production in the form of a dialogue with his fellow servant's flute. And the accordion became both the servant's paunch and a wall behind which he could conceal himself while spying on his masters.

The text

Not all of Barba's works have included live music, but every one of them has had a complex vocal score. These scores consist of songs, chants, incantations, and vocables, in which the voice is used as a sonorous (musical) instrument, augmented with naturalistic dialogue. Work on this vocal score, much like the music, is usually begun during the later phase of developing the composition improvisations, and is explored separately from the other elements of the emerging performance text.

The verbal texts in a Barba production are rarely original pieces written specifically for it. From the moment Barba considers a particular theme he begins to collect texts that he feels are relevant to it. These "found texts" usually come from a variety of sources, which can include novels, news items, poems, magazine articles, and even parts of casual conversation. Barba prepares a scrapbook in which he collects these texts as he finds them, so that slowly, over a period of months, he accumulates a stock of texts. In addition to his own collection, Barba also encourages his actors to search for material they feel is relevant to the themes and/or characters in the piece.

The group continues to collect texts well beyond the composition phase of rehearsals, but during the latter part of this period, each actor, in consultation with Barba, selects texts that s/he feels are significant to developments in rehearsals and learns them by heart so that s/he can repeat them easily. Once s/he has done this s/he begins to improvise with the tonal potential of each text, exploring its sonorous and rhythmic qualities rather than its linguistic logic.

Much as with composition work, Barba observes these initial improvisations and, after the actor has worked through them, discusses his/her choices, makes suggestions, and even occasionally writes original material more appropriate to the theme they are working on.[6] The actor then reworks his/her improvisation, exploring or rejecting Barba's suggestions, until s/he has a body of improvisations that both s/he and Barba are happy with. Once s/he has done this, s/he rote learns the improvisations in much the same way s/he learns his/her composition work, through a combination of his/her memory, notes from fellow actors, and through the use of videotape.

Thus, each actor slowly compiles a collection of scored vocal texts which is added to the ever-increasing stock of physical material and music – all of which is both separate and connected, since each element has been developed on its own but has its origins in the same thematic sources and is being developed by the same actors. These separate/not-separate elements are the raw material for the next stage in Barba's dramaturgy.

The montage

During what Barba refers to as the montage phase of rehearsals, he combines the physical, vocal, and musical elements into a single performance text. This phase begins with the construction of individual scenes. From his intuitive sense of the connections between the thematic sources of the work and the material developed by the actors, Barba selects two or more of the physical improvisations to be combined into the one scene. He then asks the actors to repeat these improvisations together many times, while

87

focusing on how each is affected by the other. The actors make minor adjustments to their original improvisations as they work together, until they feel that the individualized nature of the improvisations has been replaced by a relational tension between them. At this point Barba begins working with the actors.

Much as in creating the composition improvisations, Barba asks the actors to repeat their action sequences while he adjusts and/or makes changes to the improvisations. He might ask one actor to work in slow motion while the other continues at normal speed; he may ask one to freeze in place while the other continues; he could equally ask them to alternate their actions, or have one performer drop part of his/her action while moving another fragment of action from the beginning of the sequence to the end. Little by little, in this way, he constructs a scenic logic from what were originally separate, individual improvisations.

Barba does not limit his actors to their original composition improvisations during this stage in rehearsals. He might introduce additional hand props, he may explore musical accompaniment, or he may even ask the actors to create new sections of improvisation. There are no rules, but brief descriptions of this phase of rehearsals for two productions, *Brecht's Ashes 2* and *The Million*, give an idea of how Barba works.

Brecht's Ashes 2

Rasmussen had done an individual improvisation, lying on her back – she was making strange cooing sounds. I [Pardeilhan, playing Arturo Ui] had an action where I was in front of a bowl of water and put my face into it. Barba wanted to create a scene in which Kattrin [Rasmussen] would be raped by Arturo Ui. Actors were thinking about how this could be done without the obvious. For instance, I was working with lighting matches and trying to get Kattrin to smoke when she doesn't want to. Barba saw the two loose bits of material individually and then simultaneously. He then asked the actors instead of doing their "scenes" on opposite ends of the room to put the bowl between Kattrin's legs. The juxtaposition of images worked, creating the equivalent of rape without rape. After this only the details remained to be worked on.

(Pardeilhan in Klein, 1988:185–186)

The Million

Barba asks an actor to put on her Japanese lion-dance costume. As part of her individual training she has learnt the lion dance of the Kabuki dance-theatre, the Buyo Dance Theatre. Both costume and dance are new elements to this work.

B. [*Barba*] Colleagues! What is she?

A. [*actor(s)*] An English sheepdog.

A. A lion.

A. Was Marco Polo in Africa?

B. This performance has no longer anything to do with Marco Polo! Now, it is Voltaire's *Candide*! Africa. A Safari. Torgeir [Wethal] is on a safari after a lion.

The actor here referred to, portrays a figure which is representative of the European culture – missionary/collector/colonialist/traveler/exploiter, though no *one* aspect dominates.

B. (*to the remaining actors*) Can you find some music with Spring-associations which can be played on brass instruments?

An English folk-dance melody is played, the actress attempting to fit her lion dance to it.

B. Torgeir! Find a rifle in the store room!

The actor returns with a rifle.

B. Take some steps. Find out how to carry the rifle.

The actor improvises various sequences to the folk-dance music.

B. (*to the actress in the lion-dance costume*) You take the rifle!

She repeats her dance, this time fitting the rifle to her movements.

(Farrimond, 1981:95)

Another consideration at this point in rehearsals is how to combine the vocal material with the physical work. This linking of the physical and vocal can be done in several different ways, but all of them are essentially the same. Once Barba and the actors have a sense of the physical shape and structure of a scene, they select vocal improvisations from the stock of material they have accumulated. Since these improvisations are primarily concerned with the sonority of the texts, their suitability for a particular scene is based more on their musical relation to the themes of the piece than on how appropriate they are as dialogue which explains the physical action as part of a narrative. In fact, in several productions the company has even used made-up

89

languages in which sounds replace semantic content entirely. *Min Fars Hus*, for example, was performed in a fabricated tongue that sounded like, but was not, Russian, and the spoken text for *Oxyrhincus Evangeliet* consisted of made-up versions of Coptic and Yiddish.

Many adjustments are called for when the vocal improvisations are added to the physical score. In most instances, the actors have developed their vocal material individually, without considering dialogue-like interchange. Much as with the initial physical work on scenic montage, those in a particular scene then explore their vocal material together, while Barba watches without interrupting. Invariably there are discrepancies between the vocal and physical scores because either there is too much vocal material for the action sequence or vice versa. In this initial phase of the work, the actors attempt to address these discrepancies, and to develop an interactive vocal score through investigating different rhythms, speeds of delivery, and tonal qualities.

Eventually, Barba begins to work with the actors, suggesting adjustments to both their vocal and physical improvisations in order to fit the spoken text to the action, and to ensure a cohesive work that best serves the theme(s). He might suggest cutting sections of text, or ask the actors to speak together or alternately, or he may advise speeding delivery in some sections, slowing it in others, etc., always with the aim of marrying the physical and vocal material without one dominating the other.

It is this need for balance that Barba cites as the major reason for separating physical and vocal improvisations in the first place. He wants the actor to be able to manipulate his/her physical and vocal scores separately to ensure that one does not unduly influence the other, and to give him/her independent control over his/her two major expressive tools, his/her body and voice (Barba, 1985c).

Music is another consideration at this point in rehearsals. As each scene begins to take shape, Barba and his colleagues decide whether music is called for, and, if they feel it is, they either take material from the tunes and songs they have collected during rehearsals, or, if they decide that some other piece is more appropriate, they learn it. These musical choices are based on how effectively they feel the tunes and songs expose shades and facets of the scenic theme, independent of the physical and vocal scores. Just as the physical and vocal scores are separate but related layers of the performance text, music is viewed as another dimension of the same text rather than mere accompaniment to it.

The music in Barba's dramaturgy is closely related to his use of choral singing. Quite apart from the spoken improvisations developed during the early part of rehearsals, Barba has created entire choral scores for his productions during this scenic montage phase of the work. As early as *Kaspariana* (1967) the Odin used choral material developed collectively during rehearsals. But the importance of choral singing peaked in *Oxyrhincus*

Evangeliet (1985), where over half of the entire vocal score was either sung or chanted without instrumental accompaniment.

The production montage

Since there is no causal or clear narrative connection between scenes, their order is as open to intuitive choice as the selection of material within them. Once the group has developed as few as three scenes, Barba begins to experiment with their sequential order in the performance text. These experiments continue as Barba and his actors add more completed scenes, so that any one scene may be tried in several different places in the emerging performance text before Barba and his colleagues finally decide on its place in the production. The structuring of the production montage is not as casual as it may appear, however, since the intuitive choices of Barba and his colleagues are shaped by several factors: thematic considerations, the on-going rehearsals, and many years of experience with these techniques.

Scenography

Barba does not work conventionally with the design aspect of his productions. Most decisions about design are made collectively by the group during rehearsals, based on the themes of the piece and on the improvisations they generate. These decisions, which include everything from the design of the set to the costumes and even stage and hand props, are as much part of the dramaturgical process as the embryonic physical and vocal scores. Rehearsals may begin with some ideas of staging – dances from different countries played a large part in the initial work on *The Million*, for example, so an open dance space became part of the setting early in rehearsals. But rehearsals do not begin with a completed design concept, or a ground plan that dictates blocking.

As one might expect from Grotowski's disciple, the audience–actor relationship is a very important design consideration for Barba. Prior to *Oxyrhincus Evangeliet*, simplicity of staging was the keynote of all his productions. Set design considerations usually focused on deciding where the audience would be seated in relation to the playing area, rather than on building large complex structures on stage. These relationships were usually one of three: playing in the round (*Ornitofilene, Kaspariana, Ferai, Min Fars Hus*, and *Come! And the Day Will be Ours*); the audience seated on either side of the playing area (*Brecht's Ashes 2*); or the audience facing a slightly raised stage set in front of a plain black cloth with no curtain and most of the stage and hand properties in full view of the audience (*The Million*).

This design simplicity was abandoned for *Oxyrhincus Evangeliet*, but the process by which the set evolved during rehearsals was much the same as it had been for the less complex works. The production took place inside a huge structure made of red cloth that contained the audience as well as the actors. The audience sat on raised benches built on either side of a narrow

91

polished wood stage about 2 feet high, not unlike a very long table or kabuki hanamichi, that ran the entire 15-meter (approximately 49-feet) length of the enclosed space.

Despite the relative complexity of the *Oxyrhincus Evangeliet* set, rehearsals began with little idea of its final form. As the group accumulated a stock of improvisations and the direction of the production became a little clearer, however, Barba and his actors began to consider the best way to stage the material – a decision invariably arrived at through a combination of intuition and trial and error at the Odin. The initial investigations of the Borges story in 1982, for example, were performed with a conventional end-on staging. But as the group began to collect improvised material during the work-shop/rehearsal period proper some eighteen months later, the narrow staging was experimented with. These experiments, which included input from an Italian architect colleague of Barba's, Luca Ruzza, were initially done on floor level until it was realized that there might be sight-line problems. The group then tried working on very high tables. These proved to be technically awkward for the actors to get on and off, however, so they were abandoned for an equally narrow stage raised only some 2 feet.

These experiments with a contained staging prompted the idea of an equally contained audience. The group explored ways of surrounding an audience seated on either side of the stage. This led to the construction of performance areas at either end of the main stage, and raised platforms behind the audience where actors could also perform.

During this same period, as Barba continued to work on both the scenic and production montages, he and his colleagues recognized the emerging ritual quality of the piece. They felt that this called for a space in which they could both incorporate their audience and control lighting. Their solution to these problems was to build an entire structure inside which both the actors and the audience were contained, a structure which not only had its own lighting rig, but also allowed the actors to perform both in front of and behind the audience, and to move outside the structure. This allowed them to create various sound effects, like pounding a rock with a large hammer, various types of footsteps and running, as well as singing – all of which heightened the audience's sense of being surrounded and contained.

Even though building the set involved a great deal of time and called for a variety of technical skills, it was constructed in much the same way as other Odin sets, collectively. Both the group's technician, who is the primary set builder, and the company's touring manager began working on the set. Then, toward the end of rehearsals, when most of the design decisions had been made, the group stopped rehearsals and helped complete the task. Several of the actors are talented craftsmen and they helped construct the polished wood panels that formed the stage, built a functional guillotine, and prepared the metal rigging that surrounded the audience and stage. Some helped cut and sew the huge red curtains that were the walls and roof of the set, while others worked on the rostra and walkway to be placed behind the audience and at either end of the main narrow stage.

Final stage of rehearsal

As rehearsals near completion, final decisions are made about the content and order of scenes, characterizations are fixed, and design details finalized, so that gradually a cohesive whole begins to emerge.

Once Barba and his actors feel that this cohesive whole is sufficiently complete to be shown as a "work in progress," they perform it for a public. The initial performances are usually given in Holstebro over a two- to three-week period with no more than three performances per week. Because Holstebro is a small city, audiences are not always large for these showings. Nevertheless, they allow Barba and his group to test the newly created mise-en-scene in performance. During this period Barba continues to work with the actors, making adjustments based on notes taken during performances as well as on feedback from spectators.[7] The production then tours larger theatre centers, primarily in Europe initially, as Barba continues to fine-tune the piece for several months.

This is not to say that Barba stops working on the piece once these initial performances are over. Most of the Odin's productions remain in the repertory for a minimum of two years during which time Barba sees them often and, apart from giving notes to his actors, suggests changes, and even calls productions back into the rehearsal room to be reworked. *Oxyrhincus Evangeliet*, for example, began touring in September 1985, and, as late as February 1987, Barba took the production off the road for several weeks to rework parts of it – despite the fact that the group had decided to end the production's run in July the same year.[8]

BARBA'S DRAMATURGY

Barba regards dramaturgy as an accumulation of actions (Barba and Savarese, 1991:68). But he uses the term action in a somewhat unconventional way since he ignores psychological actions, such as questions of motivation or justification, and focuses entirely on physical actions. Dramaturgically speaking, however, these physical actions are not limited to actors' movements. For Barba, they include all aspects of the mise-en-scene: "actions (that is, all that has to do with the dramaturgy) are not only what is said and done, but also the sounds, the lights and the changes in space. At a higher level of organization, actions are the episodes of the story" (Barba and Savarese, 1991:68). Not only are the actors' vocal and physical scores dramaturgical actions for Barba, but also the lighting, sound effects, proxemics, the musical score, variations in rhythm and intensity, scenes, and even the objects used in the performance. Toward the end of *Brecht's Ashes 2*, for example, there was a scene in which a cook abandoned her cooking and walked around the stage singing. As a backdrop to her song, Brecht and a musician worked together on another song at an organ in a corner of the stage, while the rest of the cast sat in silence around a sofa in a tableau reminiscent of Berlin's decadent 1930s observing everything. The lights brightened and the *Three-penny Opera*'s Mackie Messer (one of the leading characters in *Brecht's Ashes 2*) stepped out of the tableau and announced that Brecht had returned to a recently liberated East Germany. He then danced with another of Brecht's characters who played an important role in Barba's production, Kattrin from *Mother Courage*, while displaying a copy of *Pravda* as the others cleaned the stage. The dancing became more frenzied as the cleaning neared completion, until suddenly Messer stuffed the copy of *Pravda* into Kattrin's mouth and the lights went out. Barba regards each of the components in this scene as a dramaturgical action: the spatial relationship between the performers, the rhythm of the dances and the cleaning of the stage, the way in which the copy of *Pravda* is used, the lighting changes, etc.

But these various actions only become dramaturgically significant when they are interrelated, when they are, as Barba puts it, woven together into a text (Barba and Savarese, 1991:69). This network of actions (the text) then works directly upon the spectators' "attention, on their understanding, their emotions, their kinaesthesia" (Barba and Savarese, 1991:68), and is the means through which they experience and extract meaning from the production.

Barba maintains that this network of actions can be shaped into one of two basic plot structures: concatenate or simultaneous (1985e:76). The concatenate plot structure is a linear narrative in which actions are linked together causally, as in most conventional theatre. The simultaneous plot structure ignores linearity in favor of having several actions taking place at the same time, without regard for their causal relationship – as in the scene described above, in which the cook walked around singing while Brecht and the musician worked on a new song, and the rest of the cast formed a tableau in another part of the stage.

Barba argues that literary texts, such as plays and adaptations of novels or poems, tend to favor concatenation, but that mise-en-scenes based on performance texts developed by the actors during rehearsals tend more toward simultaneity. These distinctions seem somewhat over–generalized, however, because, even though it may be true that the nature of written language favors a concatenate structure, they fail to take into account at least one other plot structure that has become reasonably common in the past twenty years, the episodic structure. The works of auteurs such as Robert Wilson, Richard Foreman, Linda Mussman, and Martha Clark, as well as groups such as the Wooster Group and Mabou Mines, though different, frequently lack linear plot development and owe little to the convention of causality, but often consist of unconnected episodes rather than simultaneous action.

Despite the fact that Barba regards the ideal dramaturgy as one in which the two plot structures are balanced (1985e:78), his rejection of realism has led to his favoring simultaneity over concatenation because of the multifaceted perspective it brings to dramaturgy:

> The simultaneous interweaving of several actions in the performance causes something similar to what Eisenstein describes in reference to El Greco's "View of Toledo": that the painter does not reconstruct a real view, but rather constructs a synthesis of several views, making a montage of the different sides of a building, including even those sides which are not visible.
>
> (Barba and Savarese, 1991: 70)

That is, the simultaneous presents various scenes from different perspectives and replaces the simple linear plot with a complex network of interrelated actions. But, unlike a painting, which is static, this networking unfolds over time, resulting in many instances during which several actions and/or scenes take place simultaneously, as in Brecht's move to Berlin in *Brecht's Ashes 2*, or a sequence earlier in the production in which Walter Benjamin was symbolically hung by Arturo Ui at one end of the stage while at the other an actor and actress (portraying Galileo and an assistant) carefully dissected a fish as they sipped wine and recited principles of physics.

Dramaturgy and the actor

The importance of improvisation in Barba's dramaturgy places the actor at the center of the creative process. This is particularly obvious in the initial stages of creating a new mise-en-scene, because it is the actor who bears the greatest responsibility for providing the raw material for the production. It is the actor who develops the initial improvisations, and it is the actor who adapts them, in consultation with Barba, into the composition improvisations that are the basis of the performance text. Roberta Sklar, Joe Chaikin's assistant director on *The Serpent*, in attempting to describe the Open Theatre's method of creating works uses a term, "active notation," which characterizes this creative role of the actor (Venza, 1970). Though there are differences between the Open Theatre's and Odin's methods of developing works, this term touches on what is common in Chaikin's and Barba's dramaturgy: it is the actors who explore and create the raw material that are the foundations of the mise-en-scene, not the playwright.

This collection of raw material in Barba's dramaturgy might be compared to the first step in the collage song-writing technique of rock singer/song writer David Bowie. One approach used by Bowie in developing lyrics for his songs is to write unconnected words, phrases, and sentences on different scraps of paper which he mixes together in a hat. He then selects clippings at random and composes his lyrics based on the order of selection.[9] This "chance," stream-of-consciousness method of writing lyrics has parallels with the Odin actors' accumulation of improvisations. In much the same way as Bowie writes and collects words and phrases that he will later rearrange into the lines of a song, in Barba's dramaturgy the actors are creating the "words," "phrases," and "sentences" which are the basic building blocks of the performance text. In both cases the "randomness" in the initial phase of creation is loosely channeled by a variety of possible structures which include a subtext of past experiences, themes that the creator wants to explore, and/or even a skeletal format such as a scenario.

The importance of the actor in Barba's dramaturgy is directly related to his concept of the body-in-life. There are essentially two levels of communication in theatre for Barba: signification and what he terms synesthesia. Signification is the domain of semiotics and includes the intended (and often unintended) meanings read into a production. The synesthetic level of performance, on the other hand, refers to the level of communication between actors and audience which defies signification, such as the effect of an actor's body tension on the audience, or an audience's response to the "feel" of a particular scene.[10]

Montage and meaning

Barba rejects linear narrative, which dominates conventional Western theatre, for what he calls its artificiality and denial of organic life. He maintains that dramaturgy should reflect the quality of any living organism by being a dialectic between order (i.e., causality, deductive logic) and disorder, "the asymmetrical and unforeseeable order which characterizes organic life" (Barba, 1985a:24).

This dramaturgy in Barba's productions is based on what he calls montage, a term derived from Meyerhold, Eisenstein, and the cinema, which he defines as "To compose (to put with) … to mount, to put together, to weave actions together: to create the play" (Barba and Savarese, 1991:158).[11] For Barba, montage includes both the linking together of separately developed actions to create each performer's score and the combining of these scores into a performance text:

> If the performer's actions can be considered as analogous to strips of film which are already the result of a montage, it is possible to use this montage not as a final result but as a material for further montage. This is generally the task of the director, who can weave the actions of several performers into a succession in which one action seems to answer another, or into a simultaneous assembling in which the meanings of both actions derive directly from the fact of their being co-present.
>
> (Barba in Barba and Savarese, 1991:160)

The improvisations that Barba and his actors prepare as the building blocks of a production are ordered intuitively. The montage is a product of what "feels right" – based on Barba's and his actors' months of rehearsals, as well as their knowledge and explorations of the thematic sources of the work – rather than on rigid adherance to the law of cause and effect.

Andrzej Zurowski suggested a model that provides a valuable insight into Barba's production dramaturgy when, in describing Tadeusz Kantor's theatre, he used the term "visual narrative". In this description, Zurowski defines visual narrative as a theatre of "non-verbal semantics based on the body or visual expression, on associative and emotional language, with the type of narration … [which] evades linear verbal logic" (1985:364–365). Following this definition, Barba's mise-en-scenes could be characterized as visual/aural narratives, that is, narratives which "evade linear verbal logic" but in which the semantics are "based on the body or visual expression, on associative and emotional language," as well as on the sonorous qualities of the voice.

Dramaturgy and meaning

Barba's method of developing a production montage is reflected in his concept of dramaturgical meaning, a concept which is better understood when viewed through the analysis of meaning suggested by the Italian theatre semiotician, Marco De Marinis (1987). De Marinis argues that meaning in all theatrical productions falls along a continuum between what he terms open and closed performances. Open performances are ones in which little or no meaning is intentionally being conveyed, so that members of the audience have a degree of freedom in choosing the meanings they read into a work, as in avant-garde/experimental productions, like Robert Wilson's 1987 production of Heiner Muller's *Hamlet Machine* at New York University, in which the conventions of plot, dialogue, and cohesive argument were replaced by an emphasis on visual composition, distortions of the normal time frame by having many scenes in slow motion, and the constant repetition of simple, apparently meaningless, actions and dialogue. Closed performances, meanwhile, are loaded with intended signification which can be read differently by different people, but which allow for a much less free reading than productions in which the writer, director, and actors have no specific ideology, socio-political comment, and/or philosophical point of view that they wish to convey to their audience. As De Marinis points out, the best examples of closed performances are genre-based theatres with an agenda, such as political theatre, children's theatre, women's theatre, and gay theatre (De Marinis, 1987:103). In De Marinis's terms, Barba's concept of meaning is open. But, unlike De Marinis, he does not limit this openness to the spectator, arguing instead that the open nature of any production is as much part of the rehearsal process as of the product it leads to.

Barba identifies three levels of meaning in his dramaturgy: the actor's meaning, the director's meaning, and the spectator's meaning (1982a:35–36). The actor's meaning stems from the links between the personal associations underlying the improvisations that are the raw material of the production, and the physical score they lead to. These associations are rarely, if ever, discussed with Barba, who focuses on the external physical and vocal tension of the actor in constructing the montage rather than on the internal, psychological source they stem from. However, despite the fact that Barba does not include these psychological components in his shaping of the production montage, the actors often retain them and draw on them in performances, as Rasmussen attests in an open letter she wrote to a spectator about her experiences as an Odin performer:

> We were working on a new play, *Come! And the Day Will be Ours.* The images of the hopes and fears concerned with our own lives enter into this play. They are there for the actors, but not for the spectators. In this play there is a scene where I am left alone, and where I feel footsteps behind me. ... "Death" walks by me and in front of me, perhaps showing the way, perhaps leaving. And it is as if I see a field: "Leave, that all this may live." At this moment I hear the pounding of a hammer, as the others at the opposite end of the room begin to nail a book down. I suppose that spectators think of soldiers who nail the latest official proclamations to wooden walls and doors, or of the crucifixion, or of those who take books, living words, and freeze them, transforming them into laws that destroy forever.
>
> When I hear these blows I remember a situation many years ago. I heard a hammer strike, and my companion said, "That's death. A carpenter is making a coffin." So when I hear this sound in the play, I kneel down with my face on the floor, and I continue praying with my hands: the things of the earth have to grow. With my hands, I try to warm that which is still closed up within the earth.
>
> When I hear footsteps approaching, when two hands lift my head and open my mouth, I feel it is the moment of an acceptance of things to come.
>
> Yet on the other hand, spectators say it is as if my face turns to stone, and is transformed into a skull. Naturally, I know that this scene is, objectively, the result of the montage, fragment by fragment, done by Eugenio with the material from my improvisation. I know that it is linked in a sequence of actions which have little to do with my own associations.
>
> (1979:11–12)

The director's meaning has its origins in both the thematic sources of the piece that he and his actors are working on, and the improvised material developed by the actors. But the meaning Barba assigns to the production rarely dictates the actor's or the spectator's understanding of the work. His meaning is based on his own personal associations which, as with the actors' associations, are rarely shared with colleagues, let alone with the audience.

Barba maintains that this dialectic between the actor's and director's meaning of a particular production enriches the audience's experience of it:

> It is tension which determines the life of the theatrical organism. Here expropriation does not pay off. If the actor allows his material to be completely expropriated by the director the actor and the director will end up with nothing in their hands but a fistful of sand.
>
> But pacifism and humanitarianism do not pay off either: if the director does not seek to expropriate the actor's creative work for himself, in a personal way, this work will remain on the molecular level, the sand in a private garden.
>
> A performance is the result of a collision which occurs in a situation of acceptance and of reciprocal confidence. The depth and extent to which the creative work of a group of individuals can develop depends on this dialectic.
>
> (1982a:35)

The open nature of Barba's dramaturgy, combined with the dialectic between the actors' and director's understanding of a production's meaning allows spectators a wide scope in choosing their reading of the work. These readings may vary greatly because of Barba's limited use of closed signification, and his emphasis on the synesthetic level of communication. But this rejection of a closed meaning structure should not be mistaken for disregarding the audience. Barba, in fact, like many of the experimentalists who began working in the 1960s and 1970s, demands more from his audience than mere passivity. He maintains that viewing a performance is action: it is work (1982a:36). Barba has been accused of making theatre that is difficult to understand, but he is not interested in productions that require no effort on the part of the spectators. The audience, just like the actors, must be active during a performance, even if the action is entirely mental:

> Seeing becomes action when there is an effort to understand, to distinguish something that one knows but does not succeed in recognizing, in order to discern the essential thing: the relationships which exist between the different events which are occurring before our eyes.
>
> (Barba, 1982a:36)

For Barba, the passive spectator is equivalent to the actor with no energy.

Barba's active spectator is involved in a creative act. Just as Barba attempts to reproduce the dynamic of creative thought in the production montage during rehearsals, he demands that, rather than being swept along by a linear narrative, the spectator make mental leaps in understanding and personal associations while watching a performance – that is, the spectator should be engaged in a creative rather than logical thought process. A typical example of this "creative process" was the Odin's early piece *Kaspariana*, which one critic described as an "open" or "labyrinth" work [which] demands not that the spectator discover any "unique meaning" that the work is supposed to contain, but that he create his own sense, that he find his own path in the complex of images and significant sounds which have penetrated him, which can be translated only by allusion or metaphor and cannot be reduced to any analysis which claims to be a substitute for the "presence" of the work of art.

(Fumaroli, 1968:54)

Fragmented dramaturgy

Fragmentation lies at the root of both the actors' and director's dramaturgy in Barba's performance texts.

The entire dramaturgy of the actor, from the time Barba begins to work with him/her on his/her composition montage until the completion of each scene, is based on a fragmentation process. Once the actor has fixed his/her composition improvisation, Barba works with him/her adjusting and re-arranging sections of it, that is, deconstructing (pulling apart) the original improvisation, by breaking it into fragments which are worked on separately, and then reintegrating these reworked fragments with the remaining sections of the original improvisation to form a physically choreographed score. This score is then combined with another actor's score developed in the same way, and adjustments are made once again. Just as with the individual improvisations, these adjustments involve fragmenting the scores of the actors by taking sections of action from one place in the sequence and placing them elsewhere, slowing down some sections, speeding up others, having one actor stop his/her action while the other continues his/hers, etc. During the latter part of this process, the vocal improvisations, which have been developed separately, are adjusted along with the evolving physical action to create an integrated physical and vocal montage. Each actor within this integrated montage has a precise physical and vocal score which Barba refers to as an "intricate mosaic of tensions" (1985c).

These various mosaics of tension are Barba's attempt to communicate with the audience at a level other than the semantic. Like performers' scores in traditional Eastern genres, the Odin actors' scores are codified. But unlike their Eastern counterparts, for whom much of this codification is traditional and/or symbolic, the Odin's codes are not objective symbols handed down from generation to generation that one can learn in order to "read" the performance. In studying Beijing opera, one learns that a certain kind of step means that the actor has just entered a house, or that to move in a circle while holding a small whip indicates that the character is riding a horse. But the Odin's codes are drawn from a combination of sources including everyday life, years of training and experience, performance skills, and from knowledge of Barba's acting principles. The audience cannot "know" these codes in the same way they can learn the codes of Beijing opera.[12]

The subjective nature of the Odin's codes establishes a synesthetic contact with the audience. Spectators are influenced by the actors' command of the pre-expressive as much as they are by the semiotically loaded meanings they "read" in a production. In Barba's dramaturgy there is a conscious attempt to address an audience's perception at the physiological and mental levels simultaneously, because he acknowledges that an actor's mosaic of tensions communicates with the spectators through both the central nervous system (i.e., synesthetically) and semantics (i.e., at the level of meaning).

Another way in which fragmentation plays an important role in Barba's construction of scenes lies in how he combines raw material from different sources in developing his scenic montages. In a scene that includes movement, spoken text, and music (or singing), for instance, each element has been developed separately. The movement has its origins in a stock of physical improvisations, the spoken text in vocal improvisations, and the music in material collected independently of the other two. Each of these components is both separate from and connected to the others since each has been developed/learned independently but each is also a product of common thematic or intuitive choices. These independent yet related elements are brought together in bricolage fashion by Barba as he constructs his scenes. Each element has a dual function: it both reveals its own connection to the theme, and is an integral part of a gestalt which contains the theme of the entire work.

Just as Barba's concatenation theory relates to Eistenstein's reading of El Greco's "View of Toledo," this fragmentation could be compared to a cubist artist's attempts to capture the essence of an object by revealing all its surfaces simultaneously. In Barba's dramaturgy each "surface" – the physical score, the spoken text, and the music – is separate, but then each is laid over the top of the others, much like the surfaces of an object. However, just as in cubist theory, each of these "surfaces" only exists in relation to all the others; by revealing them simultaneously one captures the essence of the whole.

The fragmentary nature of Barba's production montages lies in the lack of causal connection between scenes. Each performance text consists of separate independent scenes in which many of the same characters may appear, but the order of which could be altered. This is not to say that Barba's productions have a random structure which could be changed without altering the logic of the final work. When the production montage is being constructed, there is no necessity for one scene to follow another because events in the first scene cause those in the second. Each scene in a Barba production is created independently, and it is only when the production montage is put together in the latter stages of rehearsals that relationships are established between scenes.

The very origin of the term montage lies in an attempt to fragment conventional narrative structure in the theatre. It was, and still is in the way

Barba uses it, an attempt to achieve cohesion through "establishing a certain final thematic effect" (Eisenstein in Dukore, 1974:943) rather than relying on a plot to unify the production. Barba's use of montage in his production dramaturgy is designed to thwart the expectations of his audience (i.e., their expectations of a logically coherent plot structure) in order to establish a level of communication based on synesthetic factors and personal associations with material in the piece.

Similarly, Barba's inclusion of simultaneously running scenes in his performance texts adds another fragmentary dimension to his productions. This simultaneity not only fragments the sequential ordering of the scenes, but also fragments an audience's perception since spectators must either choose only one scene to watch, switch from one scene to the other(s), or attempt to watch all of them at once. The hanamichi-type stage with the audience seated on either side in *Oxyrhincus Evangeliet* provided many examples of this fragmentation. During the Grand Inquisitor's first entrance, for instance, he moved along the stage on his hands and knees dragging a large rock attached to the cape around his shoulders. As he moved to center stage singing, Joan of Arc was at one end of the stage making a speech, Antigone was at the other end doing the same, and the Hasid looked on in wonder from floor level. Given the audience sight-lines and the length of the stage, it was impossible to see the entire action at once. Spectators had to choose what to watch.

Phenomenological fragmentation

Barba distinguishes between what he terms the phenomenology of reality and the phenomenology of creative thought (1985a:20–22; 1988a:129), the former being causal, logically connected linear progression, as opposed to the latter, which is non-linear and proceeds in leaps rather than in a causally connected sequential chain. Applying this distinction to his dramaturgy, Barba (reflecting his concept of body-in-life) maintains that his dramaturgy is an attempt to invest his performance texts with "thought-in-life," that is, a dramatic structure which mirrors the dynamics of creative thought. In other words, he wants his work to "render perceptible" the phenomenology of creative thought (Barba, 1988d:129).

In practical terms, this means fragmenting conventional reality. As Barba puts it,

> the actor does not remain yoked to the plot, does not interpret a text, but creates a context, moves around and within the events. ... The linearity of the narrative is shattered through constantly changing the point of view, atomizing the known reality, and through interweaving objectivity and subjectivity (i.e., expositions of facts and reactions to them).
>
> (1988d:129)

Fragmentation has *always* been an important aspect of Barba's dramaturgy. This is because each of his rehearsal methodologies has its origins in a deconstruction/reconstruction process similar to the Schechner paradigm discussed earlier. In the group's formative years, when Barba based his productions on dramatic texts, he and his colleagues deconstructed the literary source of their work then reconstructed the material in order to create the performance text. Since 1974, the company has abandoned dramatic texts in favor of improvisation, but theirs is a most unusual approach that might best be described as deconstruction/reconstruction improvisation: each actor develops a series of composition improvisations which are deconstructed (i.e., pulled apart) by Barba, then reconstructed (i.e., adjusted, reshaped, elaborated) in order to explore new relationships and build individual scenes. In both the dramatic text and improvisation-based dramaturgy, raw material is fragmented and reconstructed.

Initially, a writer provided the raw material for the work; now the actors have taken over this task. In Barba's present dramaturgy, the actor is author while he is both dramaturge and director. In tasks that overlap and interconnect during rehearsals, Barba, as dramaturge, shapes the authors' (i.e., actors') raw material while, as the director, he transforms the material into a performance text.

Despite this duality of roles (or possibly because of it) and the differences in rehearsal methodologies and source material for productions, Barba's performance texts have retained a surprising consistency. They have always been episodic, causality has generally played a minor role in structuring the montage, plot linearity has been ignored and, even with the lack of conventional unifying devices such as plot and causality, there has always been a cohesion which owes its origins to the visual/aural narrative. In short, Barba's performance texts are based on an apparent opposition: narrative fragmentation (i.e., lack of conventional unifying devices) versus visual/aural cohesion. The power of his dramaturgy lies in the tension between the two.

5

PRODUCTIONS

During the Odin's first ten years, from 1964 to 1974, Barba created only three productions – *Ornitofilene, Kaspariana,* and *Ferai* – each of which was rehearsed and performed over a one- to two-year cycle then abandoned in favor of a new work. From 1974 to 1979, however, the Odin carried no less than five new productions in its repertoire. And with the expansion of the NTL in 1984 to include additional groups as well as Barba's encouragement of solo productions, the number of Barba-directed productions being performed at any one time during the 1980s and 1990s has remained between four and five.

Despite the number of productions in the current Odin repertoire, all of them are essentially of two types: studio pieces, sometimes referred to by Barba as secret or introverted works, and their extroverted counterpart, open-air productions intended for the streets. Despite their differences, these two types of productions share much because they are created by the same group, whose esthetics and dramaturgical methods inform both.

A STYLE

Barba's productions are in a constant state of flux. Even though he is unable to be at every performance, he invariably gives notes after those he sees. And it is not unusual for works that have been on tour for over a year to be brought off the road and reworked. When these reworkings are extensive enough, resulting from either a lengthy break from performing a piece or cast changes, they are even billed as a different version of the production – as were the four versions of *Anabasis* and *The Million.*

Barba's rejection of realism in favor of presentational productions makes great demands on the actors' movement and vocal skills. These demands are evident in an intricate choreography bordering on dance, and an equally complex vocal score – often consisting of several languages or even fabricated tongues, delivered in a style that might best be described as a combination of singing, declamation, and incantation.

This presentational quality is further emphasized by the way in which Barba uses music. Most of his works call for relatively complex scores which are an integral part of the performance text. A typical example is *Min Fars Hus* in which he used a flute and piano accordion to comment on the action and to visualize situations:

> The "voices" of the flute and the accordion, animated by two actors in the performance, commented on the action, dialoguing between themselves (they were the voices of two servants who were observing the actions of their masters). At a given moment they might be "speaking" with detachment, commenting ironically on the "passions" of the rich and noble people; then, on the contrary, they were obedient servants, working to create the setting of their masters' actions: the wind on the Siberian tundra, the noise of the horses' hooves, the flame in front of an icon in a room where a young woman had been killed.
> Through incantations and associative sounds, the actors, using the musical instruments sought to "visualize" these situations and others.
>
> (Barba, 1986a:76–77)

Barba's musical scores are not limited to the flute and piano accordion. They are played by a variety of instruments ranging from kazoos and whistles, through trumpets, various drums, guitars, recorders, bagpipes, to organs, and even the medieval hurdy-gurdy.

Consistent with Barba's presentational approach, there is little psychological exploration of character or situation in his productions. Far from realistic, many of the characters who appear in his works are larger than life archetypes who project their personalities through their costume, the way in which they move or distort their bodies, and through vocal expression in a manner much closer to Meyerhold's concept of the grotesque than Stanislavsky's notion of psychological realism.[1] Many of these Odin grotesques have proved so enduring, in fact, that they reappear time and again, particularly in the group's street-theatre work. Characters, which will be described later, such as Mr Peanuts, the masked dwarf, the kazoo-blowing top-hatted band leader, and the androgynous white-masked stilt figure with his/her smaller sister/brother have been appearing off and on in productions since 1974.

As well as recurring characters, there is also a recurring "character theme" in many of Barba's productions. Wethal, for instance, is frequently cast as a figure outside of the group. In *Ferai* he played the demigod king who was above the common people; in *Anabasis* he was a masked dwarf who led, but was not part of, the band which was a central motif of the production; in *The Million* he had the role of a priest, the only clearly identifiable Westerner in a world populated by exotic characters from a variety of cultures; and in *Oxyrhincus Evangeliet* he played Sabbatai Zevi, a figure of god-like stature to whom others paid homage. This casting is no accident, according to Barba, who regards Wethal as the embodiment of his ideal actor, that is, one who is able to separate from his role, the performer who is both a character in

105

the production and "is always himself – a figure from the outside, observing, coming, travelling, making comments" (Farrimond, 1981:113).

This duality, which serves to highlight the dichotomy between the fictional world of the production and the real world of its presentation, is further emphasized in Barba's rejection of conventional staging. In each of his productions, Barba adjusts the actor–audience relationship to create an overall metaphor, and/or to define the contact between performers and spectators. In all his early productions, for example, he placed the audience on the same level as the performers, and incorporated metaphors – such as a courtroom (*Ornitofilene*), medieval mansions (*Kaspariana*), and a Viking burial ship (*Ferai*) – into the seating arrangements. This not only established an intimacy between the actors and spectators, but also made one of the themes in each production concrete.

CRITICISM

A common criticism of Barba's productions is that they all seem alike, that once you have seen one you have seen them all. To be fair, these critics generally acknowledge a difference between the Odin's studio and street-theatre work, arguing that all the studio productions are essentially the same, as are all street pieces.

This criticism touches on a common feature of recent theatre, the difference between the interpretive director and the auteur. The interpretive director (in the line of people like Stanislavsky and Max Reinhardt), in whom the emphasis is on versatility, dominates conventional theatre. Such a director is a craftsperson able to direct a season of plays ranging from the classics and farces to romantic comedies, naturalistic dramas, and the absurd. It is his/her task to transfer the writer's words from the page to the stage with due respect to the play's themes. The auteur, on the other hand – who owes his/her origins to Gordon Craig, Meyerhold, Artaud, and Brecht – has a personal agenda which s/he explores through productions which bear little resemblance to the intentions of the playwright (unless the director is also the writer). Some of these directors, such as Richard Foreman and Robert Wilson (occasionally), write their own material. Others, like Schechner, Wilson, and Grotowski, use(d) literary material as a stimulus to their own and/or their actors' imaginations without concern for the writers' original intentions. While these directors, and others, such as Joe Chaikin with the Open Theatre and Julian Beck and Judith Malina at the Living Theatre from the late 1960s to mid-1980s, relied almost entirely on improvisation as a source of their material.

Barba is an auteur, an artist whose creativity is defined by his own body of work rather than his interpretation of the text of others. As he himself put it when one interviewer asked for his response to the criticism that all the Odin productions were essentially the same,

When you've seen one Van Gogh canvas.... It's the same thing. If that's the kind of criterion you use, there is no need to read the novels of James Joyce or Dostoyevsky, or to look at Cezanne's paintings. All you do is choose one book and you can burn the rest. In my opinion, this so-called "weakness" is actually the artist's very mode of expression.

(Hagested, 1969:56)

Another criticism often made of Barba's productions, particularly in the 1970s and early 1980s, was that, despite his concern with the social role of theatre, they lacked a political point of view. While it is true that most Odin productions have not been overtly political, many of them have dealt with socio-political issues. *Ornitofilene*, for instance, used the conflict between local villagers and an ecologically conscious group of developers to explore the Nazi occupation of the village some twenty years earlier. *Ferai*, which drew heavily on Greek and Nordic mythology, also dealt with the conflict between a democratic king who allowed his countrymen to decide their own fate and citizens who yearned for the authoritarian leadership of a dictator, while the protagonist of *Brecht's Ashes 2* was a committed Marxist.

A major source of the political criticism of Barba's work stems from a misunderstanding of his dramaturgy. Even if one accepts that some of his productions have socio-political roots, Barba's rejection of linear plot structures in favor of visual/aural narrativity means that the issues in them are not dealt with conventionally. The issues provide the themes the actors explore during rehearsals. They are not the source of propaganda or the subject of realistic scenes in which characters simulate a daily life that reflects socio-historical conflicts.

Barba believes that most political theatre runs the risk of preaching only to the converted. For him, the political act is often more potent than the political statement. Citing Grotowski's example of establishing a center for theatre research and daring to do ritualistic, quasi-mystical productions in a society in which social realism was the official artistic credo, Barba maintains that the way in which one does theatre is more telling politically than what is said on stage (Barba, 1981a:58). For this reason, he has always placed a greater emphasis on how productions are created than on the political values they express.

Some critics have attacked Barba's productions as being obscure, because of what they regard as his lack of thematic clarity. But Barba's esthetics call for a minimum of intended signification. It is not poor directing or lack of structure that leads to productions with many possible meanings. On the contrary, Barba does not want a theatre in which the production's themes are packaged in the dramaturgy.

This esthetic, with its emphasis on personal rather than collective meaning, presents a difficulty for critics and scholars alike. If meaning is emphatically subjective (i.e., intentionally left as open as possible), it is

107

difficult to discuss a work's meaning in light of what Barba and his colleagues intended the audience to take from it. To be consistent with Barba's esthetics, a critic or scholar can only discuss his/her own subjective responses to a particular production.

Keeping this problem in mind, I will attempt to avoid discussing meaning in my consideration of Barba's productions. I will focus on the sources of material used as a basis for each production, the themes used in creating them, scenarios, where available, and descriptions based on my own or others' observations, as well as published and unpublished documents about them.

STREET THEATRE

Street theatre is a generic term for Barba which includes all of his open-air productions ranging from parades and barters to more formal productions such as *The Book of Dances* and *Anabasis.* This is not to say that street-theatre productions are limited to the streets, however, since in at least one instance, *The Million,* Barba often presented the same work in theatres with only minor alterations.

Barba's street-theatre work is a product of the Odin's residencies in southern Italy during the early 1970s when, free of the rigors of the Danish climate, the group was able to train and rehearse outdoors. But Italy was not only the geographic origin of these performances: its history also provided Barba with both a technique for attracting audiences and a metaphorical structure for the productions.

One of Barba's first concerns in developing street theatre was the audience. Unlike more conventional theatre, in which there is a captive audience which is seated according to the predetermined design of the performance space, the actors must attract spectators and structure their playing area in street work.

In considering the first of these problems, Barba recalled his reading of modern Italian history, in which Giuseppe Garibaldi, with only one thousand men, swept across southern Italy in 1860 defeating several armies much larger than his own. One of Garibaldi's strategies was to have troops run through villages carrying flags which attracted the local children. These children then followed Garibaldi's soldiers creating a huge dust cloud. This dust cloud gave his enemies the impression that they were facing a very large army, which led to many of them surrendering without a battle. Barba borrowed Garibaldi's strategy to attract audiences for his street theatre (Barba, 1985c). In beginning a parade or more formal street-theatre piece, for instance, Barba often has his actors stand on rooftops or balconies blowing trumpets, banging drums, and waving flags. Then one or more rappel down the side of one of the buildings and, together with other actors, move through the streets waving flags and playing their instruments. This invariably attracts the attention of the local people, many of whom follow the actors, who lead them to the area they have chosen for the main part of the performance.

The origin of this strategy prompted Barba to describe the components of his street theatre in military terms. The actors on rooftops with flags and trumpets he terms mariens (derived from Mars, the Roman god of war); these are followed by huge characters on stilts that Barba refers to as tanks, since they are large, move slowly, and appear powerful. It is usually these characters whom Barba uses to establish and control the major performance area by forcing the crowds into a circular or semi-circular configuration, inside which the group performs. Those that follow in the rear Barba calls the cavalry. They are the ones kept in reserve until the last moment when they burst on the scene and dominate the action (Sciarrata, 1984:2).

This military analogy is not limited to the formal aspects of Barba's street theatre, since it also contributes to its content – primarily in the form of martial arts displays. Most of the Odin's street theatre incorporates stylized combat with either bare hands, flags, staves, musical instruments, or actual weapons such as machetes.

But, despite the importance of the military metaphor in both the form and content, there are other influences on Barba's street theatre which are unrelated to combat or weapons. One such influence is the European popular theatre tradition of parades and street festivals. This tradition includes live music, colorful costumes, stock characters, masks, and spectacular skills such as choreographed displays with huge colorful flags – all of which Barba and his colleagues have used in their work. Similarly, the circus-like concept of entertaining through a display of skill, something that is alien to the Odin's process-oriented studio work, plays no small part in their street performances. Rappelling down the side of a tall building while continuing to play a trumpet, for example, being able to run, dance, as well as fall and get back up again on stilts, acrobatics, and dances from various parts of the world, have all played major parts in one or more of Barba's street-theatre pieces.

THE PRODUCTIONS

There is little or no documentation on the three major street-theatre productions mounted between 1974 and 1988: *The Book of Dances, Anabasis,* and *The Million.* This is because all of them were based entirely on performance texts developed in rehearsals, they contained little or no dialogue, and no scripts were published. There was a minimal unifying theme or through-line in each, and Barba's episodic dramaturgy dominated the productions, giving them the structural quality of a variety show or circus performance in which self-contained acts are linked together in a loose-knit sequence. Equally, there is little critical material about them, except for *The*

Million, because they were rarely presented in the formal setting of a theatre attended by critics. Most criticism has been published as part of longer reports on festivals at which the Odin has performed. Typical of such critical response is a report on the 2nd International Group Theatre Gathering held in Bergamo in 1977 by Ron Jenkins, in which he briefly describes an Odin street parade that included scenes from *Anabasis*:

> An equally forceful, but simpler and more primitive form of imagery was displayed by Denmark's Odin Teatret [he is comparing the Odin's performance to a Polish group, Akademia Ruchu, and a Welsh company, Pauper's Carnival, which he described earlier] … this young troupe masterfully enacted a battle between vivid physicalizations of sound and color. In an announced street event white-masked drummers clashed with marching flag bearers. The musicians used drum beats and drum sticks to parry the attacks of the dynamically manipulated red banners. The battle was an elemental whirlpool of pounding rhythms and flashing colored cloth. On one level it was just a carnival parade stunt. But the grandeur and skill with which it was executed gave the confrontation archetypal powers.
>
> (Jenkins, 1977:1)

The Book of Dances

This production premiered in Carpignano, Italy, in July 1974 and remained in the Odin's repertoire until 1980. The cast consisted of Roberta Carreri, Tom Fjordefalk, Tage Larsen, Else Marie Laukvik, Iben Nagel Rasmussen, and Torgeir Wethal.

The Book of Dances grew directly out of the training being explored by the group during its southern Italian residency in 1974, and consisted primarily of various exercises structured into sequences which were linked together into a single performance. Most of these sequences were independent of each other, with little thought given to a unifying theme. Despite this apparent lack of thematic cohesion, there was a unity of sorts in that audiences generally viewed the exercises as different types of dances (hence the title) in which many of the same characters appeared.

The production began with members of the company in colorful costumes running through the streets and alleyways of the town carrying flags, blowing whistles, and playing drums to attract their audience. Once they had their audience's attention, they moved toward a previously chosen playing area with their audience following them. This performance space was usually set up against the backdrop of a wall or building, with the audience standing in a semi-circle around it.

Scenes included mock combat between characters with hip drums and others with long poles to which streamers were attached; solo pieces in which

110

individual actors "danced" with the same streamer poles; sequences in front of a huge black cloth backdrop in which puppeteer-type characters manipulated streamers attached to other character's arms and legs forcing them to move like marionettes, and simple "dance" scenes with figures on stilts moving to music.

It was during this period that Barba and his actors were exploring personal rhythm in their training and their experiments were carried through into the production. These experiments were not limited merely to incorporating rhythm-based training exercises, such as the snake composition improvisation described in Chapter 3. They also included explorations of the relationship between physical and musical rhythms and the use of instruments as hand props. These experiments led to a fixed musical score which called for the actors to play instruments such as a recorder, a kettledrum and various hand drums, as well as tambourines, and a simple xylophone.

This production proved very popular with audiences, as is evident from a description of it presented in a village outside of Belgrade, Yugoslavia, during the 1st International Group Theatre Gathering in 1976:

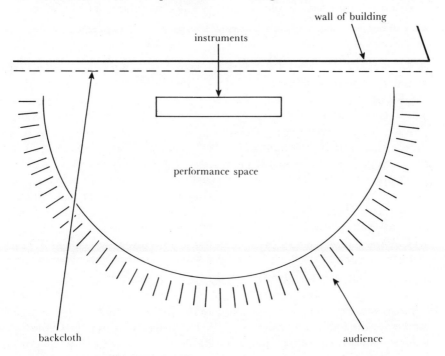

Note: When not in a scene, actors either played musical accompaniment or sat and watched those performing. They did not leave the playing area during the performance.

Figure 5.1 Plan view of a typical performance of *The Book of Dances*

111

The strange procession wound its way through the narrow streets of the "musical colony," and the Odin-ites began a succession of numbers, as if they were recalling with their movements the gestures and words of ancient pilgrims and the traveling entertainers of the Middle Ages, as if they were reviving their vocation and challenge to the public. Whirling around in virtuoso fashion on top of high stilts, three of them dialogued, changed the rhythm of the movement, took the villagers' breath away, ran into the yards and rapidly changed masks and facial expressions. In front of them went a drummer, one actress playing the harmonica, and two clowns ran among the children. The procession around the actors grew rapidly, all other jobs in the lanes and backyards were interrupted, even the sale of fresh lamb was put off till later.

When the procession reached a big meadow and dispersed on the benches and surrounding grass, it was clear that the seeds had not been sown in vain. Surrounded by the happy faces of the onlookers waiting with baited breath, the Odin Teatret continued its song and dance numbers on the grass stage. Through their skill and visible inner enthusiasm for acting, the spectators failed to notice that night was falling.

(Jovanov, 1976)

The Book of Dances has left its mark on Barba's subsequent work in several ways. It was the first of his productions to use music extensively, something that has become an important component even in the more intimate studio pieces. It was the first Odin piece in which the larger-than-life stilt-walking characters, who continue to play an important role in the group's street theatre, made their appearance. It was also in this production that two of what have become stock characters in most of the subsequent street-theatre works appeared for the first time: Wethal's dwarf figure with a half-mask, whistle, and walking cane which he uses much as a drum-major's baton; and Rasmussen's character dressed in a white training costume, with a white half-mask, and playing a kettle drum strapped to her waist.

The Book of Dances paved the way for a more ambitious project, *Anabasis*.

Anabasis

Anabasis was first performed in Barcelona, Spain, in April 1977, and remained in the Odin repertoire until 1984. During its seven years of performance, *Anabasis* went through several different cast changes and versions. The final, fourth version, performed from 1982 to 1984, had a cast of twelve, consisting of Torben Bjelke, Roberta Carreri, Toni Cots, Tom Fjordefalk, Francis Pardeilhan, Tage Larsen, Else Marie Laukvik, Iben Nagel Rasmussen, Silvia Ricciardelli, Ulrik Skeel, Julia Varley, and Torgeir Wethal.

Anabasis was more sophisticated than *The Book of Dances*. Even though it

112

drew heavily on training, scenes were not merely exercises lifted directly from the training studio. The performance text was the product of original improvisations which used training exercises as a point of departure. These improvisations focused on a loose thematic framework that justified much of the parading and mock combats that were a major part of the work. This theme, of a group of foreigners traveling through a strange land, is embodied in the title, which is taken directly from a chronicle by Xenophon, a fourth-century BC Greek writer. Xenophon tells the story of a Greek army forced to make a long journey through many foreign lands (Asia Minor in his *Anabasis*), populated by both friendly and hostile people, on their way to the sea in order to return to their homeland.

Anabasis began with the actors entering a town or village grouped together in a parade-like formation with Wethal's dwarf drum-major at the head. The group entered carrying flags, playing drums and trumpets, and singing. At a signal from Wethal they dispersed, running through the street, into buildings, onto balconies and rooftops. As several actors rappelled down the sides of buildings into the squares, others playing instruments, waved flags, and continuing their frenzied rushing through the town.

The noise and wild activity invariably drew a crowd, many of whom followed the actors to the central square or park where it had been decided that the performance would be held. The audience was directed to form a circle by the characters who, once the spectators were in place, presented a series of self-contained scenes which included several stilt figures in dance-like sequences done to music, a fight between one of the stilt figures and Wethal's dwarf, and several mock combats in which flags, musical instruments, and a machete were used as weapons. Following these scenes, the actors regrouped into their parade formation and left the square, only to be confronted by two stilt figures who produced a huge black cloth in which they enveloped the rest of the cast, ending the production.

As in *The Book of Dances*, music played a large part in the new work with the performers playing instruments such as kettle and bass drums, trumpets, cymbals, a bell, whistles, and a kazoo. Similarly, colorful costumes were again in evidence, as were larger-than-life stilt figures, and the episodic dramatic structure of dance-like sequences which included mock combats with hand props. The action called for several different rhythms and moods, most of which were dictated by the music or singing. These rhythmic moods varied from the funereal, as the group first entered in parade formation, through the frenzied running and frantic action of a military charge and call to arms, when the actors ran through the streets, to the playful, game-like quality of popular theatre, in the episodic sequences in the square or park.

It was in making *Anabasis* that Barba formulated his military metaphor for street theatre. He thought not only of the thematic analogy with an ancient Greek military expedition, but also of the actors as parts of an army protecting themselves as they moved through an alien land (Barba, 1986a:275).

Despite these militaristic overtones, neither *Anabasis* nor *The Book of Dances* dealt with warfare or told soldier's tales. They did, however, increase the number of stock characters which have continued to appear in most of Barba's street-theatre works. In *Anabasis*, Wethal's dwarf and Rasmussen's half-masked drummer were joined by two stilt characters, one a skeleton dressed in a formal dinner suit which has since become known as Mr Peanuts, and the other, an androgynous white-masked character with a flowing black and red costume, elongated fingernails, and a black feather boa. These giants were joined by a more earth-bound personality in a top hat, formal black pants and shoes, suspenders, and a white long-sleeved shirt, with a duck decoy which he/she (the masculine character was created and played by Carreri) used instead of talking.

The Million

Interculturalism was a major component of *The Million*. As the reader may recall, the production owes its origins to a three-month sabbatical during which most of the actors studied performance genres from different parts of the world. The material the actors returned with – drawn from kathakali, pentjak, legong, and the capoeira – formed the basis of the production which, as well as reflecting the specific journeys that inspired the piece, also owed much to the group's broader travels and contact with other cultures while on tour (Taviani, 1986a:266).

This focus on the intercultural is also echoed in the title, which is the nickname Venetians gave Marco Polo in response to what he told them of his travels in Asia. To the citizens of Venice "everything he described was a million times bigger, a million times more improbable, a million times more cruel than anything they had imagined" (Odin Teatret, 1984).

The Million is unique in the Odin's history in so far as it is the only production that the group has performed both as a street-theatre piece and indoors. It was originally conceived by Barba and his colleagues as a street-theatre production with spectacle, use of music, dances, and minimal dialogue. But it proved equally successful in the more intimate setting of indoor theatres.

The production was first presented in Aarhus, Denmark in September 1978 and remained in the Odin repertoire until 1984, during which time it, like *Anabasis*, underwent several cast and text changes. The final, fourth, version was performed by Roberta Carreri, Toni Cots, Francis Pardeilhan, Tage Larsen, Else Marie Laukvik, Iben Nagel Rasmussen, Silvia Ricciardelli, Ulrik Skeel, Julia Varley, and Torgeir Wethal.

The setting for all versions was essentially the same, consisting of a long, rectangular playing area with the audience seated on both sides. At one end of the main playing area was a raised stage on which the actors, dressed in Oriental and Latin American costumes, played musical instruments and from which they entered the main playing area. This was balanced at the other end of the space by a trunk full of colorful scarfs, and a lounge seat, shaded by a large parasol, which the leading character, a European priest, sat on at key points during the performance.

As with its predecessors, *The Million* made extensive use of music. But, unlike *The Book of Dances* and *Anabasis,* the music was drawn from a variety of different cultural sources. Added to the previous array of drums, trumpets, cymbals, and bells were an electric guitar, a piano accordion, castanets, and an Indonesian gamelan. The inclusion of the gamelan was indicative of the diverse nature of the score, which featured tunes with their roots in Asia, Latin America, and popular Western ballads such as "I Left My Heart in San Francisco" and "Oh Susana."

The production centered around a character dressed as a traditional Italian village priest who alternated between being audience to the main action and taking part in various episodes. The rest of the cast played a variety of exotic characters, many of whom wore half and full-face masks. These characters included Balinese dancers, a lion from the Japanese kabuki, cliched versions of a Mexican in a huge sombrero with a rifle that would not stop firing and a Moroccan in Arabic-style robes, the Hindu Monkey King, a

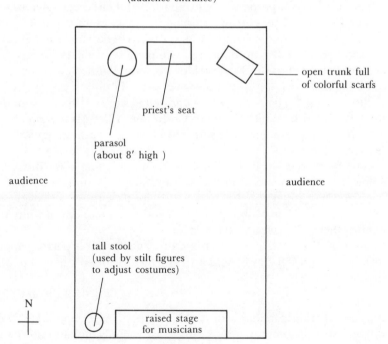

Figure 5.2 Plan view of the set for *The Million* (Watson, 1985:135)

115

macho Latino in an immaculate white blazer and matching hat, the androgynous stilt figure from *Anabasis* – who was joined by a smaller version of the
same – and a samba-dancing bear.

In keeping with Barba's dramaturgy, the mise-en-scene consisted of episodic vignettes with no linear narrative. Comedy was a priority in a performance text made up of pantomimic sequences, dances – which, in
addition to the samba, included waltzes, a candomble, the capoeira, and
a comic version of a frantic Balinese dance – and mock combats set to music.

The production was generally well received by audiences, playing to full
houses whenever it was performed in theatres during the six years it remained
in the Odin's repertoire. Similarly, critics were generally kind, if somewhat
superficial, in their analysis of the work. Ned Chaillet of *The Times* of London,
for instance, described it as "a dazzling celebration of theatricality that brings
together striking images from such places as Bali and India, with scenes played
on stilts and a wide range of world music" (1980:9), while Mel Gussow in the
New York Times compared it to circus and praised the skills of the performers:

> At the center of Mr. Barba's play is an actor playing Polo, dressed in
> black like an evangelist, speaking in English and giving a sampling of
> his discoveries abroad.
>
> With his cigar as baton, he calls the cast into action. ...
>
> What follows is a potpourri of gymnastics and choreographic turn-
> abouts that would be equally at home in circus as an experimental
> theater. The acts, not individually identified as to national source, run
> the range from ballroom dancing to comic Kathakali [there was, in
> fact, no kathakali in the New York production], with the performers
> tumbling and twirling one another over their shoulders. ...
>
> The evening is a pastiche in music as well as story – Hispanic sounds
> freely mixed with "Yankee Doodle Dandy" and "I Left My Heart in San
> Francisco," with the words, unsung, and left to our own imagination.
> Intermittently there is the punctuation of fireworks.
>
> As we realized in the troupe's contemplative opening play, "Brecht's
> Ashes 2," a commentary on the life and art of Bertolt Brecht, the
> company has athletic agility and an ability to surmount provincial
> boundaries. In "The Million," the actors also have an opportunity to
> express their talents for broad comedy.
>
> ... Even in this antic evening, the Odin Teatret has a performance
> intensity, as it offers audiences a vividly theatricalized carnival of all
> nations.
>
> (1984b:C25)

But several critics familiar with Barba's work, such as Denmark's Henrik
Lundgren, sensed something more than just comedy and an entertaining
display of skills in the piece: "there are moments of spirited rhythmical music;
the production's contrasts run the gamut from the capricious to the

aggressive, but its underlying tone is one of fertile, sharp edged irony"
(1984:3). These critics appreciated the similarities between *The Million* and
Barba's studio productions.

STUDIO PRODUCTIONS (1964–1991)

The most obvious difference between Barba's street-theatre productions and
his studio pieces is that the latter are presented in theatres or large rooms
that can be transformed into makeshift performance spaces. But, as mentioned earlier, Barba rejects the traditional separation of stage and audito-
rium by the proscenium arch, preferring instead to include the architectural
arrangement of the performer–spectator relationship as part of the thematic
design concept of each production.

These seating arrangements have led to the charge that Barba fosters an
elitist theatre by limiting the number of spectators. Most of his early productions allowed for no more than forty spectators, but with his mid-1970s
production of *Come! And the Day Will be Ours* he added additional seating to
accommodate up to 120 people. In the 1980s, this number was expanded to
as many as 180 for *Brecht's Ashes 2* and *Oxyrhincus Evangeliet*. This second
increase meant abandoning the previous seating design, of having the
audience seated on the same level as the performers, in favor of raked seating
with only the front row on the same level as the actors.

Barba's limitation on the number of spectators is clearly open to the charge
of elitism, but, to be fair, several factors have to be taken into consideration.
In the group's early years, there were very few spectators who wanted to see
the Odin's work. It was not until *Ferai*, the production prior to *Min Fars Hus*,
that Barba's work gained a following in Europe. His response to this interest
was to increase seating, and to do so again to accommodate the growing
audiences of the 1980s. However, these increases have also taken the nature
of the production into account. Despite the interest in his work, for instance,
Barba has limited the size of his audience to 100 for the latest Odin production, *Talabot*, because of scenic considerations.

It should also be remembered that Barba is an experimental director with
a clearly defined esthetic which does not appeal to a mass audience. He does
not work in a conventional theatre geared to presenting a season of plays for
subscribers in a major cultural center like Copenhagen, Berlin, or Paris. His
theatre interests a limited number of people and it is for these few that he makes
his theatre. He neither is, nor wants to be, part of the cultural mainstream.

Barba's studio works can be roughly divided into three periods: the first
years, from the group's formation to the early 1970s; the developmental
period, from the early to the late 1970s; and the mature years, from the late
1970s onward. The three productions Barba directed during the first years,
Ornitofilene, Kaspariana, and *Ferai,* were all based on scripts or scenarios
written prior to rehearsals. The developmental period marks the group's first

117

experiments with collective creation. During this period, the improvisations that eventually became *Min Fars Hus* and *Come! And the Day Will be Ours* were as much about the group and its individual members as they were about the material that inspired them. Barba's mature works, *Brecht's Ashes 2*, *Oxyrhincus Evangeliet*, and *Talabot*, on the other hand, are the result of a more subtle evolution in which the montage is a product of the group's and each individual actor's meeting with the themes, characters, and the fictional world explored during rehearsals, rather than an expose of the group itself.

Regardless of these developments and the personal nature of the Odin's productions, one of the most common observations made about Barba's studio work is that it bears a close affinity to religious ritual. Barba denies any such connection, maintaining that this is a projection of people's own predilections onto his work (Hagested, 1969:56), and ignores a fundamental component of religious ritual which his productions lack, namely a canon of beliefs and faith which have their root source in a supreme being (Farrimond, 1981:113–114).

Barba's productions may not be based on a belief in God, but his assertion that audiences only perceive religious connotations in his works because of how they choose to see them ignores the fact that many of his studio productions use techniques and images found in Christian and other religious rituals. Productions such as *Ferai*, *Min Fars Hus*, and *Oxyrhincus Evangeliet* used incantation and chanting similar to that in both the Catholic and Orthodox faiths, while Barba's focus on the musical, synesthetic quality of language rather than its cognitive aspect has parallels with the role of language in rituals like the Latin Mass or Sanskrit Hindu rituals where the majority of participants understand few words in the ceremonies. Similarly, much of the physical action in Barba's studio productions is far removed from the physical action of daily life and is frequently perceived as having symbolic rather than mimetic value – as do many of the actions in religious rituals. *Ferai* and *Oxyrhincus Evangeliet* were performed with dim church-like lighting, and the latter even used candles hung by chains from above – a form of lighting found in Orthodox churches. Images such as the Last Supper of Christ and his crucifixion were used in *Oxyrhincus Evangeliet*, hardly surprising when one considers that the entire production was constructed as a liturgy (Klein, 1988:211), a structure that echoed an earlier Barba production, *Kaspariana*, which was described by at least one critic as "an atheistic mass" (Fumaroli, 1968:55).

Barba's studio productions have not been as universally celebrated by critics as his street theatre, the major objection being that these works are difficult to understand. Ron Jenkins, writing about *Come! And the Day Will be Ours*, for instance, says:

The same company presented an intensely physical performance of a play about the rape of American Indian culture by modern society. It was a haunting multi-textured chant of music, movement, and words. Barba and his company reached to the roots of an ugly phenomenon and gave it the form of a sinister black mass. The result was outstanding theater despite its sometimes excessive obscurity.

(1977:1)

This comment was echoed in Ned Chaillet's review of *Brecht's Ashes 2* in *The Times* of London:

There is still a large measure of the company's original introspective style on display in one stream of their work, and it is very evident in their new production, *Ashes of Brecht* [the production was presented under this title in Britain], a somewhat obscure meditation on exile. ... *Ashes of Brecht* is intensely demanding and would benefit from more blatant revelation of its intricate scheme.

(1980:9)

These accusations of obscurity have their origin in Barba's esthetics. He wants the spectator to be involved in a creative act along with the actors. He also wants his works to stimulate associations, to prompt members of the audience to establish their own narrative/emotional logic in what they see.

THE PRODUCTIONS

Even though there are differences between Barba's street and studio productions, they are structurally similar. Both consist of individual scenes that have little or no causal relationship to each other. Both rely on the visual/aural narrative. And both, when described, tend to read much like a list of apparently unconnected images and scenes in which many of the same characters reappear. This disjunction is less evident in Barba's first three productions, because of their literary origins. In these pieces, the linear narrative is more evident than in his subsequent works.

Ornitofilene (The Bird Lovers)[2]

This, Barba's and the Odin's first production, was based on a play especially written for them by one of Norway's most famous contemporary writers, Jens Bjorneboe, an early supporter of the group. Barba originally intended to mount a realistic version of the play but when he received the script, he discovered it had fourteen roles and there were only four actors in the company. With the agreement of the writer, Barba and his actors reworked the script during rehearsals, establishing the model of a collectively created dramaturgy which Barba has used ever since.

The production was first performed in Oslo, Norway, in October 1965. It was performed some fifty times in Norway and other parts of Scandinavia

119

until the group moved to Holstebro in the summer of 1966, when they had to abandon the production because one of the actors, Tor Sannum, decided against leaving Norway.

In addition to Sannum, the cast included Anne Trine Grimnes, Else Marie Laukvik, and Torgeir Wethal. The set, designed by Barba and Ole Daniel Bruun, resembled both a meeting hall and courtroom. It consisted of nothing more than desks and chairs in which the actors and spectators were interspersed in a space approximately 36 feet by 55 feet – an ideal size for touring to even relatively small villages since these are roughly the dimensions of the average school gymnasium in Scandinavia.

The production, presented in Norwegian, was set in a small village where a group of wealthy tourists has decided to build a modern hotel which will bring money and employment to the poverty-stricken region. The investors make only one condition, that the villagers give up hunting the local birds. The people are outraged, not only because this is one of their only pastimes, but because it was these same outsiders who, some twenty years before, came to the village as soldiers of the Third Reich and tortured and killed many of the local people. According to one critic, the production, which explored

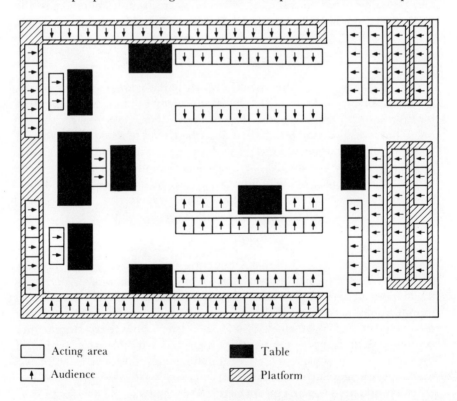

| | Acting area | | Table |
| | Audience | | Platform |

Figure 5.3 Plan view of the stage for *Ornitofilene* (Barba, 1986a:30)

120

the contradictions of yesterday's killers being today's protectors and the victims of the past being nature's present-day enemies, evoked the Nazi pogroms as well as the violence of both war and peace (Taviani, 1986a:247).

Despite the conventional narrativity of Bjorneboe's play,the production was far removed from psychological realism. Barba made extensive use of chanting and singing, as well as role swapping, in full view of the audience, with minimal costume changes. The production was full of rich poetic images, including a psalm used as a judge's accusation against a condemned prisoner, an executioner beating himself while his prisoner flinched from the blows as he recited from a letter written by a partisan condemned to death, and three actors using their hands as puppets who answered a cross-examination on justice and injustice acompanied by a chant about the violence of history.

Unfortunately, I have been unable to locate any reviews of *Ornitofilene*. A lack of published material on the first production by an unknown group is understandable. But, this omission may be as much a product of failed research as a dearth of material, since Barba assured me that a well known Danish critic, Jens Kruuse, saw the production and wrote about it.

Kaspariana

For his next production, Barba commissioned a noted Danish poet, Ole Sarvig, to write a scenario based on the Kaspar Hauser story. This tale, which has been used in novels, plays, and films as a metaphor of natural man's struggle against socialization (Innes, 1981:180), concerns the true story of a young 16-year-old boy who was found wandering the streets of Nuremberg in 1828, after having been kept in isolation since birth. Many people took an interest in this boy who could neither read nor write, seeing him as a symbol of man's innocence. His mysterious murder, five years later, after he had learned not only to read and write but also to cheat, lie, and hate, came to symbolize the crushing of the human spirit under the pressures of social conditioning.

Kaspariana, which premiered in Holstebro in September 1967 and remained in the group's repertoire for a year, marked the first formal collaboration between Barba and his literary advisor Christian Ludvigsen, the professor of literature at Aarhus University, who was to play an important role in Barba's next work, *Ferai*. The production had a cast of seven which, in addition to the three actors who had come from Norway (Grimnes, Laukvik, and Wethal) included two Swedes, Jan Erik Berstrom and Lars Goran Kjellstedt, as well as Iben Nagel Rasmussen and Dan Nielson, both from Denmark.

Ludvigsen's collaboration with Barba was not *Kaspariana*'s only significant legacy. It was the first of Barba's productions to tour outside of Scandinavia (to Italy), and, though it was not hailed as a masterpiece, the production was regarded highly enough to be invited to the Theatre of Nations Festival in Paris (but was never presented on account of the student unrest of May

1968). Its Italian performances were also Barba's first contact with a small group of Italian theatre intellectuals, who included Taviani, Franco Ruffini, Nicola Savarese, Fabrizio Cruciani, and Claudio Meldolesi. Over the years this has developed into an important relationship for Barba personally, as well as for his work in the third theatre movement and at ISTA.[3]

The *Kaspariana* set, designed collectively and constructed by Bernt Nyberg, again relied more on the arrangement of the audience and performance space than on more conventional scenery. Unlike *Ornitofilene*, the scenography for *Kaspariana* was based on what Barba describes as a medieval model (1986a:32), with the audience seated around the main performance area, which was contained by several wooden ramps that served as "mansions." The entire space was painted black, except for the mansions which were white. These mansions, unlike their counterparts in medieval theatre which were static, could be moved, rearranged, and pulled apart. They were also used as personal armor; as set properties (one was draped in cloth and transformed into a throne); and even as musical instruments – they were made of fluted timber which made sounds when hands or objects were dragged across them.

The production, which has been described as an atheistic mass (see p. 118), featured psalms, incantations, symbolic rather than realistic movement, and even the appearance of Christ himself. Like its predecessor, the performance text was based on improvisations rather than on a dramatized version of the writer's scenario. This performance text has been published and, even though it gives the impression of a work that is somewhat more oriented to the linear narrative than the production actually was, it does provide the best understanding of Barba's production:

(1) The actors put on their costumes, commenting on the day and the times: it is a period of meanness and triviality which will be forgotten by posterity or, on the contrary, will our successors remember it with nostalgia? There is talk of the event of the day: a public execution.

(2) Food is served while the details of the execution are discussed. On hearing that the victim's head has fallen, the psalm "How beautiful are the blue heavens" is sung.

(3) Stifled cries are heard and lead to the discovery of a young man: Kaspar. The crowd watches his attempts to stand and speak. They fall upon him like a bird of prey, but they only soothe him.

(4) Kaspar's social birth: he is clothed and given a name. The community welcomes him into their midst with the psalm: "Behold in awe, my child, the true God."

(5) Kaspar is told the saga of the king who has sent his beloved son out amongst his subjects only to be killed by them.

(6) Kaspar learns to walk helped by a woman who sees in his unsteady stride the first steps along the road leading to destruction.

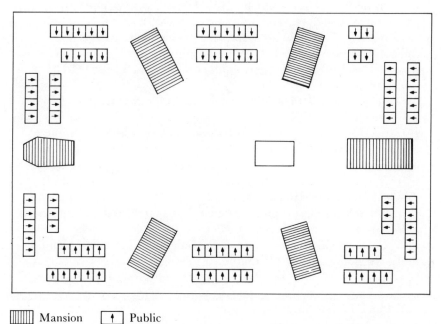

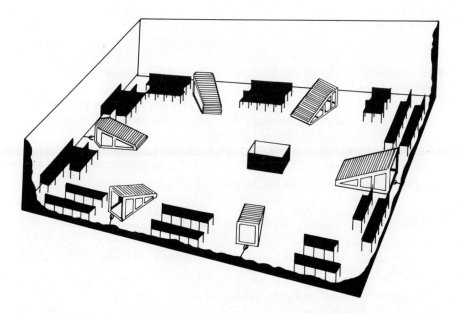

▥ Mansion   ⬚ Public

Figure 5.4 Plan view and sketch of the set for *Kaspariana* (Odin Teatret, 1973:46)

123

(7) Knowledge (a chorus which mixes Hebrew, Sanskrit and Greek) is passed on to Kaspar. He is violated with words: a prayer, a false syllogism (Jews are bad, Christians are good, we are Christians, we are good), a categorical imperative which commits one to nothing (to be sincere toward oneself and others) and a quotation from literature ("To be or not to be").

(8) The appearance of a woman makes the dignified teachers forget their pupil.

(9) Attention is once more focused upon Kaspar. He is "enthroned" like an object on exhibition, a monument, a totem. Hope is projected onto the young man – our future, our posterity – but only disappointment results. Kaspar has forgotten all he has learnt. His master's disillusionment turns into despair and panic. They beg him to remember, threaten him, prompt him. When Kaspar finally utters the false syllogism, everybody is happy. The event must be celebrated.

(10) A ball is held, but only reveals personal failures. Kaspar, planted motionless on his pedestal, mutters random fragments of his lessons: "Christians are good ... be sincere towards yourself.... To be or not to be.... "

(11) Since Kaspar did not join in the festivities, he is considered ill. Everybody makes the same diagnosis: he needs a woman.

(12) The bride is washed and clothed. Everybody waits excitedly. But instead of using the woman as a mere sexual object, Kaspar experiences love. Howling like jackals from whom a bone has been stolen, the others kill the child born of the union and separate the lovers.

(13) Kaspar looks for help in the *Book of Books.* But the Man from Nazareth says: "I have not come to bring peace, but the sword. I have come to divide a son from his father, to set brother against brother...."
The crowd reappears claiming that struggle is the genesis of all things. Like a medieval knight, Kaspar is consecrated man of arms. He is left alone to face another man while the homicidal knife is raised to carry out the last and most extreme experience.

(14) The lights go out. "Beautiful is the earth, beautiful is God's heaven, beautiful is the pilgrimage of the soul towards its celestial home." The psalm concludes *Kaspariana.*

(Barba, 1986a:33–34)

Critics and scholars, aware of Barba's earlier connection to Grotowski, tended to see the work in relation to Barba's more famous mentor. In his review of *Kaspariana,* Marc Fumaroli, for example, felt that Barba's and Grotowski's work sprang from much the same roots:

> For Barba and Grotowski, the theatre comes not from the world of Law, but from the world of Love, and a true *caritas* is created between the actors who signify and the spectators whose subconscious receives the

signs, in a common, fraternal revelation of their destiny as men vowed to misfortune, destruction, and death, permanently alienated from liberty and truth.

(1968:55)

Christopher Innes, though not suggesting that Barba's and Grotowski's work was identical, saw Barba's originality as greatly influenced by both Grotowski and expressionism:

His [Barba's] continuation of Grotowski's research into the psycho-physiological basis of acting led to the formulation of a "new theatrical language" – or so he claimed, although in fact it strongly resembled the iconographic style of early expressionistic silent films in using archetypal gestures, postures and facial masking to transform "spontaneous" emotions into "pure" states of Fear, Pain, Desire.

(1981:178)

Innes also regarded the production as having a strong connection to myth, ritual, and religion:

Myths are used as images of "the worn out stereotypes that make up our habitual social conduct" to reveal these as inherently primitive, repressive and violent. Against them are set "ritual" behavior patterns, "biological reactions that spring up in extreme situations," where the socially conditioned gestures of everyday life are transformed into a "natural physical language," a sacerdotal sign language of hieratic attitudes ... the main problem with a play like *Kaspariana*, which has also been referred to as an atheistic mass, is that the challenge to religion presupposes a climate of belief that no longer exists.

(1981:178, 180)

Fumaroli, the critic who described *Kaspariana* as an atheistic mass, echoed these links with myths and ritual by comparing the production to kathakali:

This mutability of dramatis personae and of the stage elements obeys the profound laws of myth and of dream. It demands a dramatic style which owes much to Kathakali, another theatre of metamorphosis where the actor can be in turn or simultaneously animal, god, demon, rain or wind, and must by his own inspired magic create the cosmic dream space where the great hieroglyphics of destiny can appear.

(1968:52)

Ferai

Ferai is the production that established Barba's international reputation as a director. Following its premiere in June 1969 in Holstebro, it toured extensively around Europe, culminating in its invitation to the 1970 Theatre of Nations Festival in Paris, where it was the hit of the festival.

The production began with Barba and his literary advisor, Ludvigsen, researching two myths: the ancient Greek legend of Alcestis, the princess who sacrificed herself for the sake of her husband; and the saga of the Danish king, Frode Fredegod, who was so revered by his people that, in order to retain the political and social harmony of his reign after he died, his soldiers removed his intestines, salted his body, and carried him around the kingdom in a chariot as a symbol of national unity.

Following their research, Barba commissioned Peter Seeberg, a Danish novelist and screenwriter, to write a play that combined the two myths. Barba's and Ludvigsen's knowledge of the source material, coupled with the lyrical nature of Seeberg's script, and the fact that it had only four roles for a company of eight, led to more changes in the original text than had been made in either of Barba's first two productions. But these changes were done in close collaboration with the writer, who, along with Ludvigsen, attended rehearsals for several months and was actively involved in suggesting changes and even rewriting the original text.

All of the Scandinavian languages were used in *Ferai* (Danish, Norwegian, Swedish, and Finnish) since most of the actors spoke in their native tongue. Apart from Laukvik, Rasmussen, and Wethal, who had been in the previous

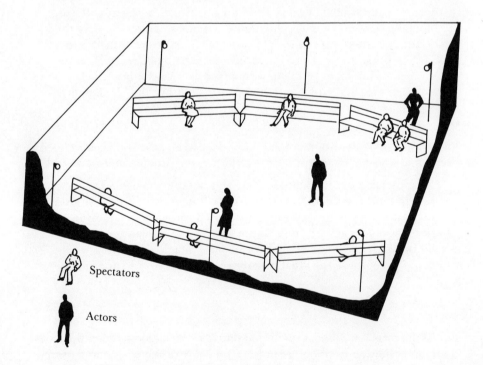

Spectators

Actors

Figure 5.5 Sketch of the set for *Ferai* (Barba, 1986a:36)

126

production, these perfomers included five newcomers to the group: Ulla Alasjarvi, Marisa Gilberti, Juha Hakkanen, Soren Larsson, and Carita Rindell.

The scenic design of the production was simpler than for either *Kaspariana* or *Ornitofilene*. The audience was seated in two single rows of benches facing each other in a semi-elliptical shape that metaphorically represented a Viking ship and the nave of a church. The performance, which took place both in front of the audience and behind the seats, centered on three objects: a knife – which at different times in the piece served as a whip, a saber, a royal scepter, and a ritual object; an ivory egg – which also had mutiple uses and meanings including a royal orb, the skull of the dead king, and the head of a child; and a blanket which, when laid on the floor, defined the central acting area.

Ferai was as removed from realism as Barba's previous productions with its use of a chorus, incantation, and stylized movement. But critics, like Fumaroli, maintain that its dramatic montage was more logical than *Kaspariana*. The plot, for instance, can be described in a few words. An elderly king, Frode, dies and Admetos, a younger man, takes his place and wants to make changes in the kingdom. The people react and in the ensuing conflict Admetos' wife, Alcestis, commits suicide. This description, however, gives no idea of the complex subtleties, symbolic implications, or the role of the chorus in Barba's performance text. Fumaroli's eyewitness account, which he divides into four stages, gives the most thorough understanding of the production.

First stage: after the funeral rites for the dead king Frode and a duel which selects Admetus as the new king, Admetus invites his people to a new era of equality and love. The people enjoy their new-found liberty by organizing an orgy, then plot against the new king in hope of returning to the old order.

The second stage is the wedding night of Admetus and Alcestis, daughter of King Frode. Fully dressed, the two actors play not the exterior act, but its interior content, the exchange of two memories, of two unique experiences. Exchange, but with it fundamental misunderstanding: the queen projects a paternal fantasy on the king and tries to make him virile and violent; Admetus projects a maternal fantasy on the queen and identifies her with the kingdom he wants to free from the tyranny of the dead father. This misunderstanding is expressed by counterpoint between the lyrical dialogue and the rough movements of the actors, who crawl on the ground. The queen is impatient, provocative, possessed by ancient, unsatisfied desires; the king is vibrant and tender, like a child.

Third Stage: the misunderstanding between the king and his people and between the king and queen becomes a Gordian knot. The people, after several futile efforts to assassinate Admetus, disinter the body of King Frode and carry it in triumph throughout the kingdom. An actress of the Chorus is ceremonially draped in the shroud of the corpse and

127

carries the ivory egg in front of her face as the death mask, and the Chorus carries her in procession from one end of the acting area to the other, while the royal couple silently pace their domain, crossing the procession without seeing it, as if they occupy a different space. The queen in turn becomes nostalgic for her father; when the Chorus shows her the disinterred corpse, which now has the form of a small mummy, she first is horrified and repulsed, and then takes the mummy and carries it: the Virgin holding the infant Jesus or the Pieta.

Fourth stage: Admetus, who witnessed the preceding scene in silence, sticks his knife into the head of the mummy-doll, that is, into the ivory egg. This act awakens the queen, the people also are disillusioned, but hasten to reincarnate the old king in a new way by acclaiming the Choragus his heir. The Gordian knot is tied again; rather than a rivalry between a living king and a dead king, there are now two living kings. The queen decides to cut the knot, and commits suicide before the two kings and the Chorus. She chants nursery rhymes in a low voice, then cries and groans, evoking the sounds of both childbirth and love. Death becomes birth. She rises up and throws off her shoes and heavy djellaba, shakes out her long blond hair, and bidding farewell to the earth, she leaves the theatre, singing a prelude to her apotheosis. The king mourns her, seizes the suicide knife and moves toward the Chorus and Choragus. When they hear him play a flute air on the knife handle, they begin dancing about him and all leave the theatre led by the king, by the same door Alcestis used.

(1969:49–50)

Critics such as Innes and Fumaroli, who were by now relatively familiar with Barba's work, saw connections between *Ferai* and *Kaspariana* in their myth-like, religious quality and ritualized action. Innes found *Kaspariana* to be the more successful production of the two:

The intention was to present a complex of expressionistic images with multiple meanings which each spectator could decipher in terms of his own experience, though this was more effective in *Kaspariana* because the metaphors were more familiar.

(1981:179)

Fumaroli, on the other hand, felt that *Ferai* was the work of a more mature director and company:

Kaspariana was an expressionistic nightmare in black and white, staged with virtuosity which hid the weaknesses of the young actors. *Ferai*, created with a more coherent and fully trained troupe, allowed the director to play a less evident role; Barba's work is evolving toward greater rigor, precision, and economy.

(1969:49)

But both agreed that the most successful element in the production was Barba's use of symbolic props. As Fumaroli put it in discussing the knife:

> In *Kaspariana* the metamorphosis of scenic objects was astonishing but gratuitous; in *Ferai* this knife [that the Queen commits suicide with and which later transforms into a flute] not only creates a link for the various emblematic tableaux, but through its metamorphoses it symbolizes the evolution of the situation. We feel we have seen this knife before, perhaps in Bosch's "Garden of the Earthly Delights," where it is one of the most enigmatic elements.
>
> (1969:53)

This link between the themes of the production and the props was echoed by Innes:

> The play is a conflict between male and female principles epitomised in the three props, which formed the only material or scenic aids in the production – the masculine symbol of a knife with leather thongs that was used as a whip representing political repression, as a sabre for the duel, a royal sceptre and a flute; the feminine and passive symbol of a blanket, used to represent the subjugated kingdom, swaddling clothes, the dead body; and an ivory egg symbolizing both life and death, a skull and the fertile womb.
>
> (1981:179)

Min Fars Hus (My Father's House)

Min Fars Hus, which premiered in April 1972, was the first of Barba's productions created entirely from improvisations. The production was based on Fyodor Dostoyevsky's biography and novels, though it was not so much an illustration of them as a piece grounded in the group's history and its members' reactions to Dostoyevsky's life and works. In fact, the theatre scholar who has followed the Odin's work most closely over the years, Taviani, regards *Min Fars Hus* as the most personal of the company's productions because he maintains that it dealt as much with personalities and relationships in the group as it did with the actors' reactions to Dostoyevsky (1986a:252).

The production, which was very successful, toured throughout most of Western Europe and remained in the Odin's repertoire until 1974. Ever conscious of their expanded touring schedule, which took the group to many countries with different languages, and the fact that there was not a common native language among company members, Barba focused much of his energy in rehearsal on language, deciding eventually to work with a fabricated Russian which he and the actors developed together. This language, which was based on tonal and rhythmic variations rather than on linguistic

129

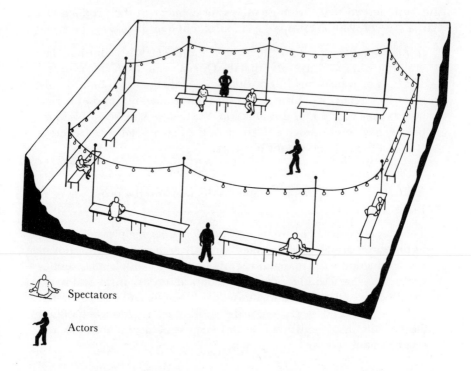

Spectators

Actors

Figure 5.6 Sketch of the set for *Min Fars Hus* (Barba, 1979:177)

signification, contained several Russian words but primarily consisted of nonsense words that sounded Russian. Thus all the actors had equal skills with the new language and all audiences had equal access to it.

The production had a cast of seven: Jens Christensen, Ragnar Christiansen, Tage Larsen, Else Marie Laukvik, Iben Nagel Rasmussen, Ulrik Skeel, and Torgeir Wethal. Like Barba's earlier works, it used the audience to define the performance area, which for *Min Fars Hus* consisted of a rectangular space on the periphery of which were plain wooden benches for the spectators. The sole source of light for the production was a simple garland of lights above the spectators' heads.

In creating *Mins Fars Hus*, Barba and his actors were drawn to particular events in Dostoyevsky's life. The group discovered that many of these events – such as his relationship with his father, his introduction to St. Petersburg's intelligentsia, his imprisonment in Siberia, his epilepsy, his passion for gambling, and his bizarre affairs of the heart – were reflected in his writings in events like Prince Myshkin's and Smerdiakov's epilepsy, the emotional pain of the love triangle which appears in several novels, and the animosity toward a father in the Karamazov brothers' confessions (Barba, 1986a:39).

This biographical and literary material was the source of personal associations for the actors which were explored through improvisation during rehearsals. Some of these associations included the link between Dostoyevsky's isolation in Siberia and the Odin's own isolation in Holstebro, their parallel inability to reach their public: in Dostoyevsky's case because his books were banned by Stalin, in the Odin's because it was a small group on the geographic periphery of European culture. On a more personal level, the relationship between oneself and one's parents was explored through Dostoyevsky's descriptions of the relationship in *The Brothers Karamazov*.

As rehearsals progressed, these explorations tended to focus more on the group's and the actors' personal histories than on Dostoyevsky's life. As Taviani described the production, "it has no text, no story, no reference points constituted by precise facts, known and recognizable by the spectators. It is not *on* or *by* Dostoyevsky, it is simply *dedicated* to Dostoyevsky" (1979:22).

Min Fars Hus marked both a confirmation of Barba's emerging directorial style and a major development in it. As with his previous works, the piece had little to do with realism, employing a stylized use of the performers' bodies and voices. In keeping with the use of props in *Ferai*, the production included a set prop as a major visual motif. In this instance, a black cloth was used intermittently to define and characterize space visually by performers who spread it out on different parts of the floor in various shapes and textures (sometimes smoothly, at other times wrinkled, sometimes folded, etc.).

Influenced by developments in their training, especially the composition improvisations which the company was working on at the time, the actors' physical work consisted of dance-like choreographic scores. Barba's focus on the sonorous quality of vocal expression rather than its semantic value continued, through incantation, singing, and dialogue that favored rhythmic and tonal variations in speech over subtextual considerations – all in a language which was incomprehensible to its audience.

This emphasis on the musical quality of language was taken a step further in *Min Fars Hus* with the introduction of musical instruments. During the lengthy rehearsals, one actor learned to play the flute, several others learned to play recorders, and yet another studied piano accordion. These instruments became an integral part of the production, not only in their conventional roles of providing mood music or as an accompaniment for songs and dances, but also as a substitute for words in several dialogues, and as a means of defining character: the flute became like a long nose which was played in such a way that it transformed the actor into an anteater, while the accordion was both the paunch of a Russian aristocrat and a wall from behind which he could spy on others (Barba, 1986a:76–77).

In addition to these developments in his dramaturgy, Barba's structural approach to his work also underwent a major change in *Min Fars Hus* that continues to influence both his studio and street-theatre pieces. This change, which primarily owed its origins to the fact that improvisation had replaced the role of the writer in rehearsals, was the rejection of any semblance of a

131

linear plot. The production montage of *Min Fars Hus* consisted of a sequence of apparently independent episodes dominated by visual and aural imagery.

Despite the success of *Mins Fars Hus*, many regarded it as a difficult production because of its break with traditional theatrical norms (Taviani, 1986a:252–253). Others, particularly critics in Poland, where the production was presented in 1974, attacked it as being merely an imitation of Grotowski. Yet others, familiar with both Grotowski's productions and Barba's history with him, praised *Min Fars Hus* as the work of an original artist with roots in the experiments of the Polish Laboratory Theatre (Osinski, 1986:143).

This conflict among the critics raises what could be another study in itself, the question of Grotowski's legacy in Barba's esthetics. To address the question briefly, Barba acknowledges Grotowski's importance for him:

> In the theatre, people always like to strut their originality and repudiate their true parentage, the tradition that spawned them. This feeling is totally alien to me. If there is one man I consider my master it is Grotowski. He brought me into the profession, and I have the greatest respect for what he is doing. His fundamental ideas, his method of working, and his professional conscience are a constant challenge to me.
>
> (Hagested 1969:55)

But Grotowski maintains that all he did was provide a foundation for Barba's theatrical work:

> Barba worked with me from 1960 to 1963 – when I was unknown in Poland, in Europe, in the world. From the example of the Polish Laboratory Theater probably he saw the possibility of highly precise technical work. But from the very beginning he developed his own technical skills which evolved in a direction different from the Polish Laboratory Theater.
>
> (Schechner, 1984:103)

Regardless of what Grotowski says, there are similarities between his own work and Barba's, similarities born of Barba's commitment to an esthetic he began to formulate while he was working with Grotowski: the rejection of linear narrativity in both their works, for example; the importance of choreographed physical and vocal scores; limiting the number of spectators to ensure a personal contact between the performers and those who see their work; structuring the actor–audience relationship differently for each production; and minimal use of lighting and recorded sound.

Equally, however, Barba's methodology has moved away from Grotowski's model. Consider this description of rehearsals for *Kaspariana* by Rasmussen:

> We worked training in the morning – performance work started late in the afternoon. The work started with improvisation, one must make

an improv., and be able to repeat it. ... Everything Torgeir (Wethal)
was doing was already taking the direction of being in performance.
Eugenio worked for periods alone with Torgeir in the same way that
Grotowski worked with Cieslak on *Constant Prince*. His manner of
working was that he would work alone with Torgeir and later come
back and work results with the group.

(Klein, 1988:72)

This is quite different from the way Barba works today. Since the later
rehearsals for *Min Fars Hus*, the raw material of Barba's performance texts
has become the individual improvisations of *all* the actors.

The importance of improvisation for Barba is another example of the way
in which his work has developed differently from that of his mentor. Improvisation has become the sole source of the performance text for Barba,
whereas, excluding his last piece for the theatre, *Apocalypsis cum Figuris*,
Grotowski always began working with a script which he adapted during
rehearsals.

In many ways the different emphasis placed on the actor–role relationship
in Grotowski's and Barba's work encapsulates the difference between their
esthetics. For Grotowski the role is the means by which the actor reveals
his/her inner self to the audience: "The important thing is to use the role
as a trampoline, an instrument with which to study what is hidden behind
our everyday mask – the innermost core of our personality – in order to
sacrifice it, expose it" (Grotowski, 1968:37). Grotowski sees this "sacrifice" as
a quasi-religious act which transforms the actor into a holy performer
(Grotowski, 1968:34). Barba, on the other hand, views the role as being only
one part of a duality. The actor portrays the role but at the same time s/he
must adhere to the principles of acting underlying the pre-expressive mode
in order to project his/her personal presence. In Barba's esthetics, the actor is
not involved in revealing the inner self or in a "religious" act, s/he is simply
both the actor and the character. This duality is revealed through a mastery
of the unique approach to training developed by Barba and his colleagues.

Come! And the Day Will be Ours

Come! And the Day Will be Ours was first performed in May 1976 in Caracas,
Venezuela, and remained in the Odin's repertoire until 1980. The production, which was based on the late nineteenth-century clash of cultures in the
North American West between European immigrants and native American
Indians, took its title from a line in a letter written by General Custer prior
to the Battle of Little Bighorn in 1876. It interwove three basic strands that
have appeared intermittently in Barba's work: the political, portrayed in the
power struggle between the two ethnic groups; the intercultural, which was
primarily explored through music in the production – as the Indians began

133

to incorporate the white man's instruments and songs into their own musical heritage and the settlers, in turn, adapted Indian music to create a folk tradition of the West (it should be remembered that this was two years before the first version of *The Million*); and the metaphor of journey as a unifying thread of the dramaturgy (which was to reappear in *Anabasis* and *The Million*) in both the journeys of the immigrants and what Barba described as the Indians' journey to cultural destruction (1979:133–134).

As in *Min Fars Hus*, the personalities of the company played important roles in the production – so much so, in fact, that, as with its predecessor, the actors in *Come! And the Day Will be Ours* were not identified as specific characters but were rather associated with an object, an instrument, or a color: "the one in white," Else Marie Laukvik; "the one with the book," Torgeir Wethal; "the one with the drum," Iben Nagel Rasmussen; "the one with the violin," Tage Larsen; "the one with the banjo," Roberta Carreri; and "the one with the guitar," Tom Fjordefalk. These roles were further divided into two groups of three each, the "civilized," consisting of Larsen, Laukvik, and Wethal, and the "not civilized," made up of Carreri, Fjordefalk, and Rasmussen. This division was further reflected in the languages used in the production, since the immigrants spoke in their respective Scandinavian tongues, which gradually became a heavily accented English as they became pioneers in their move West, and those playing the Indians spoke in a language based on indigenous American languages such as Quechua and Cheyenne.

By now a trademark of Barba's studio productions, the seating for the audience defined the performance space. This seating consisted of a double row of benches in a circular shape with entrance/exit passageways at either end which were decorated with arches. In the center of the performance space was a pole topped with a wheel-shaped frame surrounded by lights. According to Barba, the entire set was designed to reflect both a Buffalo Bill Wild West Show and an Indian sun-dance circle (1986a:190).

Despite the socio-political nature of the source material, *Come! And the Day Will be Ours* was as removed from the conventions of realism as its predecessor, *Ferai*. Once again, the production consisted of fragmented episodes developed from improvisations based on the group's responses to material they researched on the clash between the Indians and the European settlers, and on what they saw reflected in this meeting of cultures in their own experience as a theatre group. As in the previous works, singing, chanting, the sonorous use of the voice, and choreographed movement bordering on dance were used extensively. And, as is clear from the way in which the characters have been described above, music also played an important role in the production, both as accompaniment for its many songs and dances and as a way of conceptualizing identities and social relations. The "one with the drum," for instance, was a native Indian shaman who wore her hip drum throughout the production and used it as

134

a means of communicating with the gods, while the European guitar was not only played by the immigrants but was also taken up by one of the Indians near the end of the production and played poorly as a "foreign" instrument. Similarly, one of the European pioneers transformed an Indian song into an insipid piece of folklore.

The success of *Ferai* resulted in an expanded touring schedule which, for the first time, included Eastern Europe and Latin America. This touring schedule exposed the Odin to new ideas, techniques, and a broad range of cultural influences at a time when changes were also taking place in the group's work as a direct result of the recently completed Italian residencies. These travels and creative ferment led to the personal experiences of the actors becoming an even more important factor in the production than in *Ferai*. In the program notes for the first performances of *Come! And the Day Will be Ours* Barba discussed the many personal factors that shaped the performance:

> Different threads became interwoven during our work, creating new images which astonished us and sometimes perturbed us. There were the experiences of some of us gathered while traveling in Latin

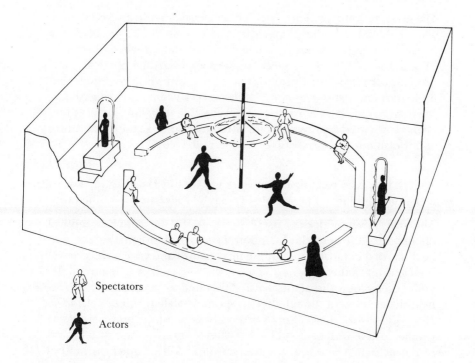

Spectators

Actors

Figure 5.7 Sketch of the set for *Come! And The Day Will be Ours* (Barba, 1979:177)

135

America and the far East; the ten months spent by our group in southern Italy; our own personal experiences of working in a group. ... There was also our awareness as a theatre group establishing links, meeting people with whom it has something to exchange, but nevertheless continually living in isolation.

(1979:135)

These factors were so important to Barba's conception of the piece that elsewhere in the same program notes he described the production as a border between representation and testimony. That is, the performance text (representation) was a fixed score, a rigid structure through which the actors attempted to reveal both their individual responses to the thematic roots of the production that shaped their improvisations in the first place and their personal experience of performing the work (testimony) (Barba, 1979:134).

As mentioned earlier, Ron Jenkins described *Come! And the Day Will be Ours* as "outstanding theater, despite its sometimes excessive obscurity" (1977:1). But not all critics agreed with his assessment, as can be seen in Michael Coveney's review of a performance at the 1976 BITEF Festival in Belgrade, Yugoslavia:

The assault on the audience yielded a maelstrom of confused images about colonialisation [*sic*], religious tyranny (with Mao's red book as a form of new bible), therapeutic howling, an ecstatic freaked-out *mestiza* who, in the middle of the piece, undergoes a startling physical transformation, an aggressive violin player and a girl in white, Edwardian undergarments who goes completely berserk while muttering Shakespearian fragments. There is no comprehesible story-line, just crashing changes of mood-gear as the actors dredge in some private motivation and thrash out an expression of it. It left me cold.

(1976:12)

A more balanced reading of the work was that by David Zane Mairowitz, who characterized it as an example of what he calls "theatre of the body":

The play never addresses itself, however, to the cultural/political dilemma [of the genocide] ... both history and indignation seem to be discarded in favour of multiple impressions and visceral responses. It is clear that a theatre whose spine is the actor will be a theatre of the body, even when the actors have elaborated a "text" during the rehearsal period. So although there is sporadic dialogue in *Come! And the Day Will be Ours*, it is a drama of bodies and voices, more or less in psychic league with each other, but often criss-cross, one sure hazard of gut acting. It is not a question of pure skill so much as natural emoting freed from the restraints of story.

(1976:21)

Brecht's Ashes 2

Barba's next production, *Brecht's Ashes*, had two distinct incarnations: the first in 1980, *Ashes of Brecht*, which was halted the following year when Brecht's heirs withdrew permission for the Odin to use Brecht's works; and the second, *Brecht's Ashes 2*, which remained in the Odin's repertoire from 1982 to 1984, based on Brecht's life (as was the original), and the Chinese poems, medieval ballads, and works of contemporaries like Tucholsky and Muhsam that were the sources of inspiration for much of Brecht's writing.[4]

The second version became the more famous of the two because it remained in the repertoire longer and toured more extensively. This version was performed by a company of nine, four of whom were appearing in their first studio production: Toni Cots, Francis Pardeilhan, Silvia Ricciardelli, and Julia Varley. The other five were veterans of Barba's studio works: Roberta Carreri, Tage Larsen, Iben Nagel Rasmussen, Ulrik Skeel, and Torgeir Wethal.

The production, which was performed with the audience seated on either side of the stage, marked a large increase in seating, with space for up to 180 spectators. In order to accommodate so many people, Barba employed raked seating, which certainly allowed for a larger audience but also broke with his previous intimate stagings. This break with his own scenic tradition was not total, however, since the physical relationship between the actors and audience retained his production concept of the architectural metaphor by reflecting Brecht's concern with distancing his audience from the fictional world on stage.

Regardless of the increase in the number of spectators, Barba retained his convention of a minimal set. On the outer edges of a large, open performance area were eight small coffee tables and chairs in which members of the audience were seated. Between the coffee tables on one side of the stage was a small stove with a frying pan and large cooking pot. At one end of the playing area was a table and 44-gallon drum, both of which were covered with a black cloth. Similar black cloths were used to cover the organ and tower-like structure at the other end of the stage.

Brecht's Ashes 2 saw Barba return to some of his theatrical roots. Apart from the fact that the life of an artist had been the inspiration for his first production based entirely on improvisation, *Min Fars Hus*, Brecht held a special place in Barba's and his company's history. One of his major reasons for beginning his formal theatre studies in Poland had been his interest in Brecht's concept of theatre as a political tool. And, even though he has moved far from Brecht's dramaturgy, he is still committed to the concept of theatre as a socio-political weapon. In addition to this ideological link, Barba is on record as saying that he sees parallels between Brecht's life and the Odin's experience. They share a knowledge of what it is to be an immigrant, for example, Brecht in his wanderings before and during World War II, the Odin as a group of actors from many countries led by an Italian based in the

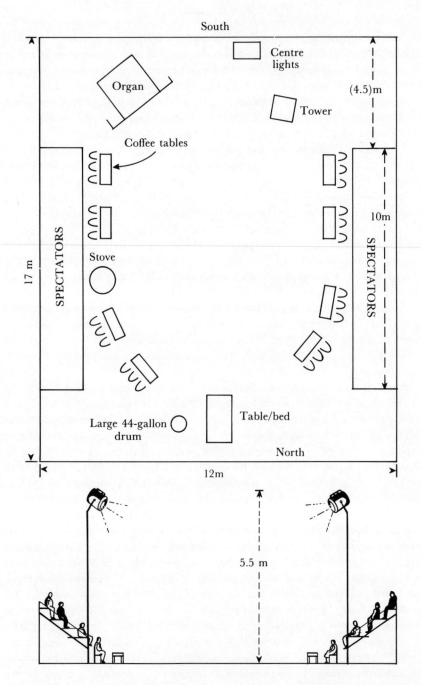

Figure 5.8 Plan and elevation views of the stage for *Brecht's Ashes 2* (Odin Teatret, 1982)

hinterland of western Denmark. And both know exile from the cultural mainstream which forces one to rely on inner fortitude rather than the attention of others for creative strength – Brecht working on his plays in exile with little chance of them being performed, and the Odin continuing their research in Holstebro which had little meaning for anyone but themselves (Barba, 1981a:59; 1986a:220).

Despite the source material for *Brecht's Ashes 2*, the production was again as removed from realism as Barba's previous two improvisation-based works. But the personal component that had been so significant in *Min Fars Hus* and *Come! And the Day Will be Ours* was far less evident. The work focused on how the group responded to the material rather than on the tension between Brecht's life and the group's personal history. This reorientation was nowhere more evident than in the fact that for the first time since Barba began creating his works entirely from improvisation, the actors played designated characters which included, among others, Brecht himself, Walter Benjamin, and Helene Weigel, as well as Brechtian creations such as Arturo Ui from *The Resistible Rise of Arturo Ui*, Kattrin, the deaf mute daughter of Mother Courage, and Mackie Messer from *The Threepenny Opera*.

The production, which was mostly performed in the language of the host country (English in Britain, French in France, etc.), with several characters speaking German from time to time, was a fantastical journey through Brecht's history, an unusual history, however, in which events in Brecht's personal life were interwoven with the worlds he created in his writings. Brecht's departure from Berlin in 1933, for example, was prompted by the Cook from *Mother Courage* who, in an obvious reference to the Nazis' book-burning rituals, set fire to a book in her frying pan and danced around the stage to a cacophonous mixture of classical music and march tunes as the pages were consumed in flames. In a similar vein, it was Arturo Ui, the incarnation of Nazi brutality in Barba's production, who murdered Walter Benjamin. And Mackie Messer stuffed a copy of the Soviet newspaper *Pravda* (which means "truth") down Kattrin's throat, almost choking her, as they danced in celebration of Brecht's triumphant return to East Berlin in 1948.

These, and other powerful images, such as Ui's rape of Kattrin, and a bizarre parade, located somewhere between a funeral procession and Hieronymus Bosch's concept of hell, in which Ui and and an actress carried a cat's skeleton around the stage while "singing" in pained screams, were set in a quasi-cabaret atmosphere realized through the coffee-table setting, a number of up-tempo German songs, and a Brechtian-style jazz score played on the organ.

Despite the emotive imagery and music, the entire piece was framed against the backdrop of Brecht's alienation theory, with constant reminders that the people on stage were actors portraying characters. The members of the cast introduced themselves and the roles they were to play in the opening scene of the production; for instance, several members of the cast played different characters with only minor costume changes done in front of the audience, and part-way through the piece, Brecht and Helene Weigel stepped out of the scene to have a cup of tea and comment on the action.

In the Odin's only appearance in North America, *Brecht's Ashes 2* was performed at La Mama ETC in New York city in 1984, as a companion piece to *The Million*. The New York critics were divided over the production. Mel Gussow in the *New York Times* likened it to Grotowski's work and praised it as an evening of physical theatre:

> As produced by this Danish-based troupe, the evening is a provocative crossbreeding of theater, politics and biography, and it is also a demonstration of collective performance art.
>
> In common with his former colleague, Jerzy Grotowski, Mr. Barba takes a laboratory approach to the interrelationship of cultures and myths. Drawing freely on his work with Grotowski, Mr. Barba offers an evening of kinesthetic theater, in the double sense of the word – art in action ... as author and director, Mr. Barba bears the firebrand of Brecht. Potential didacticism is avoided by the fierce collaborative determination of the nine-man cast, alternatively speaking English and German and undertaking a regiment of roles. The actors have been well-schooled in mime, dance and the martial arts; they are also adept at playing various musical instruments.
>
> The precision in performance also carries one past the elliptical sections of the script. After a visceral 90 minutes, we are left with a portrait of Brecht as an artist harassed but unyielding.
>
> (1984a:C21)

Michael Feingold of the *Village Voice*, on the other hand, felt that Barba's legacy was not limited to Grotowski, and, even though he found Barba's images effective, he felt that *Brecht's Ashes 2* was cold and unfulfilling:

> The main point about Eugenio Barba is that his images are alive, and stick in the mind, which means a piece like *Brecht's Ashes 2* can be enjoyed even if you're apathetic to its materials or dubious about its intellectual premises. The work is image-work first and last, owing something (predictably) to Grotowski, to Kantor and other Eastern European directors, perhaps most of all to Brecht himself, who really began for Europe the disassembling of the naturalistic stage.
>
> Not that sources are everything: Barba's images are original in their combination of simplicity and simultaneity. He's a collagist and satirical cartoonist with theatrical passion, in this piece pulling a character from one Brecht work, a prop from another, an action from a third, then setting the three off in a distorted dance down one end of the stage while he starts up a similar combination with antithetical elements at the other. ...

Like his subject, Barba's achievement is paradoxical and divided against itself. His images are rich and arresting enough to interest any audience, but the intellectual matter they bear is schematic and unfulfilling. The piece lives to revel in Brecht's contradictions as if he were a dissertation instead of a human being; it stages a theoretical argument in image form as if the function of the theater were literary criticism.

(1984:79)

Oxyrhincus Evangeliet (The Gospel According to Oxyrhincus)

Oxyrhincus Evangeliet, which premiered in March 1985 and remained in the repertoire until 1987, marked another step in the Odin's move away from reflecting the personal history of the group in its productions. This move was most evident in the emphasis on character in rehearsals, an emphasis which was reflected in the importance of interrelated character realities in the production. Each character in *Oxyrhincus* – which included, among others, Antigone, Sabbatai Zevi (a false Messiah), Ecce Homo (the Prodigal Son), and Zusha Mal'ak (an Hasidic tailor) – related to those around him/her in terms of his/her own world. As one scholar points out, Zevi was Creon in Antigone's story as well as father to the Prodigal Son (also called Polinices – Antigone's brother – in the production) in the Son's story; in Zevi's world, these were all his followers drawn from the cangaceiros (Brazilian outlaws) that populated his kingdom of faith, a kingdom that was confronted with medieval Jewish lore in the shape of the tailor (Klein, 1988:186). As Barba himself put it when an interviewer suggested that Ecce Homo was a Christ figure:

You [the interviewer] say it is Christ. And I reply: it is and isn't Christ. In the production he is called Polinices, Antigone's brother. And both were children of Oedipus, who, having found the truth, blinded himself. He is at the same time the Prodigal Son who returns to his father's house to submit to him, while Polinices returns to Thebes, his birthplace, to attack it. The production is a tangle of threads in which opposites are interwoven.

(1985h:7)

The importance of characters in the piece was further emphasized by the fact that for the first time in a Barba production each actor was credited in the program as playing a named, single character. Antigone was played by Roberta Carreri; Jehuda, the Grand Inquisitor, by Tage Larsen; Else Marie Laukvik played Zusha Mal'ak, the Hasid; Francis Pardeilhan was Ecce Homo; Julia Varley played Joan of Arc; and the false Messiah, Sabbatai Zevi, was played by Torgeir Wethal.

Despite the dramaturgical complexities this emphasis on character generated, which were further compounded by Barba's montage techniques and his rejection of linear narrative, the basic premise of the production was relatively simple. An Hasidic tailor arrives in the capital of Armageddon where South American outlaws are building a spiritual city under the guidance of their Messiah. This world of the false Messiah is populated with an array of characters who are both the outlaws and the figures of history or fiction whose names they bear.[5]

The production took its title from a former Coptic city in old Egypt, Oxyrhincus (modern-day Behnesa), where some of the oldest known Christian manuscripts were found early this century. These, and other Gnostic manuscripts found in 1945 at Nag Hammadi, were part of the inspiration for the production, along with the early rehearsal work on Borges' novella *The Dead Man*, and the associations these two sources conjured up for Barba in the world of the popular Brazilian outlaws described in the novels of writers such as Euclides da Cunha and the films of Ruy Guerra and Glauber Rocha.

These two strands, of the Brazilian outlaws and early Christian manuscripts, were brought together for Barba through several avenues of research that he and his actors worked on in rehearsals: the Vargas Llosa novel *The War of the End of the World*, in which a Christ-like figure establishes a city populated by outlaws and the poor in the hinterland of Bahia, Brazil only to have it destroyed and its inhabitants slaughtered by the army; Antigone's revolt against authority; the figure of Joseph Stalin as the archetypal totalitarian despot; and the image of the characters who populated the work meeting at the foot of Christ's cross (Barba, 1985a:30–32). All of these sources, and the associations they led to, helped shape a performance text which incorporated the messianic in its thematics, and whose dramatic structure was based on the Catholic Mass (Barba, 1985h:2).

In contrast to his previous three studio productions, the actors played no musical instruments but chanting as well as choral and solo singing played a major role in the work, and the sonorous potential of the voice was constantly challenged by dialogue that focused on the phonetic rather than semantic. This focus was enhanced by the fact that the entire production was presented in two fabricated languages: a language which sounded like Yiddish but contained only a few genuine Yiddish words, spoken by the Hasidic character; and a simulated Coptic based on a combination of Coinic Greek (the language spoken in Oxyrhincus) and Coptic – the language of the Christian manuscripts that inspired the piece.[6]

The long narrow stage, described in Chapter 4, which provided the main performing area, limited the physical action of the piece. The dance-like quality, that had been a feature of most of Barba's previous works, was not lost entirely, but it was more contained than in his earlier productions. *Oxyrhincus* relied heavily on choreographed movements of the upper torso, arms, and hands, as well as tableaus at either end of the stage.

Oxyrhincus was a major break from the scenic simplicity of Barba's previous studio works. It was set inside a huge structure made of red cloth that

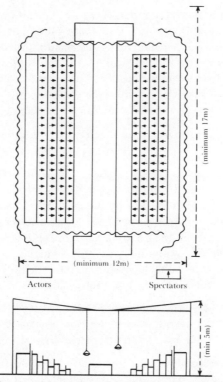

Actors   Spectators

Figure 5.9 Plan and elevation views of the set for *Oxyrhincus Evangeliet* (Odin Teatret, 1985)

surrounded both the performers and their audience. The hanamichi-type stage, which was approximately 2 feet above the floor, ran through the center of the structure with a narrow space between it and the first row of the audience who sat on raked seating on both sides of the stage. Despite this raked seating, most of the spectators were either at the same height as the actors or looking up at them because the action took place on the raised stage, in narrow aisles behind and above the back rows of seating on both sides of the house, or in the towers at both ends of the stage. This distortion of conventional sight-lines helped create a larger-than-life quality in the characters which was enhanced by their rich, brightly colored costumes, body padding to make people appear larger than they were, as well as genuine South American gaucho chaps, leather hats, and even a whip.

Critics were touched by the perverse religious quality of *Oxyrhincus.* Mario Scali, for instance, saw the production as a reflection of the Odin's own "religion of rebellion" that spectators had to surrender to in order to understand:

> To plunge into *Oxyrhincus*, forgetting all that you know, is the only way to benefit from this performance, from the wild imagery, where each character collides with the others. They have nothing in common if

143

this is not a rebellion. Each person represents a human itinerary but at the same time they are bound by that which binds the actors of the Odin: this religious spectacle brings its religion outside of itself. Each person's rebellion on the long table is the revolt of those at the Odin, "those who refuse to be buried alive," or walled up in a congealed set theatre which is forever rehashing the same themes.

(1985:34)

Jean Francois Peyret saw it as a religion of nightmares in which the spectator is trapped:

Upon entering the room, my religion, that which waited for me, was achieved so to speak. I had the uneasy feeling that I was, as Montaigne would have said, "a mouse in a trap." ... All those unusual characters, each like a prisoner of his own fable, appeared from all over, from behind, from in front, from the curtains, trampling on the table which was for me already something sacred, screaming, singing, in that strange incomprehensible language, all dancing in front of my eyes as if I was in a dream, hallucination, nightmare.

(1984:1)

Other critics, like Ugo Volli, compared it to *Brecht's Ashes* and found it an even "colder" production which had a disturbing effect on its audience:

There is no possibility for an emotional relationship with these nearly unrecognizable, atrocious and evasive characters. One cannot sympathize. If then *Brecht's Ashes* was in third person, but very warm, participatory, sympathetic, *Oxyrhincus* is, on the other hand, a suggestive but cold production. It is as though ice is covering, hiding an incandescent nucleus of anger, and this sensation has a particularly disturbing effect on the audience.

(1986:10)

In her excellent analysis of *Oxyrhincus* Stacy Klein maintains that this distance was the very catalyst to the spectator's imagination:

Repeated images of death, perverted sexuality, and torture do not touch the spectator. It is all shown as a game from which the dying wake up miraculously only to be killed and tortured again. It is indeed given the same moral distance as that given to the participants of our own world, through the mass media and television, from the horrible events of our time. In *Oxyrhincus* we are participants in this game – we watch and feel nothing, we watch and do nothing – we do not care. ...

At the same time, however, we always remain aware of our participation, through the mirror image of ourselves by the other spectators and through being surrounded by the action which takes place below us, above us, and beside us. And we understand, subconsciously, the

144

performance dialect of distance – a distance which at the same time creates coldness and provides the opportunity for our imagination to flow.

(1988:209)

Talabot

Talabot, the Odin's next production, premiered in August 1988 in Holstebro and began touring Europe the following month. The original cast consisted of Cesar Brie, Naira Gonzalez, Jan Ferslev, Richard Fowler, Iben Nagel Rasmussen, Julia Varley, and Torgeir Wethal. Brie and Gonzalez left the company in early 1990, however, and were replaced by two actors studying with Carreri, Falk Heinrich and Isabel Ubeda. *Talabot* remained in the Odin's repertory until September 1991 and, apart from its performances in Denmark, toured in Sweden, Norway, France, Italy, Switzerland, Austria, Poland, Mexico, Peru, and Chile.

Talabot owes its origins to the writings of a contemporary Danish anthropologist, Kirstin Hastrup, who conducted much of her field work among isolated villages in Iceland. In her book *The Challenge of the Unreal* (1987), Hastrup uses her experience in Iceland to consider the personal implications of what it is to be an anthopologist living in, and at the same time studying, a foreign culture. Barba read and was touched by Hastrup's book. He contacted her and explained his interest in developing a production based on her life. She agreed to cooperate with Barba, at which point he conducted several interviews with her, and also asked her to write a series of autobiographical texts.

The initial rehearsals for *Talabot* were done in Chicxulub, a town in Yucatan, Mexico, over a three-month period in early 1988. During the first part of these rehearsals, each actor was asked to stage three excerpts from Hastrup's writings and/or taped interviews. These stagings were done very quickly, each one taking no more than a few hours, and the actors not even bothering to learn lines of text. Despite the fact that few of these early explorations of Hastrup's life found their way into the final production, these improvisations were important because, in developing them, the actors used many hand props, such as shells, a scarf, and an axe, which became central to Barba's mise-en-scene.

As one might expect of Barba, Hastrup's autobiography was simply a point of departure for his production. Certainly incidents and characters from her life, including herself (played by Varley) and her father (played by Fowler), appear in the piece, but they are joined by others that have as much to do with Barba's imagination and his theatrical history as they do with Hastrup's anthropology. Using an experience of Hastrup's, in which she maintains that she met one of the Huldrefolk (hidden people) of Icelandic mythology, Barba introduced what he describes as "the 'hidden people' of Nordic legend ... [and] the dead from the history of our times" (Odin Teatret,

145

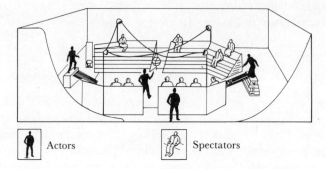

Figure 5.10 Plan view and sketch of the set for *Talabot* (D'Urso and Barba, 1990:216)

1988:2). These characters included: the Danish explorer Knud Rasmussen (played by Ferslev); a Trickster (played by Rasmussen) who was a grotesque, shamanic figure with magical powers; the French actor, director, and writer Antonin Artaud (played first by Brie and later by Heinrich) whose theatrical theories have influenced a generation of experimenters since his death in 1948; and Fidel Castro's colleague, the Argentine revolutionary Ernesto (Che) Guevara (played by Wethal).

The set for the production was relatively simple compared with that of *Oxyrhincus Evangeliet*. It consisted of two ramps and raised platforms at either end of the playing area, which was defined by four raked seating modules. The main action took place in the elliptical playing area in front of the modules, while the space behind them served as a "backstage" area which actors used to change costumes, collect and store props, and from which they provided musical and vocal accompaniment to the action – all in full view of the audience. There was no set furniture, though there was an extensive use of hand props, lavish costumes, and a collection of colorful masks worn by the "mythical" characters. Lighting was very simple, consisting of bulbs in reflector dishes which were hung from wiring that criss-crossed the playing area.

Continuing in the vein of *Oxyrhincus Evangeliet*, *Talabot*'s mise-en-scene relied on simultaneity and a complex interweaving of thematic associations rather than a concatenate, linear plot. As David Shoemaker, who published an excellent description and analysis of the production in *New Theatre Quarterly*, put it: "The action of *Talabot* is characterized by unexpected changes of direction, breaks in the text's linear development, and a composition based on montage and the interweaving of two or more simultaneous actions" (1990:307). This simultaneity, and the complex universe Barba created, in which anthropology, autobiography, Nordic mythology, and the archetypes of his imagination all met, owed much to the four frames of reference he identifies in his working notes published in the program for the production. Apart from Hastrup's biography and field work, these frames of reference included a page from an essay on commedia dell'arte by Edward Gordon Craig, a psalm, *Confession*, by the Danish poet B. S. Ingemann, and the title *Talabot*. This latter reference was particularly rich with associations for Barba because, as well as being the name of the first ship Barba worked on in the Norwegian Merchant Marine, it was the name of the French engineer, Paulin-Francois Talabot, who led the "French Brigade" during the planning of the Suez Canal, and it is a word in the Mayan language of the Yucatan which means both "to reach the seashore" (tal'bot) and "to come to agitate the body" (talah bot) (Odin Teatret, 1988:3–5).

Incidents from Hastrup's field work in Iceland, including her attendance at an all-male sheepshearers' party and her work in a fish-packing plant where the drunken men she shared her accommodation with teased her threateningly before soaking her in beer, were intercut with intimate, revealing incidents, such as the conflicts with her father that culminated in his death, and her grandmother's funeral.

Guevara's story unfolded through scenes that depicted him as both a sickly provincial teenager and a charismatic revolutionary. His death scene, which is done with Guevara in the traditional commedia "Capitano" costume and ends with him coming to life in an explosion of sound and music as he dances to the accompaniment of "El Condor Pasa," for instance, was preceded by an incident from his youth in which he was mistakenly invited to a formal dance hosted by the wealthy father of the girl he was in love with at the time. At the party he managed to dance with his sweetheart to a romantic, lyrical waltz before, at the screeching behest of the father dressed as the commedia character Brighella, being beaten and evicted from the gathering by the musicians.

These juxtapositions of symbols and what appeared to be unconnected scenes continued throughout the production, as in Artaud's famous "The Theatre and the Plague" speech at the Sorbonne, which was presented as a vulgar, violent outburst by a masked Artaud at one end of the stage, while Hastrup sat at the other end struggling to give voice to her emotional and mental anguish over the break-up of her first marriage.

All this was interwoven with songs, music, and a Trickster who moved in and out of the action throughout the piece, orchestrating scenes as if she/he/it had the power to bring memories and nightmares to life on stage – a peculiar stage life in which Hastrup and her father spoke the language of the country in which the production was being presented, Guevara spoke Norwegian, and Artaud a mixture of the local language and Italian.

Talabot was generally well received by the critics. It was particularly successful in Scandinavia because of the production's focus on Hastrup and Iceland. But, as always, critics had difficulty in categorizing Barba's work because of his rejection of conventional plot structures, and the importance physical expression plays in his theatre. Some, in Stockholm particularly, even labeled *Talabot* experimental dance theatre. This difficulty was echoed by Shoemaker: "Confronted by the barriers of language and the nature of the Odin's dramaturgy, an audience accustomed to a steady diet of conventional naturalism may find that much of *Talabot* is inaccessible, at least on initial viewing" (1990:307). Penny Simpson of the South Wales *Echo* suggested that one way of understanding the production was to focus on the visual motifs rather than the narrative:

> Red twine, masks, shells and a silk scarf are some of the more elemental means used by the Danish theatre company Odin to weave together striking images in their show *Talabot*. ... With music played on accordions, harps and guitars, these objects link together a woman anthropologist's life story with the history of her post-war generation.
>
> Scattered like leaves are portraits of figures like the revolutionary Che Guevara, theatre pioneer Artaud and Chairman Mao, whose ghostly presences inform Odin's interpretation of the anthropologist Kirsten Hastrup's life. Other ghosts have a more physical manifestation and enter into scenes played out between Kirsten and her father. ... But that's as far as the facts take you – the rest requires keeping a sharp eye out for the recurring motifs (the shells and the scarf) which propel you into a maze of images, that bring into explosive contact diverse figures from the past and the present.
>
> (1990)

In agreeing with Simpson's assessment of the visual in *Talabot*, the Swiss critic, Rene Zahnd, also touched on the importance of sound in the production:

> In the production, a lot of importance is given to singing, the voice, and to sound effects. These sound landscapes, which are a testimony to the wonderful skills of the performers, bewitch the spectators. But the essential component of the production is visual. The costumes are beautiful, the objects are often handled as if they were amulets, the masks create an imaginative world, and the mise-en-scene surprises and continually forces the attention from one corner of the stage to the other.
>
> (1989)

Many of the Italian critics took up Barba's own description of the production in the program in which he states that *Talabot* is "A story of the generation of 1948" (Odin Teatret, 1988:2), by which he meant those born in 1948 and living their maturity through the second half of the twentieth century. Some, like Odoardo Bertani of Modena's *Avvenire*, described it in more poetic terms as depicting "the defeat of a dream" (1988), while Fanny Monti from *Romagna* saw *Talabot* as "a journey through history with the Trickster as mediator" (1989).

6

THE INTERNATIONAL
SCHOOL OF THEATRE
ANTHROPOLOGY

Despite the importance of productions for Barba and his colleagues, they are only one aspect of their work. Training and performance research have always been major concerns at the Odin, concerns which culminated in the foundation of the International School of Theatre Anthropology (ISTA).

ISTA, which Barba established in 1979, is a most unusual school that has no classrooms or students, meets only periodically, has no curriculum, and has no graduates. Nevertheless, it is one of Europe's most important theatre research institutions.

ISTA is based at the NTL in Holstebro, Denmark, and remains under Barba's direction. Holstebro is only an administrative center, however. The primary work of ISTA is done during the public sessions held from time to time at the request of particular funding bodies. These funding bodies are responsible for financing, locating, and administering the session they have commissioned, while Barba provides the expertise, the specialized personnel, and designs the program.

ISTA's public sessions bring together traditional Eastern master performers and their Western counterparts, as well as relatively young, inexperienced actors and directors from the Euro-American tradition, and a team of intellectuals including theatre scholars, anthropologists, psychologists, biologists, and critics. These sessions are primarily a combination of workshops, seminars, and lecture/demonstrations during which Barba and his colleagues research performance.

A CONTEXT FOR ISTA

It is no accident that ISTA was born in the 1970s and matured during the 1980s, a fervent period of experiments in the theatre and interdisciplinary scholarship centered around interculturalism. In the academic world it was during these years that the work of scholars like Richard Schechner, Victor Turner, Clifford Geertz, Irving Goffman, and Barbara Myerhoff – all of which drew heavily on the connections between performance and anthropology – gained ascendancy. And in the theatre, Grotowski, Barba's teacher, was

149

engaged in his "Theatre of Sources" work, which compared various ritual performances from different cultures. Peter Brook and the actors of his Paris-based company, the International Center for Theatre Research (ICTR), were involved in a search for theatrical universals in the center's production *Orghast*, in Brook's African journey, and in *Conference of the Birds*. The Japanese director Tadashi Suzuki was creating productions derived from a combination of sources which included classical Greek tragedy, ancient Japanese ritual practices, noh, and contemporary Western-influenced experimental theatre techniques. Barba's ideas echoed those of his contemporaries.

Despite its historical context, ISTA is very much the product of Barba's personal experience and preoccupations. One of the major features of the early ISTAs, for example, was workshops in which participants developed their own training exercises from improvisations rather than being taught new skills, an approach based on Barba's autodidactic training system.

The role of Oriental performers at ISTA also owes its origins to events prior to 1979. Barba first visited the kathakali training school in Kerala, India, in 1963 and both took exercises from it back to Grotowski and evolved his own philosophy of training based on what he saw when he founded the Odin Teatret. Despite the fact that Barba did not return to India for almost another twenty years, he maintained a dialogue with Asia through his invitation to various Oriental performers during the 1960s and 1970s – including artists from noh, kyogen, Balinese dance-drama, chhau, bharatanatyam, and odissi dance – to conduct workshop/seminars for Scandinavian actors in Holstebro, and through inviting these and other master performers from the East to teach at the third theatre gatherings he directed in Belgrade (1976) and Bergamo (1977).

In fact, even though these two gatherings were designed as points of contact and workshop/training sessions for members of the independent group theatre movement, they provided a model for ISTA. Apart from Asian performers conducting workshops primarily designed to help Western actors develop their own training programs – an important component of the first two ISTAs particularly – many other features of ISTA can be seen in these earlier gatherings. The "community" concept, of people brought together in a relatively isolated setting where they work, sleep, and eat together, began with the third theatre gatherings and has been carried over into ISTA. Similarly, master performers from the West teaching and leading workshops was an integral part of third theatre meetings that has subsequently played a major role in ISTA, as has the lecture/demonstration, also a feature of third theatre gatherings, in which actors, directors, or theatre groups show and explain their training and performance techniques. Including performances for the general public in the ISTA program was a continuation of similar programming at third theatre meetings. And the attempt to combine intellectuals and theatre practitioners in one forum had its origins in the meetings in Belgrade and Bergamo where scholars such as Taviani, Franco Ruffini, and Nicola Savarese, who have since become members of the permanent staff of ISTA, were asked to attend the gatherings to observe, document, and advise.

THE ISTA PROGRAM

There were six ISTA sessions between 1980 and 1991: the first in Bonn, Germany (1980), followed by meetings in: Volterra, Italy (1981); Blois and Malakoff, France (1985); Holstebro, Denmark (1986); Salento, Italy (1987); and Bologna, Italy (1990).[1] Despite developments, changes, and thematic differences, most of the ISTAs have consisted of a three part-program: a private workshop/research session for invited participants; a forum open to theatre practitioners, scholars, and scientists unable to take part in the private work; and a series of performances for the general public.

The private, closed sessions have always been the most important part of ISTA. It is in these that the major research, discussions, and teaching have taken place. In the first two ISTAs, the emphasis in this part of the program was on teaching. The pedagogues taught either their techniques or the principles underlying them to young performers. There were lengthy seminars in which directors worked on scenes from *Hamlet* under Barba's guidance at both ISTAs, and at the Volterra gathering Barba conducted a series of workshops using Edward Bond's play *Narrow Road to the Deep North* in which he demonstrated his directorial methods. The teaching sessions were augmented with seminars on improvisation, training, the connections between games and performance, Italian theatre, and the development of performance texts from literary sources such as novels. These seminars were led by various experts and master performers who, as well as ISTAs' permanent intellectual staff, included Rasmussen, Cots, and Larsen from the Odin; Orazio Costa – who, along with Giorgio Strehler and Luchino Visconti, was one of the founders of post-war Italian theatre; Clive Barker – from Warwick University and author of *Theatre Games* (Methuen, 1977); Keith Johnstone – an expert on improvisation from the University of Calgary; Dario Fo; and Grotowski.

There was a shift in emphasis in the closed sessions during the following two ISTAs (France and Denmark) from teaching to lecture/demonstrations, so much so, in fact, that the entire Holstebro ISTA, which combined the closed and open parts of the program, consisted of little else.

The lecture/demonstration continued to be an important component in the 5th and 6th ISTAs, as did the teaching seminars of the earlier meetings. But Barba introduced a workshop/rehearsal model in ISTA V that dominated its closed session, as it did at the following gathering. In these workshop/rehearsals, which explored the creation of intercultural performance texts, Barba and his team of performers and musicians from

151

India, Bali, Japan, and the Odin developed mises-en-scenes which incorporated their various culturally based performance techniques. In Salento, these workshop/rehearsals began with Goethe's *Faust*, while in Bologna the point of departure for the work was nothing more than a theme, "the voyage."

The open forums at ISTA invariably last no more than a few days, and are primarily designed to allow those unable to attend the longer, closed meetings access to the ISTA research, Barba's ideas, and various scholars' responses to ISTA. These sessions have always taken the form either of lecture/demonstrations or more conventional conference-type symposia.

All of the ISTAs have included open lecture/demonstrations, mainly led by Barba. In these lecture/demonstrations, pedagogues present fragments of performance which are used as the frame of reference for discussions of the principles underlying the techniques and codification that constitute their particular performance form. A typical example is a lecture/demonstration Barba conducted with Panigrahi at the open session in Bonn: Barba first asked Panigrahi to do a short dance with full musical and vocal accompaniment, following which he got her to repeat the dance without accompaniment. He then asked her to repeat the piece once again without musical backing, but this time requested that she stop and hold her body position at particular points in the dance in order for him to analyze the techniques underlying the odissi choreography. In doing this, Barba pointed out various elements embodied in the form, including the constant, yet precise, shifts and counterbalances in muscular tension; the changes in weight distribution; the continual alterations in the center of gravity; and particularly, the use of precarious equilibrium in choreographic elements such as the tribangi.

The conferences/symposia have been a part of several ISTAs since they were first introduced in Volterra with a series of symposia on theatre anthropology. Following Volterra, there have been similar open sessions on the connections between semiotics and theatre anthropology (Salento), and performance techniques and historiography (Bologna). These symposia have included such eminent scholars as Patrice Pavis, Marco De Marinis, Monique Borie, Frank Hoff, Ron Jenkins, Masao Yamaguchi, Raquel Carrio, Franco Ruffini, and Ferdinando Taviani.

The performances at each of the six ISTAs have primarily been social affairs in which the Asian and Western pedagogues have presented performances for the public. Invariably, these performances have been given throughout the region in which the particular ISTA was taking place. In Volterra, for instance, performances were presented in different parts of Tuscany and as far south as Rome, while in Holstebro the ISTA performances were presented in various parts of Denmark.

At several of the ISTAs, the performances have included barters. In Salento, barters between the ISTA performers and the local community included two on religious music in which Hindu Indians, Lutheran Danes, and Catholic Italians shared their musical traditions, and another based on the theme of trance, which combined a Balinese trance ritual with the Salento trance dance, the tarantella. And in Bologna, there was a barter in an abandoned factory near the main railway station in which the young Arab immigrants who live there presented songs, performance art pieces, and skill displays such as walking and jumping on broken glass in response to dances and improvisations by the ISTA artists.

It has become something of a tradition at ISTA that these performances and barters culminate in what Barba calls a Theatrum Mundi. The Theatrum Mundi is a huge performance in which the Asian performers and musicians combine with their Odin colleagues to produce an intercultural spectacle under Barba's direction. In Salento, for example, there were two such events, one in a large Italianate theatre in the provincial capital, Bari, and another in the courtyard of a medieval castle in Copertino. In Bologna, the congress culminated in a Theatrum Mundi in an open-air theatre in the center of the city which included not only all the ISTA performers but also all of the participants.

ISTA I – BONN

Like so many events in Barba's and the Odin's history, ISTA was a combination of vision and circumstance. Following the third theatre gatherings in Belgrade and Bergamo, Barba wanted to mount a program along similar lines but with somewhat different goals. He was interested in comparing the techniques of Eastern and Western performers in a workshop situation, in order to test his hypothesis that, as well as being very unlike each other, they also had much in common. He also wanted to organize a gathering that focused on teaching young directors and actors in an intercultural setting, rather than in one dominated by concerns such as group dynamics and devising strategies for artistic survival in an unsympathetic environment. In addition to these aims, he was keen to formalize the role of the intellectuals at such meetings by asking them not only to document the workshops but to also take an active part in the research. As luck would have it, Barba met someone willing to finance his ambitions.

Following the Bergamo meeting, he was asked by the director of the Kulturamt der Stadt (State Ministry for Culture) in Bonn, Dr. Hans Jurgen Nagel, to mount a similar gathering in the city. Barba refused, but explained to Dr. Nagel that he had plans for a much larger gathering with a different format which would cost three times as much. Barba held out little hope of Dr. Nagel's raising the money but, much to his surprise, Dr. Nagel contacted him several months later to inform him that he had in fact raised the money and also found the ideal location for the meeting.

Barba, who had given little thought to the details of such a gathering

153

(including what to call it) because he had not expected the money to be forthcoming, began designing what was to become the basic format of this new organization. Firstly, he needed a team of master performers from both traditional Asian theatres and the West. The latter presented few problems since several of his own Odin actors, namely Cots, Torben Bjelke, and Rasmussen, shared Barba's intercultural concerns and were keen to be involved. He also had many contacts in Asia because of the various workshops he had arranged during the 1960s and 1970s. He invited odissi dancer Sanjukta Panigrahi and her musicians, with whom he had remained in touch following her Holstebro seminar in 1977. He asked two Beijing opera performers, Tsoa Chun-Lin and Lin Chun-Hui, from the Fu-Hsing Dramatic Arts Acadamy in Taipei, Taiwan, which he had visited on several occasions. He invited I Made Pasek Tempo, who had been Cots' teacher in Bali, along with his group of dancers and musicians. And in his search for a kabuki actor in Japan, Barba was introduced to the nihon buyo performer and master teacher Katsuko Azuma, whom he invited along with her musicians.

Just as the master performers presented few recruiting problems, so the intellectuals Barba wanted to take part in this new project were easy to gather, since he had either known them personally for several years or had been introduced to them by trusted colleagues. He invited what he referred to as a "scientific team," which included professors Ruffini, Fabrizio Cruciani, and Ugo Volli, all from the theatre department of Bologna University (Italy); professors Taviani and Nicola Savarese from the theatre department at Lecce University (Italy); Professor Moriaki Watanabe from the theatre department at the University of Tokyo (Japan); a psychologist and neurologist from the University of Copenhagen (Denmark), Dr. Peter Elsass; Professor Jean-Marie Pradier, a psycholinguist from the University of Rabat (Morocco); an anthropologist from the University of Aarhus (Denmark), Dr. Mette Bovin; and Dr. Ranka Bijeliac-Babic, a researcher from Saint Anne's Hospital in Paris (France). As well as this core group, others were invited to open sessions, including the biologist Dr. Henri Laborit and Grotowski, both of whom were asked to address participants.

Barba wanted to invite directors and actors from the third theatre since their autodidatic approach to training was an ideal basis for the type of research he planned to conduct. In keeping with the international nature of the upcoming meeting, he also wanted to draw participants from as many different countries as possible. Advertisements were placed in theatre journals and publicity flyers sent to most of the theatre groups who were part of the third theatre network. Barba then interviewed applicants over a period of several months in different parts of Europe, until he finally selected a group of forty-nine participants representing some twenty-two countries.[2]

While Barba was busily involved in selecting those who were to take part in the first ISTA and deciding the program, Dr. Nagel was finalizing administrative details. The meeting was to be held from October 1 to 31, 1980 in a school no longer in use in the suburbs of Bonn (Hauptschule an der Dune in Stettinerstrasse 21), and was to be financed from a variety of sources including the Kulturamt der Stadt Bonn, the Sekretariat fur Gemeinsame Kulturarbeit Wuppertal (the Wuppertal Secretariat of Joint Cultural Activities), the German Commission of UNESCO, the Ministries of Foreign Affairs of Germany, Italy and France, the Danish Ministry of Culture, and the Japan Foundation.

Needless to say, in mounting a gathering on the scale of ISTA for the first time there were problems. The heavy schedule did not suit everyone, for instance, which led to several people leaving the gathering altogether. But these were relatively few, and after their departure the rest of the participants remained for the entire meeting.

Another problem was the imbalance of experience among participants. Some of the directors and actors had worked in the theatre for many years, while others were relatively new to the profession. Since the participants were not separated according to levels of experience, this imbalance led to problems for the pedagogues because they had to gear their teaching to different levels within the same class. The *Hamlet* workshop/rehearsals suffered from similar problems too because there were several instances of inexperienced directors working with very experienced actors and vice versa, as well as varying levels of experience in the casts assigned to the directors.

During the latter stages of the meeting, Barba also became aware of another limitation in the program: having participants work for only one week with each of the Oriental masters. It was never Barba's intention that participants should learn nihon buyo, odissi, Balinese dance-drama, or Beijing opera, since he feels that it takes years to master these forms, and learning them properly involves extensive exposure to the socio-cultural milieu that produces them. He wanted participants to appreciate the principles underlying the body techniques that are common to each of the forms, and then apply and/or adapt these principles to their own training and performances. Unfortunately, in moving from teacher to teacher every six days, as the program called for, participants were so preoccupied with learning the basics of each new form that it was difficult for them to focus on what was common to the forms, let alone see the relevance of what they were learning for their own work.

Barba also felt that, even though he had been able to establish a more formal relationship between intellectuals and practitioners at Bonn than in the third theatre gatherings, ISTA had not fully tapped the potential of this relationship. He felt changes in the program were called for in order to allow scholars, scientists, and artists to work together more productively.

Despite these and other lesser problems, such as the need to streamline administrative procedures, the Bonn ISTA was a success. It was the first time that Asian masters, Western performers, and scholars had focused their attention collectively on interculturalism on such a scale in Europe (or possibly anywhere). The Asian pedagogues felt that they had gained an invaluable degree of reflexivity about their art (Azuma, 1986; Panigrahi, 1986). Participants, such as the Odin actress Carreri and the young German director Christoph Falke, discovered material that they would continue to explore for years to come (Carreri, 1985; Falke, 1985). Pradier altered much of the content and approach to his teaching based on his experience (Pradier, 1986). Articles about the congress appeared in journals throughout Western Europe and Latin America.[3] The Italian theatre semiotician Ruffini published an entire book on the meeting (1981). And Barba himself had come to realize the importance of the pre- expressive.

With these publications and the personal testimonies of participants, ISTA generated a great deal of interest both inside and outside Europe, an interest that encouraged Roberto Bacci, the director of the Centro per la Ricerca e la Sperimentazione Teatrale in Pontedera, Italy to begin organizing a similar meeting to be held the following year in Italy.

ISTA II – VOLTERRA

The second ISTA session was held in Volterra, Italy, in another abandoned school, the Conservatorio di San Pietro, from August 8 to October 8, 1981. As with the Bonn meeting, Barba designed and arranged the program, while the administration was coordinated by the organizers of the gathering, Roberto Bacci and his Pontedera theatre. As for the previous ISTA, funding was raised from several different sources, in this instance from a consortium of local and district administrative bodies: the Commune of Volterra, the District of Tuscany, and the Province of Pisa.

The Volterra meeting was a much grander affair than its predecessor. Apart from extending the length of the program from one month to two, there was a lavish increase in budget which allowed the organizers to accommodate not only all the participants and pedagogues but a large number of guests who came and went at different times during the meeting. The second ISTA also had a greater public profile than the meeting before it. Apart from participants eating in local restaurants (in Bonn, everyone ate in a kitchen adjoining the workrooms), the stream of official guests who came and left the gathering did much to break down the cloistered, monastic quality of the first session, an openness which was further emphasized by the number of public performances presented in Volterra and the surrounding Tuscany region by the Oriental artists, as well as by European and Latin American groups attending ISTA.

In keeping with this policy of expansion, there was a marked increase in scientific research. In Bonn, several of the scholars and scientists had given seminars for anyone who was interested. Apart from continuing this semi-formal contact between the intellectuals and participants at the second ISTA,

Barba asked a number of the scientists to design experiments to test some of their hypotheses about performance.[4]

As well as taking advantage of the increase in funding at Volterra to expand ISTA's program, Barba also attempted to address some of the problems of the previous congress. In order to avoid imbalances in participants' experience, for example, Barba invited only actors who had worked for several years in group theatre, and he redesigned the directors' workshops so that only seasoned directors led rehearsals while their less experienced colleagues observed.

Barba also redesigned the classes with the Oriental masters in order to help participants focus on the principles underlying the forms, rather than on learning the forms themselves. Instead of participants moving from one group to another after working with one pedagogue for a limited period of time, they were assigned to groups which were led by the same master performers throughout the entire two months of the meeting.

In order to make the relationship between the intellectuals and artists more productive than at Bonn, Barba concentrated the work of the Volterra congress on a single theme, "Improvisation." This is not to say that other things were not considered, but, by concentrating ISTA's work on one aspect of performance, Barba focused the research interests of the performers and the intellectuals. Even though the groups might explore the theme differently, each could therefore also work with the other for the benefit of both.

Despite these changes from the first to the second ISTA, the basic structure of the meeting established in Bonn was retained in Volterra. Participants were to be intellectuals and theatre practitioners. The gathering's major work was to take place in workshop/training sessions led by various teachers, including the Oriental and Western masters, as well as Barba himself. Panigrahi and Azuma, as well as professors Taviani, Ruffini, Cruciani, Volli, Savarese, and Pradier were asked to take part again, establishing a core staff that has been involved with ISTA ever since. And the division of the congress – into a lengthy, closed session and a much shorter public gathering open to actors, directors, and scholars unable to attend the longer meeting – was to be retained.

ISTA came of age with this second meeting. Between the Bonn and Volterra sessions, over 200 people had taken part in ISTA – actors, directors, scholars, and scientists who took their experiences back to their homelands and into their work. The length and scale of the Volterra gathering had greatly expanded on the first meeting. ISTA's profile, with so many performances and seminars for the general public, was established in Italy. Through the publication of Barba's writings and those of others on theatre anthropology, ISTA was also becoming better known in the rest of Europe and in the United States.

But, regardless of ISTA's achievements and the interest it had generated, the economic downturn and political climate of the early 1980s, which led to cutbacks in arts funding throughout Europe, made the mounting of another meeting difficult. In fact, it was to be four years before another ISTA congress, four years during which many of Barba's ideas and interests had changed – as was reflected in the program of the 1985 meeting.

ISTA III – FRANCE

The next ISTA, held from April 12 to 21, 1985, was divided between two locations in France, the Chateau de Chambord in Blois – a provincial town some 80 miles southwest of Paris – and at Theatre 71 in Malakoff, a Paris suburb. The adminstrative coordinator was Patrick Pezin, an actor, director, and publishing editor of the theatre journal *Bouffonneries*, who had attended the Volterra ISTA. Pezin coordinated financial and logistical support from a variety of sources from within France including the regional administration, La Direction du Developpement Culturel (the Directorate of Cultural Development), L'Action Francaise Artistique (French Artistic Action), Le Ministere de la Culture (the Ministry of Culture), and L'Office National de la Diffusion Artistique (the National Office of Artistic Diffusion), as well as from the Danish Ministry of Culture. His administrative assistance was drawn from La Compagnie du Hasard, a theatre group based in Blois, and from the staff of Theatre 71.

Unlike the Volterra ISTA, which was essentially a larger version of the Bonn gathering, the French meeting was a marked departure from what had happened in the past. It was much shorter than either of its predecessors. The practical sessions with the Oriental and Western masters were curtailed, and lecture/demonstrations began to take precedence over training.

Barba retained the thematic concept introduced at Volterra, making the theme of the French meeting "Narration," but it was not explored in the same depth as the improvisation theme had been at the second ISTA. This was no doubt due to the brevity of the meeting, but it was compounded by the fact that only a few of the intellectuals who had been at past ISTAs attended the French gathering. The permanent staff of scholars in France consisted of only Taviani, Savarese, and Pradier, while the invited guests included Volli, Watanabe, and two people from Mexico who had not previously been involved with ISTA: the journalist and theatre critic, Patricia Cardona; and Professor Armando Partida from the National University in Mexico City (UNAM).

Some of these changes were due to limited funds, but others reflected a change in Barba's thinking. He was no longer so interested in researching the pre-expressive as he was in exploring what he terms the actor's use of energy, that is, how a performer activates and shapes energy – through changing posture, adjusting the center of gravity, and altering degrees of muscular tension – to create his/her performance score. In Barba's view, this new research interest called less for workshops, in which Western actors and directors had the opportunity to explore performance and dramaturgical principles that function across cultures, than it did for a detailed study of how master performers tap and structure performances from what amounts to distortions of their everyday use of the body and voice.

Since there had been no ISTA meetings during this shift in Barba's thinking, he had not yet had the opportunity to explore it together with his team of performers and intellectuals. Consequently, the program and format of the French meeting represented something of a transition in ISTA that was only to be fully realized at the following gathering. This gathering was to be somewhat akin to a large public session consisting of lecture/demonstrations before an audience of some 200 invited specialists. All practical training was to be abandoned, and the theme of the meeting was to be all-important.

ISTA IV – HOLSTEBRO

The fourth ISTA session was held between September 17 and 22, 1986 at the Odin Teatret's headquarters in Holstebro, Denmark. It was administered by the NTL and funded by the municipality of Holstebro, the Japan Foundation, the Japanese Bureau of International Educational Relations, and the Indian Council for Cultural Relations. Unlike the previous two meetings, in which research had often extended beyond the theme of the particular meeting, the Holstebro theme, "The Female Role as Represented on the Stage in Different Cultures," dominated the entire event – an event led by twenty-nine Asian and European pedagogues which attracted 137 participants, from twenty-one countries.

The pedagogues included what were by now two of Barba's closest ISTA collaborators, Panigrahi and Azuma, both of whom brought musicians, singers, and additional performers with them. Panigrahi was accompanied by her guru, Kelucharan Mahapatra, and an 11-year-old Gotipua (i.e., a young male odissi dancer), Gautam, who studied with Mahapatra. Azuma brought a female colleague from her school, Kanho Azuma, and a kabuki onnagata (a male performer specializing in female roles), Kanichi Hanayagi, with her.

In addition to Panigrahi's and Azuma's companies, there were four Balinese dancers – Swasti Bandem, Ary Bandem, Desak Laksmi, and Ketut Suryatini; two kathakali performers – Sankaran Namboodiri and K. N. Vijayakumar; and two Chinese opera groups, one with Tracy Chun, Yvonne Lin, and Helen Liu from the Fu-Hsing troupe in Taiwan, and another from the People's Republic of China made up of Mei Bao-Jiu, Mei Lan-Fang's son who, like his father, specializes in female roles, and Pei Yan-Ling, one of China's leading Hebei opera actresses.

Barba's original intention was to counterbalance these Eastern pedagogues with actresses from the three major Western performer-training traditions: those trained within acting families, as had been the tradition

159

prior to the formation of modern training institutes; the conventional modern training in theatre schools; and the autodidactic training of groups such as Grotowski's and Barba's companies, which developed during the 1960s. Unfortunately, Franca Rame, who learned her craft as a member of one of Italy's oldest theatre families, was unable to attend the congress because of illness, as was Bibi Andersson, who had trained at the National Drama School in Stockholm. This left Sonja Kehler, a graduate of the Teaterhochschule Leipzig, and the Odin actress Rasmussen to represent the West's approaches to female roles.

The pedagogues dominated the lecture/demonstrations which took place in the Odin Teatret studios on the outskirts of Holstebro. These studio sessions took up the entire day, and were closed to all but the invited participants and performers.

The demonstrations constituted the largest part of the the daily program. These demonstrations were three- to four-hour sessions, during which most of the pedagogues described their early training and used short performance pieces to illustrate the techniques and dramaturgy of their particular form. The descriptions of training were basically lecture/demonstrations while the performance pieces focused on the blurred distinctions between male and female in many theatrical forms. These presentations consisted of males playing females, females portraying males, and actresses playing females who display male characteristics.

Unfortunately, a combination of factors, including reluctance on the part of some performers, language problems, and scheduling conflicts, allowed most of the pedagogues to talk only briefly about their techniques of gender portrayal. And Barba did not speak during these demonstrations, except to say a few brief words at either the beginning or end of each session.

Discussions were reserved for the "reflection" section of the program, a one- to two-hour period set aside each day specifically for dialogue between participants.

There was more contention among those attending the Holstebro ISTA than there had been at any of the previous meetings. This was primarily due to the fact that the majority of those invited were scholars and critics, that is, a group more accustomed to discussion and debate than making theatre. To be fair to participants, Barba's mistake was in believing that all of those he invited shared his interests. Many did, but many others wanted to see their own agendas explored – leaving Barba open to criticisms such as those by the American critic, Erika Munk, who, in two bitter, personal attacks in the *Village Voice* (1986a) and *Performing Arts Journal* (1986b) accused him of being anti-feminist, stifling debate by giving prominence to lecture/demonstrations, and manipulating the schedule toward his own research interests without concern for questions that interested others.

In addition to Munk's criticism, there were a number of scientists and academics who raised the question of linguistic precision. Several of the scientists maintained that Barba's concept of energy is vague because it cannot be measured or transposed into a mathematical formula, while some theatre academics, anthropologists, and sociologists had similar misgivings with Barba's use of the terms "strong" and "soft" to describe different qualities of energy, since they felt that terms like "strong" and "soft" lack precision.

Barba and his closest colleagues were understandably concerned by the conflicts at the Holstebro meeting. Discussion and the exchange of ideas had always been a part of ISTA but, in this instance, many of those leading the debate were at odds with what Barba and his core ISTA staff wanted to examine. This conflict resulted in neither those wanting to pursue the socio-historical contexts of female representation nor Barba and those concerned with performance techniques that cut across cultural boundaries being able to focus on their research interests.

In the months following the Holstebro meeting, Barba continued a lively correspondence with his closest ISTA colleagues on the format of the next session which was already in the planning stages for the following year. Eventually, it was decided that it was best to return to the balance between intellectuals and practical theatre people which had been the model prior to Holstebro, since it had always engendered a productive and harmonious working atmosphere. Barba's research interests might have changed but his methodology had not.

ISTA V – SALENTO

The next ISTA was held in a summer school 7 miles outside Otranto, a small town in the southern Salento (commonly referred to as the boot heel) region of Italy, from September 1 to 14, 1987. It was organized by Mediterranea Teatro Laboratorio, a theatre group based in Lecce, the nearest large city, together with Nicola Savarese, the director of the Performance Section of the Department of Social Systems and Communications at the University of Lecce, under the sponsorship of the Ministry of Foreign Affairs and the Ministry of Performance and Tourism. Funding was provided by the usual variety of sources, in this instance the Puglia Region (i.e., the regional council), the provincial government of Lecce, the Puglia Public Theatre Consortium, and the Lecce Chamber of Commerce.

Consistent with Barba's decision to redress the balance of participants, more than half of those invited were young Italian directors who led third theatre groups in the southern half of the country. He also invited several experienced Italian directors from group theatre including Potlach's Pino di Buduo, and Roberto Bacci from Pontedera's Centro per la Ricerca e la Sperimentazione Teatrale, as well as several theatre workers from Chile, Turkey, and Yugoslavia. To this group of practitioners he added some thirty scholars, scientists, and critics, mostly drawn from Italy, many of whom were familiar with his work at ISTA. In all there were some seventy participants from fifteen countries representing Europe, as well as Latin and North America.

Barba's team of pedagogues included his perennial colleagues Panigrahi and Azuma, along with their musicians and singers. Azuma also brought two fellow performers, Haruchiho Azuma and the onnagata who had been with her in Holstebro, Kanichi Hanayagi. Barba invited the Dharma Shanti company from Bali, made up of eleven performers and musicians, led by I Made and Swasti Bandem, as well as seven members of his own Odin Teatret.

As with all meetings since Volterra, Barba focused the work of the meeting around a theme, in this instance "Theatre Dialogue: The Actor's Tradition and the Spectator's Identity." Unlike previous gatherings in which there was a balance between intellectuals and practitioners, however, Barba did not establish a core staff of scholars and scientists to help direct research during the closed session. Rather, he had all the intellectuals work together on an equal footing during the Faust workshop/rehearsals that dominated this part of the program.

These workshop/rehearsals began with Barba asking participants to devise scenarios which they felt captured the essence of the Faust myth. He then combined several of these scenarios and used them as the basis of a performance text that he developed with his international cast of pedagogues. Asking each performer to explore his/her role and the situations in the text through his/her own cultural form, he developed a version of the Faust story which combined artists from nihon buyo (Azuma playing Faust), odissi dance (Panigrahi as Mephisto), kabuki (Hanayagi, the onnagata from Azuma's company played Gretchen), and the Odin (playing minor roles as required), as well as Indian, Japanese, and Western musicians, all under his own direction, which has its roots in the European experimental tradition.

The "Spectator's Identity" theme was addressed during the open section of the program, which took up much of the second week. During this period, the pedagogues from Asia and the Odin gave performances and were involved in barters around the Salento region. These "meetings" with the local community were part of a larger study, begun six months before, of Salento audience patterns by Piergiorgio Giacche, an anthropologist from Perugia University who had been a participant at several ISTAs.

ISTA VI – BOLOGNA

The sixth ISTA was held in Bologna, Italy, from June 28 to July 18, 1990. The session's title, "The University of Eurasian Theatre," reflected the fact that for the first time ISTA was officially sponsored by a university, the University of Bologna. The connection was further echoed in the theme of the gathering, "Performance Techniques and Historiography."

The meeting was organized by Pietro Valenti, the director of the Modena-based theatre group Centro Teatrale San Geminiano, and Renzo Filippetti, the director of Bologna's Teatro Ridotto, with assistance from Elisa Dal Re and Monica Vaccari of the Bologna Town Council Division of Information and Public Relations. The cultural coordinator for the session was Franco Ruffini from Bologna University. The ISTA was financed by the usual consortium of organizations which in this case included: the University of Bologna, the Cultural Department of the Bologna Town Council, the Italian Ministry of Culture, the Danish Ministry of Culture, the Japan Foundation, the Saison Foundation, and the Town Council of Holstebro.

There were over eighty participants representing nineteen countries invited to Bologna, either as full participants or special guests who took part in only the second week of the meeting. These participants were joined by the usual group of guest artists who included Panigrahi and her ensemble, a group of nihon buyo performers from the Azuma School, accompanied by the onnagata Hanayagi Kanichi who had taken part in the previous two ISTAs, a troupe of actor-dancers from Bali, and several members of the Odin Teatret.

The closed session, from July 1 to 8, was held at the Villa Guastavillani, a large villa set in a small park on the outskirts of Bologna. During this week of seclusion the program consisted of lecture/demonstrations, seminars, and a lengthy intercultural workshop/rehearsal, similar to the Faust workshop in Salento, called "The Crossing." The other part of the program, which was open to the public, included lecture/demonstrations, two international symposia, several barters, and a series of performances in Bologna.

Despite the number of lecture/demonstrations and seminars on subjects ranging from Latin American theatre to the pre-expressivity of the trained voice and the connections between dramaturgy and choreography, the most intense work during the closed week in Bologna was reserved for "The Crossing." In his opening remarks at the beginning of the project, Barba explained that he wished to continue his explorations of intercultural dramaturgy begun in Salento, but that in doing so, he wanted to avoid one of the major problems that arose in the work on Goethe's *Faust*, that is, beginning the project with a classical text familiar to those in the West and virtually unknown to the Asian performers. In order to give scholars, scientists, and invited theatre workers a greater insight into the creative process, he devised a performance text in which they played roles as well as helped develop the scenario upon which it was based.

ISTA – A LABORATORY FOR THE STUDY OF PERFORMANCE

ISTA could be compared to Grotowski's concept of a "theatre laboratory," that is, a research center, analogous to a scientific laboratory (Grotowski,

163

1968:127). Both Grotowski, at his Polish Laboratory Theatre, and Barba, at his NTL, established such centers in which they and their performers research(ed) the actor's art through a daily regimen of study, exercises, improvisation, and experimentation. Unlike the NTL, however, where the research into training methods and the acting process is Eurocentric, the major thrust of research at ISTA is comparative, comparing Eastern and Western acting techniques with the goal of discovering elements common to both.

Grotowski's "theatre laboratory" was not his only influence on ISTA. In a list of thanks at the end of the 1986 version of his article, "Theatre Anthropology," Barba cites Grotowski's 1976–1982 "Theatre of Sources" research (a major aim of which was to discover whether ritual techniques from one culture were efficacious in another culture) as a stimulus and guide to his own ISTA investigations:

> I can conclude these thanks by remembering *my* master, Jerzy Grotowski: it is with joy that once again I have been able to measure myself with his work, to take stimulus, confirmation and questions for theatre anthropology from his researches in the "Theatre of Sources."
>
> (1986a:156)[5]

Regardless of the connections Grotowski and Barba make between scientific research and researching the actors' art, both are careful to point out that theatre is not a science (Grotowski, 1968:127; Barba, 1982b:5). The comparisons are analogous, just as they are at ISTA, an organization concerned with one of the most ephemeral of phenomena, creativity, and a creativity which is doubly ephemeral, performance, because it only exists in the moment of its execution. Unlike the writer or painter, whose creative endeavors leave sentences and works of art that are separate from their creator, there are no printed words to ponder or a finished canvass that we can analyze to recapture the actors' portrayal of a role following the final curtain. Performance leaves no trace, save in the memory of the spectator and the artist's body.

ISTA is very much Barba's child. It stems from a question that has been with him for most of his life in the theatre: the question of "Why, when I see two actors doing the same thing, I get fascinated by one and not by the other" (Barba, 1985b:12). This interest in presence, with the actor's ability to fascinate an audience regardless of the genre, style, or content of the piece being performed, has always been a concern in his work at the Odin and in his informal observations of Asian theatre. ISTA has allowed him to focus his attention entirely on this question, and to broaden his inquiry to include the formal study of forms from outside his own culture. In doing this, he has developed a conceptual matrix, theatre anthropology, which it is necessary to understand in order to appreciate ISTA fully.

Theatre anthropology

Barba defines theatre anthropology as "the study of human beings' socio-cultural and physiological behaviour in a performance situation" (Barba and Savarese, 1991:8). In formulating this definition, Barba admits that he is drawing on the original use of the term "anthropology." But the fact that he has focused his attention in theatre anthropology on the physiological aspects of performance, even to the extent of openly stating he was not interested in socio-cultural issues at all during the Holstebro ISTA, hints at the special use he is making of the term "anthropology."

Theatre anthropology is not merely an extension of cultural anthropology. It is a separate field that, at best, owes its origins to cultural anthropology. As mentioned above, theatre anthropology, unlike cultural anthropology, does not claim to be a science. In fact, as early as 1969, ten years before he founded ISTA, Barba is on record as saying that, even though the theatre can draw on the human sciences, like anthropology and sociology, it cannot be identified or equated with them (Hagested, 1969:58). In his definitive article, "Theatre Anthropolgy," republished as recently as 1991, he states that theatre anthropology serves to analyze and inform performance, not discover scientific facts:

> Different performers, at different places and times and in spite of the stylistic forms specific to their tradition have shared common principles. The first task of theatre anthropology is to trace these recurrent principles. They are not proof of the existence of a "science of the theatre" nor of a few universal laws. They are nothing more than particularly good "bits of advice"; information useful for scenic practice.

> (Barba and Savarese, 1991:8)

The way in which research is conducted at ISTA is a clear indication that theatre anthropology is not a conventional science. The work at most of the sessions has essentially followed a five-part model:

1 "Subject" – The theme chosen as the main area of research for each ISTA.
2 "Research Methodology" – How the research will be conducted. In the early ISTAs the major method was practical training, whereas the lecture/demonstration has tended to dominate more recent gatherings. At the Salento and Bologna ISTAs Barba also introduced the exploration of intercultural dramaturgy, in the work on *Faust* and "The Crossing."
3 "Findings" – Discoveries made during the research, either from observation or by taking an active part in training sessions and workshops. These findings have been essentially of two kinds: the formal discoveries that Barba and others have written about, such as the pre-expressive and extra-daily behavior discussed in Chapter 2; and personal findings made by individuals which influence their work, such as Carreri's studies with

Azuma at the Bonn ISTA which led to her exploring the connections between nihon buyo and her own training for at least five years after the meeting (Carreri, 1985).

4 "Testing Findings" – This part of the process is closely linked to "Findings" because the same methods of observation and experience are used in both. A finding is confirmed either by observing it many times, or by testing it in training workshops and/or performance. Unlike the previous three stages, this research usually extends beyond the individual meeting because, as in the Carreri example cited above, an actor, director, or scholar may continue to test what s/he has come across at ISTA for a considerable time after the event.

5 "Application of Findings" – The findings made at ISTA are intended to have application outside of the sessions, which links this stage in the research to the one before it. The major difference between the two stages is that at this point in the process the findings have been confirmed and are no longer the focus of the research. They are used instead to analyze and/or explore other things like: the Odin's use of training principles, described in Chapter 3, which owes a great deal to Barba's concept of the pre-expressive and his studies of Eastern performance; and Patrice Pavis' article, "Dancing With Faust: A Semiotician's Reflections on Barba's Intercultural Mise-en-scene" (1989), in which he considers intercultural performance semiotically, based on his experiences at the Salento ISTA.

Despite the empirical nature of this research model, it is at best only quasi-scientific. It does not attempt to follow the major research strategy of the hard sciences. Neither Barba nor those who work with him have ever tested the central hypotheses of theatre anthropology by isolating all the relevant factors and testing each one of them separately, as scientists do in the laboratory.

Theatre anthropology is an interpretive discipline echoing the way in which anthropologists Clifford Geertz and James Clifford describe their work. Geertz characterizes his concept of understanding culture as:

> ... essentially a semiotic one. Believing with Max Weber, that man is an animal suspended in webs of significance he himself has spun, I take culture to be those webs, and the analysis of it to be therefore not an experimental science in search of law but an interpretive one in search of meaning.

> (1973:5)

This view is reflected in Clifford's assertion that all ethnographic writings, including those about performance, are "constructed, artificial ... cultural accounts" (1986:2) which are "the invention, not the representation, of cultures" (1986:2).

Geertz suggests a model of interpretive anthropology based on a term borrowed from Gilbert Ryle, "thick description." In explaining thick description, Geertz cites Ryle's example of three boys rapidly contracting the eyelids of their right eyes. In one this is an involuntary twitch, in the second a conspiratorial signal to a friend; the third boy, meanwhile, is parodying the first for the amusement of his cronies. If one were to describe the actions simply, they are identical, but on closer examination (thick description) they are quite different (1973:6–7).

Geertz's interpretive model – thick description, analysis of the thickly described material, and hypotheses based on the analysis (1973) – could be used to describe Barba's ISTA methodology. Performances from different cultures are examined in order to understand "the tangible domain of the actor's material presence, the rules which determine his theatrical bios and which make it possible for him to manipulate this bios in a craftsmanlike way" (Barba, 1986d:12), as in the lecture/demonstration at the public session of the Bonn ISTA, described earlier, in which Barba worked with Panigrahi. In this lecture/demonstration, Barba gave a thick description of Panigrahi's movements as she performed them in slow motion, analyzed the way in which she adjusted her body to perform the movements, then considered these adjustments in light of his pre-expressive hypothesis.

The effectiveness of Barba's interpretive model has been challenged, firstly for what Phillip Zarrilli characterizes as questionable reflexivity, and secondly because of what some regard as the limited role of dialogue between Barba and participants at ISTA. In writing about the Holstebro congress Zarrilli says:

> I find myself stimulated by the issues which Barba probes, but troubled by the lack of reflexivity in his workshops and writing. ...
>
> Most of us need to practice a greater degree of reflexivity in our approaches to performance enactment and process. If Barba did so he could speak much more clearly about the experience and poetics of performance practice – the central issues of his concern.
>
> (1988:102–104)

In making his criticism, Zarrilli maintains that Barba is deaf to the "ideology implicit in [his] way of thinking" (1988:104), and that Barba's analysis tells us more about his own understanding of performance than anything else:

> If I ask for whom was the "myth of technique" broken, for whom is the "energy" "seductive," for whom is "energy" "invisible," I would answer: first, for Barba. Instead of getting a portrait of "performance," what we get is Barba's construction of his own view of performance through the Others [i.e., Asian performers] he studies.
>
> (Zarrilli, 1988:103)

But what is "a portrait of 'performance'"? Surely what Zarrilli asks for is an objective truth, something that describes (is "a portrait of") performance in objective rather than subjective terms. However, as Geertz points out, this desire for objectivity contradicts the very nature of an interpretive discipline:

> In the study of culture, analysis penetrates into the very body of the object – that is, we begin with our own interpretations of what our informants are up to, or think they are up to, and then systematize those. ...
>
> In short, anthropological writings are themselves interpretations, and second and third order ones to boot.
>
> (1973:15)

The interpretive nature of theatre anthropology is probably best characterized by Taviani, who describes it as a "hand-made theory." Taviani's definition of a "hand-made theory" is one which "maintains traces of the 'author's' hand and establishes a dialogue with the 'reader' based on allusions, suggestions, and ruptures" (Pezin, 1986:28).

Barba's reflexivity may be questionable if compared to that of a social scientist, but he is not a social scientist and theatre anthropology is not a social science. Barba characterizes theatre anthropology as a

> study of [the] principles of the extra-daily use of the body. This study implies a reversal of traditional concepts: it is not the assimilation of technical know-how but "learning to learn," "learning to understand." To understand the principles which govern the processes that take place in our organism and make it "live" in a theatrical situation.
>
> (1986d:10)

The focus of theatre anthropology is the actor's process. As Barba puts it, "at ISTA the focus is on the 'practical exploration' of theatrical work" (1988e:9). Its findings are primarily for actors and directors. And these findings are every bit as interpretive as theatre anthropology's methodology, which Barba points out in describing the learning situation at ISTA:

> This situation presupposes the discovery of principles – or "good advice" – in order to construct a working base on the technical, pre-expressive level, as a means to stimulate one's own creative process. One must choose one's own points of departure, not from this or that tradition or style, but from a set of "rules" one establishes for oneself.
>
> (1986d:12)

Theatre anthropology is process- rather than product-oriented. The research phase of the work, whether in workshop/training sessions or lecture/demonstrations, focuses on the performer's process rather than on the content of particular plays or dances. It is for this reason that most of the detailed studies at ISTA use fragments of performance rather than full-length works since, apart from time limitations, Barba and his colleagues are less interested in *what* the actor does than in how s/he does it.

Similarly, ISTA's discoveries, like the pre-expressive and performance principles, are processual tools. They are not universal laws that apply regardless of person or circumstance. They are pieces of "good advice" which performers must explore for themselves.

The lack of dialogue between Barba and other participants during ISTA's exploration of these pieces of "good advice" became an issue at the Holstebro meeting to which many scholars and critics unfamiliar with ISTA were invited. This was one of Munk's criticisms of the congress, and her views were echoed by Zarrilli:

> Barba's voice remains single, essential, comprehensive, and authoritarian; all that comes before it is subsumed by practical interest in the qualitative, lyrical dimension of the performance act. Bits and pieces of anecdotal information solicited from the performers are woven into Barba's lyrical tapestry. ... What troubles me is the solitary, universalizing voice precluding a dialectical process of investigation.
>
> (1988:103)

In his reply to Zarrilli Barba answered these criticisms by saying:

> As far as my "voice" is concerned, I know that some consider it as "solitary" and "authoritarian." For others it is simply responsible. Most people come to ISTA with the desire to be confronted with the research I am conducting. It would be both comfortable and incorrect not to allow this confrontation to take place in the most profound way possible, giving as an excuse the necessity of a plurality of voices. It would also be comfortable and incorrect to seek a compromise. My task consists in assuming to the limit the responsibility of answering those who are interested in my work without blocking the initiatives of those who are more interested in other persons or in other experiences.
>
> (1988e:9–10)

Elaborating on this point, Barba grants that there may have been misunderstandings among those unfamiliar with ISTA who expected to have a program of seminars, debates, and the presentation of papers. In addition to this, he describes two forums organized by participants outside of the main program in which the "dialectical process of investigation" was pursued.

Regardless of who is "more correct," Barba or his critics, several objective facts cannot be ignored. Prior to the Holstebro ISTA, Barba's team of scholars, critics, and scientists consisted primarily of people who knew his work. Following the controversy at the Holstebro meeting, he returned to the more familiar ISTA model of a core intellectual staff he had worked with previously, complemented by a few scholars or critics unfamiliar with ISTA.

Whether it is true or not, this move has left Barba open to criticism similar to that made by Zarrilli and others at the Holstebro meeting, namely that he wants to limit the "dialectic process of investigation" by not inviting those who disagree with his approach and theories.

Aware that I might be considered one of the core group of intellectuals, having attended three ISTAs (1986, 1987, 1990), and therefore open to the charge of bias, I nevertheless disagree with those who say Barba is attempting to limit debate at ISTA. He organizes ISTA on the principle he stated in his reply to Zarrilli, "most people come to ISTA with the desire to be confronted with the research I am conducting." This research forms the core of each ISTA. But at the Salento gathering following Holstebro, there was much discussion between Barba and scholars in private and during the lecture/ demonstrations of the second week about the nature of his research, and over thirty hours were devoted to discussion following "The Crossing" workshop in Bologna. Besides these discussions, there were two international seminars at each of the last two ISTAs at which many scholars, who are not particularly close to Barba, presented papers. And, in fact, the program of the two-day meeting in Bologna, "Performing Techniques and Historiography," including subject areas and who was to present papers, was decided by participants, not Barba.

Theatre anthropology is eclectic. Through scholars like Elsass and Pradier it draws on physiology and biology to explain physical techniques. Cultural anthropology may be its inspiration, but it also owes a debt to history and sociology in its attempts to provide a context for its comparative studies of different performance genres. Theatre anthropology also draws heavily on Barba's and his pedagogues' practical experiences. In fact, it is their work in the theatre, their performance knowledge stored over the years, that is the foundation upon which all studies at ISTA are based. And, like all creative endeavors, intuition plays no small part in how these practitioners, Barba included, arrive at their conclusions.

ISTA's methodology

ISTA's methodology involves three major components: interculturalism, intraculturalism, and a research process which brings together scholars, scientists and theatre practitioners.

ISTA emerged during a period in which there was a lively interest in interculturalism among certain scholars and theatre people. The fact that Barba founded an organization with the express aim of discovering aspects of performance that function across cultures, though unusual, was thus not out of step with its times. What is unusual about ISTA is its concern with aspects of performance that *underlie* expression. This concern led Ruffini to describe theatre anthropology as a study not only of the transcultural but also of the pre-cultural:

Theatre anthropology postulates that the diverse cultural scenes are one and the same pre-cultural (and transcultural) milieu ... that underneath (or better within) the different cultural behaviors [of performers] there is a common pre-cultural foundation. This pre-cultural foundation is at the center of theatre anthropology's research.

(Pezin, 1986:35)

Unlike Barba, many of those in the theatre who share his intercultural interests have focused their attention on cultural universals. At his center in Paris, for instance, Peter Brook has devoted a large part of his time to discovering a universal theatre language (Smith, 1972; Brook, 1973; Heilpern, 1977). And much of Grotowski's work since his "Paratheatrical Period" in the early to mid-1970s has been concerned with researching how ritual techniques function across cultures. This is not to say that Barba ignores cultural expression. But his research at ISTA has focused almost exclusively on what he calls the pre-expressive and how actors "shape" their energy, both of which precede cultural expression.

The premise underlying Barba's explorations of the pre-expressive and of energy is that all human beings are biologically essentially the same. No matter which culture an actor is from, his/her body consists of a certain mass, a trunk, and extremities, has a center of gravity, and opposing groups of muscular tensions that s/he uses to walk, stand up, sit down, dance, etc. And, regardless of a performer's genre — be it topeng, odissi, noh, or corporal mime, these biological givens are the physical tools s/he has to work with. Each form may require the performer to combine or use these tools differently, but often there are common biological principles underlying the uses of the body. The noh actor must bend his knees and keep his hips locked throughout most of the performance, for instance, while the odissi dancer must frequently bend his/her spine into a horizontal "S" shape while standing on one foot. But, as Barba's research has revealed, these very different socio-cultural body techniques are based on similar common principles: both alter the normal center of gravity, both require the performers to adjust their day-to-day pattern of muscular tensions in order to retain balance, and both result in an other than ordinary distribution of body weight. It is these common principles that underlie the performer's culture-based expression. These are the pre-expressive factors that inject "presence" into everything the performer does on stage. These are the bits of "good advice" that any actor anywhere can use.

This concern with biological principles is the basis of Barba's studies of codified forms at ISTA. These forms, which include many of the traditional Asian genres as well as mime and classical ballet from the West, have precise, repeatable stripes of action which contain many of their form's codes. The ability of performers from each of these genres to repeat stripes of action many times precisely allows Barba and his colleagues to make a systematic

171

study not only of the genre's codes but, more importantly, of the "good advice" embedded in the codes. The study then aims to compare the "advice" in one form with the "advice" in another to see if there are "recurrent principles" common to both.

In comparative cultural studies there is a tendency to use the "host" culture as the point of departure for a study of the "foreign" or "other" culture. Most Western commentators when discussing ISTA, for instance, emphasize the East–West/Asian–European dichotomy, as if all the Asian (foreign) performance cultures are much the same, as are all the Western (host) performance forms. In making this distinction, these commentators ignore the intracultural research done at ISTA; that is, the comparisons made among traditional Asian performance genres and similar comparisons in Western performance. There are huge differences in the performance cultures of Japan, India and Bali, and even though nihon buyo, odissi, and legong tend to be grouped together as examples of traditional Asian theatre at ISTA, a large part of its research focuses on comparing these forms to each other. Barba and his colleagues have made similar, though briefer, studies of Western theatre, in which they have compared codified Western forms, such as corporal mime, with the techniques of the Odin-trained actors.

An important factor in both the intercultural and intracultural comparisons at ISTA is that the research is conducted by intellectuals and practitioners working together. ISTA provides the framework for a working relationship between these two groups, who all too often work in isolation despite their common interests. As Taviani put it in a meeting at the close of the Holstebro ISTA:

> We so-called intellectuals and those who work in the theatre have a common denominator at ISTA, we are both researching principles. The practical people are seeking the principles actively. Actors are seeking principles for their training, for performance; directors for rehearsal, for the mise-en-scene. Those, like myself, we are devising ways of seeing, exploring ways of observing so that we recognize the principles the others know through doing. This new way of seeing becomes a means of research, a way of analysing.

(1986b)

ISTA, being dominated by its founder's insatiable curiosity about theatre, has always focused on the questions that interest him. The pedagogues are essential to these interests because they possess the performance codes that he uses as the basis of his studies. In the early meetings, the pedagogues were mainly involved in teaching either their forms or the principles underlying them. More recently, they have replaced teaching practical skills with demonstrations and discussion. Granted, this change is partly due to a shift in Barba's interests, but it is also a product of the reflexivity engendered by their ISTA experience which allows them to show and explain elements of their form in a way they could not have done prior to their involvement with Barba.[6]

Since one of ISTA's major goals is to inform Western training and performance, the actors and directors who attend sessions are an integral part of its reason for being. They are the ones who will bring their experiences into the theatre by adapting or directly applying what they learn in their creative work. This adaptation and application provides material for an ongoing process of exploration which has the potential to influence the work of those exposed to it well beyond any one particular session – as Barba himself implies when he describes ISTA as an "apprenticeship in understanding" (1986:114), that is, each session may be an apprenticeship, but mastery only comes with time.

A BRIEF, NECESSARY
AFTERWORD

Despite the fact that *Towards a Third Theatre* was only published in 1993, the manuscript was accepted by Routledge some eighteen months beforehand. Recent as this may seem in the grand sweep of history, most of the research for the book had been completed even earlier, in the latter part of 1990. In the last few days of September this year (1994), the Odin celebrated its 30th year of existence. The last four of these years being as productive as any in its history, this afterword, as its title implies, is a thumbnail sketch of Barba's and his colleagues' endeavors since the previous chapters of this book were written.

TRAINING

The Odin performers continue their daily training routines. And, even though there have been no major changes in the company's training since 1990, there has been a move to make its methods more accessible to performers who are not members of the company. In addition to the workshops that the group conducts while on tour, the past four or five years have seen an increase in the number of training opportunities for outsiders at the Odin itself. In 1990, the Odin, in conjunction with the University of Pennsylvania, mounted a month-long summer session consisting of a week of lectures at the University of Copenhagen and three weeks of practical work with Roberta Carreri at the Odin. In a similar, though unrelated development, the company now organizes a week-long open session at their Holstebro studios called "Odin Week" twice a year, one in the fall and another in the spring.

PRODUCTIONS

The Odin's current production, *Kaosmos: The Ritual of the Door*, is Barba's next major work following *Talabot. Kaosmos*, which premiered in April 1993 in Temuco, Chile as part of the International Theatre Institute Festival, has a blending of Odin's veteran actors with several new faces. The core Odin performers Torgeir Wethal, Iben Nagel Rasmussen, Roberta Carreri, and Julia Varley are joined by Jan Ferslev and Isabel Ubeda from *Talabot*, Frans Winther and Kai Bredholt (two musician/actors who have worked in several of the Odin's recent smaller productions), and newcomer Tina Nielsen. As in the previous three Odin pieces, the actors play specific roles, but in the vein of *Come! And the Day Will be Ours*, these roles are generally identified by function or relationship rather than by name. Bredholt, for example, portrays "the sailor who has seen a mermaid," Carreri plays "the mother who searches for her child stolen away by Death," Ferslev is "The Doorkeeper," while Ubeda is "The Doorkeeper's twin sister." Nielsen plays "the village bride," Rasmussen portrays "the man from the country," Varley is "Doña Musica, who comforts those who laugh until they cry," Wethal plays "The Man-who-does-not-want-to-die," and Winther is "the disinherited son of the Devil."

Kaosmos – which in addition to Chile has been performed in Argentina, Brazil, Wales, England, and throughout continental Europe – has its roots in several thematic sources. According to a note in the program, Barba dates the origin of the production to a discussion with an old Hungarian man in a café following an Odin performance. The man recited a poem, *The Seventh*, by Attila József which on hearing, as Barba puts it, "I understood immediately that this poem would become the thread of my next performance" (1993: 14). In keeping with the complex weaving of thematic-based improvisations during Barba's rehearsals, this poem was soon jointed by other areas of dramaturgical exploration. A year or so following their meeting, the old Hungarian man sent Barba a manuscript entitled "The Theatre of the Mountains and the Ritual of the Door" which was to become central to the work. This in turn led to investigations of Franz Kafka's *Before the Law* and Hans Christian Andersen's *The Story of a Mother*.

Kaosmos views the entire cycle of life from birth to death through a kaleidoscope of Beckettian pessimism; it portrays a world of perpetual waiting filled with insignificant anecdotes, brutal actions, and carnal lust which is unique in Barba's canon. Nevertheless, there are many echoes of his earlier works in the piece. Music, singing, and a powerful physical score are a large part of the mise-en-scene. The dramatic text is a polyglot of English, Spanish, Italian, Norwegian and Danish as each of the actors speaks in his or her own native tongue. The performance text is marked by powerful imagery which includes a Doorkeeper dressed in black carrying a shovel strung with a single wire which reverberates with a haunting melancholy tone when he plucks it, a mariner with a piano accordion and a voice that sears the depths of the sea in search of the mermaid that has sent him insane, a violin player in an eighteenth-century coat and hat with his face obliterated by a sheaf of wheat, and a chorus of lewd women who sing and strut the length of the stage like punkish whores defying both life and death.

In keeping with most of Barba's works, the set is simple. The audience is seated on either side of the stage in raked seating. At each end of the stage there is a white cyclorama in front of which there are two simple white benches. Behind one of the cycloramas are several lights and candles which are used to create shadow effects on it during the performance. The few other set props are brought on by the actors as they are required.

As in several earlier Barba productions, a prop plays a central role in the mise-en-scene. A large white door, that The Doorkeeper guards and in front of which The Man-who-does-not-want-to-die awaits entry, dominates the piece. It begins as an imposing door but, during the performance it is removed from its frame and at different times transformed into a coffin, a sailing boat, an altar, and finally a grave.

In addition to his productions with the main company, Barba has become increasingly involved in directing smaller pieces in the past few years. This interest in material outside of the full Odin company has its origins in the early seventies when Barba worked with several of the group's young apprentices refining their small-scale touring production of *Johan Sebastian Bach*, a piece originally developed by older members of the Odin while in residence in southern Italy. The formation of Rasmussen's company Farfa in 1980, and the incorporation of the smaller companies Basho and The Canada Project into the Nordisk Teaterlaboratorium (NTL) in late 1984 added impetus to this trend. Even though Barba was not involved in Farfa's early work, he was eventually persuaded by Rasmussen to direct its mid-eighties production of *Matrimonio con Dio* (Marriage with God). When the former Odin actor Toni Cots formed Basho, Barba directed its first production, *El Romancero de Edipo* (The "Romancero" of Oedipus), and when Richard Fowler, the head of The Canada Project, developed his one-man piece, *Wait for the Dawn*, Barba also directed it.

Despite the fact that Basho and The Canada Project are no longer part of the NTL, they were the immediate harbingers to the increased number of works directed by Barba in the late eighties and early nineties which involve only parts of the full Odin Company. These latter productions include *Memoria* with Else Marie Laukvik and Frans Winther, the one-woman pieces *Judith*, with Roberta Carreri, and Julia Varley's *The Castle of Holstebro*, the Farfa production *Itsi Bitsi* performed by Iben Nagel Rasmussen, Jan Ferslev and Kai Bredholt, as well as five lecture/demonstrations explaining the Odin's training, techniques, and dramaturgical methods: Carreri's *Traces in the Snow*, Wethal's *The Paths of Thought*, Rasmussen's *White as Jasmin* and Varley's *The Echo of Silence* and *The Dead Brother*.

All of these pieces share one thing in common. Unlike the full-scale Odin productions which are initiated by Barba, these works were generated by the performers themselves. The pieces are a combination of ideas by the performers, original improvisations, fragments of training research and/or dramaturgical materials developed for earlier productions that for one reason or another were discarded. Barba rarely observes improvisation sessions for these pieces, and the actors spend much of their rehearsal time working without him. It is only when they have developed what they regard as a meaningful body of material that they show it to him and he begins to work with them. Barba is much more the conventional director in these productions; he shapes the mise-en-scenes but he is not as intimately involved in constructing their dramaturgy as he is in his work with the full company.

ISTA

There have been two public ISTA sessions since the Bologna gathering in 1990, the first in Wales from 4–11 April, 1992 and the second from August 11–22, 1994 in Brazil.

The Welsh meeting, which is the only ISTA to take place in an English-speaking country, was organized by the Cardiff-based Centre for Performance Research headed by Richard Gough. The gathering was split between the usual closed session (April 4–10) in Brecon, a small town in mid-Wales, and an open session on the 10th and 11th of April in Cardiff.

The closed session, entitled "Working on Performance East and West," brought together thirty-five British and international directors who observed a series of workshop/seminars led by Barba, Sanjukta Panigrahi and her musicians, the kabuki onnogata Kanichi Hanayagi, and the Dharma Shanti company from Bali, as well as a reasearch team made up of Nicola Savarese, Fabrizio Cruciani, Franco Ruffini, Ferdinando Taviani, Patrice Pavis, Jean Marie Pradier and Susanne Vill, an opera singer and scholar from Bayreuth University who had attended the Bologna ISTA. Beginning with the theme "the refusnik – the individual who does not follow the norms, opinions or doctrines of authority," Barba and his colleagues developed an intercultural mise-en-scene with the performers that focused on the work of the director.

The Cardiff part of the gathering was presented under the title of "Fictive Bodies, Dilated Minds, Hidden Dances." It consisted of workshop/demonstrations headed by Barba along with his international team of performers, a series of lectures by the research team which examined commedia dell'arte, scenic space, and the ideas of Stanislavsky and Artaud – all in light of ISTA's performance research, as well as a seminar of questions on ISTA's findings and methodologies.

The Welsh meeting was the most provocative ISTA since the 1986 gathering in Holstebro with Barba and his colleagues being challenged by many of the directors and scholars who attended. Interestingly, the major criticism was one that had also been raised in Holstebro, a lack of space in the program for dialogue between Barba, his team, and participants. This lack of dialogue was compounded in Wales by the fact that many of the directors who attended the Brecon session were experienced professionals who felt that they would have learned more from this session had they been able to work with Barba and his Asian performers rather than merely observing them.

The 1994 conference, held in Londrina in southern Brazil, was the first ISTA mounted outside of Europe. It was organized by Nitis Jacon and her staff from the International Festival of Londrina (FILO) in collaboration with the municipality of Londrina, Londrina State University, as well as the Parana State government and the federal Ministry of Culture. The theme of the gathering was "Traditions and Founders of Traditions," and its thrust was as far removed from the previous ISTA as Brazil is from Wales. The Londrina meeting saw a return to the teaching concerns of the first ISTAs in Bonn and Volterra. This was especially true in the closed session, held at a ranch-style hotel, the Estancia Aguativa, in the countryside some sixty miles from Londrina between the 12th and 17th of August. During this part of the conference, the majority of participants, who were young performers and directors from southern Latin America, attended daily classes in odissi dance, kabuki theatre, Balinese dance, Odin training techniques, and orixas dance (aesthetic dance based on the ritual trance dances of the Brazilian candomble). In addition to these teaching sessions, participants observed Barba's dramaturgical and directorial methods in open rehearsal sessions he conducted for a Teatrum Mundi that was presented on the closing night of the gathering in Londrina. All of the Asian and Western master performers teaching at ISTA took part in this final presentation including Panigrahi and her ensemble, Hanayagi along with another kabuki actor, a nihon buyo performer, a singer and musician, as well as a group of Balinese dancers and musicians headed by Swasti Bandem, the Odin performers, and Augusto Omolu, a Brazilian dancer from Bahia along with his musician/drummers.

As in most ISTAs, the closed meeting was followed by a short public session. This part of the conference, held in Londrina from August 18–21, consisted of performances by the various performers, several lecture/demonstrations by Barba and the troupe of international artists, as well as a series of lectures by ISTA veterans Savarese, Ruffini, Pradier, Pavis and Vill who were joined by two Danish academics, Kirsten Hastrup (an anthropologist from Copenhagen University) and Janne Risum (from the theatre department at Aarhus University).

Despite the financial difficulties and administrative problems of mounting such a large conference in South America, far from ISTA's Danish headquarters, the Brazilian gathering was a success. And, given Barba's commitment to Latin America, it is likely that there will be further such meetings. In the meantime, however, Barba and his colleagues have already begun preparations for an ISTA in Umeå, northern Sweden to take place in May 1995, and for what will likely be the largest public ISTA ever, a thirty-five day conference being organized in conjunction with Copenhagen University as part of the city's celebration of being designated the 1996 artistic capital of Europe.

THE FESTUGE

Possibly the most interesting development in Barba's work over the past few years has been the "festuge", a festival of theatre and music performances, art exhibitions, public lectures, and demonstrations by local community groups, that he and the Odin mounted in Holstebro, first in the summer of 1991 and again in September 1993.

Holstebro is a small, relatively isolated town in western Denmark of some 30,000 inhabitants. It is hardly a cultural center like London, Paris or even Copenhagen. Barba and his colleagues, in conjunction with the enlightened support of the arts by the town's various municipal governments over the past thirty years, attract the interest of artists and scholars from all over the world. But the Holstebro festuge is not, nor is it intended to be, yet another major European international summer festival. This is a community event, a festive occasion for the people of Holstebro with the majority of the activities performed by them.

The festuge is a product of many factors, not least of which is the Odin's attempt to reach out to the community that has supported it since the mid-sixties. But, community aside, the festuge has its roots in Barba's history, in his concern with the social role of theatre that in earlier times led to his street theatre as well as barters, and in his intercultural research which, in its broadest terms, is predicated on a meeting and sharing between cultures.

The historical precursor to the festuges was the 1989 celebration of the Odin's twenty-fifth anniversary. This event, which ran from November 13–30, was a festive affair intended for the entire community. The company organized music concerts, exhibitions, dance and theatre performances for both adults and children, as well as film and video screenings, lectures, and seminars. The public, celebratory nature of the anniversary was a great success, and the seed of an idea was planted.

Two years later, from September 6–15, 1991, the Odin organized a more ambitious project than the anniversary, the first festuge. This festival was mounted around a single theme, "Culture Without Frontiers," had a motif performance, *Vandstier* (roughly translated as paths in the water), which continued twenty-four hours a day for nine days, and called for greater participation on the part of the community than the anniversary celebrations had done.

The theme, "Culture Without Frontiers," was inspired by the 500th anniversary of Columbus' discovery of the new world. As the press release for the event described it, the festuge was concerned with the "Danish Columbus," those Danes who had spent time abroad and had returned to their native land ". . . enriched by experience and with a new perspective, which gives impulse and 'life' to society at large" (Odin Teatret/Nordisk Teaterlaboratorium, 1991).

These Columbuses were symbolized in the *Vandstier* project, which

179

centered on a fifteen-meter viking longship that was constructed in a parking lot by the Danish group Pro Forma Hotel under the direction of Kirsten Delholm. The ship, which was built continuously throughout the festuge, was taken to a park in a ritual procession on the last day of the festival and buried. Every four hours during its building, a performance of sorts was presented in the parking lot. These "performances" were primarily by the local community and included displays by the housewives' union, by firemen, as well as by the archers' and rowers' clubs, the tae kwon do group, and a presentation by the militia and a visiting kathakali actor. In the latter a group of recruits arrived in their underwear and dressed in front of the spectators, transforming themselves from youths into soldiers in camouflage gear with blackened faces while, next to them, the kathakali actor prepared himself for his work, dressing and applying his character make-up for performance.

Performances were not limited to the parking lot. Throughout the festuge, actors appeared in different parts of the town. Several met the trains that arrived during the festivities with songs and dances, others woke early and greeted the town bakers with short skits, some even went to a session of the local community council where, in the tradition of the court jester, they admonished the mayor and his councillors with clown-like humor.

In addition to more formal theatrical presentations by the Odin and the Italian theatre group Teatro Tascabile, the festuge organizers arranged a symposium in which Danish politicians, administrators, journalists, an anthropologist, and a professor of literature discussed the role of Danish culture and national identity in a Europe in which frontiers are gradually disappearing.

The second festuge, which was held from September 4–12 1993, was even more ambitious than the first. As well as presentations by local community groups, performances, a seminar linked to its theme, and performances by Teatro Tascabile, the festivities included the Peruvian group Yuyachkani, Sanjukta Panigrahi and her ensemble, art and photography exhibitions, musical presentations, several barters between the professional performers and local communities, as well as an intercultural opera based on the Indian Sanskrit play *Shakuntala*. The intercultural concerns of the previous festuge were echoed not only in the opera but also in the theme of this second festival, "Mixed Marriages – Knud Rasmussen" (the latter being a polar explorer of mixed Inuit and Danish origin well known in Denmark).

The 1993 event saw interculturalism foregrounded in a way it had not been in the previous festival. The foregrounding was most evident in the increased number of groups from different countries taking part, the focus on marriages between Danes and foreigners that was the theme of the festuge, and most importantly in the *Shakuntala* production. This production, which was the centerpiece of festivities much like the building of the longship had been in 1991, was directed by Barba and presented by the Odin in conjunction with the Holstebro Music School. It was composed by the

180

Odin's Frans Winther and Raganath Panigrahi (one of India's leading musicians), had a libretto by Winther, and a cast that consisted of traditional opera singers and a chorus, as well as the Odin actors, and Sanjukta Panigrahi. An episode was rehearsed each day and performed that night with a presentation on the final evening of the festuge in which the entire *Shakuntala* tale was performed through integrating and editing the previous nightly episodes.

Arguably the most innovative interculturalism in the festuge, however, was the way in which Barba and his colleagues encouraged different Holstebro community organizations to work together, many of them for the first time, promoting a meeting of cultures at the community as much as national level. More than 115 organizations helped prepare the festuge. Some of these were immigrant groups from the Middle and Far East that have settled in Holstebro and its surroundings, but most were local Danes who rarely met to share their interests. The festuge prompted contact and interaction, if only for the duration of festival week.

The festuge is the nearest Barba has ever come to admitting a home. He and his Odin colleagues spend much of their professional life on tour, presenting workshops in different parts of the world, or mounting ISTAs far from Holstebro. Barba, the Italian living in Denmark, working with a group of actors from a variety of national backgrounds, who in 1988 referred to his only country as his body, "the only place where I always *am*," as he put it (1988a: 293), has not ceased his professional quest. But he has transformed the quiet gratitude and respect he has for the town that has supported his work for so many years into an open acknowledgement. Both of the festuges mounted so far bear the inevitable hallmarks of Barba's theatre journey which has taken him from its beginnings in Poland, through Norway to Denmark, Europe, Asia and Latin America. But every journey since 1966 has begun and ended in Holstebro. The festuge is Barba's way of saying thank you and celebrating the atavistic link between the Odin and its Holstebro home.

Ian Watson
New York
January 1995

NOTES

INTRODUCTION

1 This workshop took place from late July to mid-August in 1968. It was part of a series of annual workshops begun in 1966, the first two of which were only open to Scandinavians.

2 There are differences between Danish, Norwegian, and Swedish, but educated people from each country can read and understand the others' languages. The material in *TTT* was therefore accessible to all Scandinavians.

3 For more information on the Magdalena Project see Basnett, 1989.

1 BARBA: THE EARLY YEARS

1 A few examples of the many lectures and workshops Barba has given since the late 1970s give some idea of the importance of this aspect of his work to Barba. He has presented papers at Hosei University, Tokyo: "Noh and Western Theatre Practice" (1979); the University of Munich: "Science and the Theatre" (1980); and the University of Montreal: "From Stanislavsky to Theatre Anthropology" (1983). He has taught courses in acting and directing in Bhopal, India (1983); at New York University (1984); and at the Istituto de Bellas Artes in Mexico City (1984).

2 Barba is referring to his years with Grotowski in Opole, Poland, and his visit to the kathakali training school at Cheruthuruthy in Kerala, India, both of which are described in more detail later in this same chapter.

3 Grotowski's group did not officially become a laboratory theatre until 1966, after its move to Wroclaw. But the company began its research into the nature of acting much earlier, during rehearsals for *Dr Faustus* which premiered in April 1963 (Kumiega, 1985:69).

4 The English version of this article, "The Kathakali Theatre," was published in the *Tulane Drama Review* in 1967. See Barba, 1967.

5 For a discussion of these attacks on Grotowski in his early years in Opole see Osinski, 1986:36–62.

6 The article attributed to Grotowski, "Doctor Faustus in Poland," (1964) was actually written by Barba (Barba, 1985c). When it was republished in Grotowski's *Towards a Poor Theatre* Barba was correctly cited as the author (Grotowski, 1968).

7 Grotowski, along with Ryszard Cieslak and Rena Mirecka, was invited to lecture and/or give demonstrations about his work in France, Italy, and London between 1964 and 1965. For details see Osinski, 1986:80–89.

2 THEATRE THEORY: SOCIOLOGY AND THE ACTOR'S TECHNIQUE

1 Despite the fact that Brook's African journey took place prior to Barba's barter experience, Barba denies any influence from Brook in his ideas on barter. In a 1973 interview, Brook maintained that the primary goal in undertaking the journey was to explore the universal nature of the performer–spectator relationship (Brook, 1973:50). But, regardless of the differences between Brook's and Barba's goals, what is historically noteworthy is that viewing performance as cultural exchange was being explored by two important figures in the theatre simultaneously and independently. The idea was "in the air."

2 For more information on these experiments see: Barba, 1979; Biner, 1972; Grotowski, 1968; and Schechner, 1973.

3 For more details on forum theatre and on Boal in general see Boal, 1979, and Schechner, 1990.

4 This is not to say that performers trained in traditional Eastern forms have never used their techniques to explore new works. The Japanese noh actor, Katsuhiro Oida, for instance, has been a member of Peter Brook's ICTR in Paris since its inception in 1970 and has brought much of his earlier training to the company's original works such as *The Ik* and *The Conference of the Birds*.

5 This deconstruction/reconstruction concept owes something to Richard Schechner's use of the terms in describing the workshop/rehearsal process. In this process a script is "deconstructed" (i.e., explored and altered through improvisation) in order to create a performance text which is a "reconstructed" version of the original text. See Schechner, 1985:261–293.

6 Grotowski maintains that the role is the means by which the actor reveals his true self in performance: "The important thing is to use the role as a trampoline, an instrument with which to study what is hidden behind our everyday mask – the innermost core of our personality – in order to sacrifice it, expose it" (1968:37). And, in his book *Environmental Theater* Schechner discusses what he calls the environmental theatre performer which he describes as one in whom "both the role and the performer are plainly perceivable by the spectator" (1973:166).

7 For a more thorough description of Grotowski's concepts of actor and audience catharsis see Grotowski, 1968:34.

3 TRAINING

1 The "cat" exercise is adapted from an original kathakali training exercise brought back to Opole by Barba. This kathakali exercise is itself based on an older exercise drawn from kalarippayatt, an Indian martial art which is one of the major sources of kathakali. For details on the connections between kalarippayatt and kathakali see Zarrilli, 1984b: Chapter 2. For a description of Grotowski's cat exercise see Grotowski, 1968:135.

2 Meyerhold's biomechanic exercises were set patterns of physical action which all his actors learned and could repeat together. For a description of these exercises see Gordon, 1974:73–88.

3 Barba's introduction of composition exercises echoes a similar development in Grotowski's training, "exercises in composition" (Grotowski, 1968:142). Some critics have assumed that since Barba was Grotowski's assistant he merely copied these and other exercises from his teacher. This is not true, however, as is obvious if one compares Grotowski's composition exercises (Grotowski, 1968:142–145) with Barba's composition exercises described in this chapter. A detailed study of

the relationship between Barba and Grotowski is outside the scope of this book but the term "composition" as it relates to actor training originated with neither Grotowski nor Barba. Composition was part of the curriculum of Polish (via Russian) and French theatre schools of the period which referred to classes primarily concerned with movement and physical expression.

4   There have been brief periods since this time in which the actors have trained together collectively. William Farrimond, a researcher who followed the Odin's work for several months in early 1981, describes such a period in which Barba led a month-long training session that included the actors working together with props and even doing scene studies on *Hamlet*. But, as Farrimond himself points out, this was a most unusual experiment for the Odin (1981:57).

5   The shift away from the psycho-physical was a change in emphasis rather than a change in substance. Even though the psycho-physical has all but been abandoned in training, it continues to play an important part in developing improvisations during rehearsals.

6   These notes were made during a training session open to several people visiting the Odin. In the group's early days no one was allowed to observe training, but since their training methods have become so well known and there is a demand to see them first hand, guests are invited to some sessions. It should be noted, however, that there is a difference between training when observers are present and when they are not. What difference observers make is difficult to measure, but it is something that the company is aware of since most sessions remain closed, and there are times during intensive training periods and rehearsals when people are not even allowed to visit the Odin.

7   Barba cites Grotowski alone as an inspiration for his intercultural studies, but it is interesting to note that he and Grotowski were not alone in their concerns. To name but a few: Peter Brook had begun his work at the ICTR in Paris during this period; Tadashi Suzuki in Tokyo was already working on the connections between traditional Japanese performance and Western-influenced modern theatre; and Richard Schechner had begun his work with the Performance Group – which, among other things, used rituals from different cultures as a basis for some of its work, and he had published *Theories of Performance: 1970–1976* (1977) – a main theme of which is the cross-cultural nature of performance.

8   Practitioners of these forms do not usually talk of principles underlying their work. In performance they merely reproduce what they have been taught. When interviewed in 1986, for example, both Sanjukta Panigrahi and Katsuko Azuma, Eastern performers who have worked at ISTA since its first session in 1980, denied ever thinking of their art in terms of principles until after they had worked with Barba (Panigrahi, 1986; Azuma, 1986).

9   For an explanation of Grotowski's ideas on resonators, which formed the basis of the Odin's work, see Grotowski, 1968:153–165.

4 REHEARSALS AND DRAMATURGY

1   *Akropolis* was based on Wyspianski's play of the same name. *The Tragical History of Doctor Faustus* had its origins in Christopher Marlowe's *Faust.* For details on the group's adaptations of these plays see: Kumiega, 1985:Chapter 4; Osinski, 1986:66–82.

2   Barba and his colleagues rarely allow observers in rehearsals. I have been fortunate enough to see some. This description is based on a combination of these observations, published and unpublished accounts of rehearsals, and interviews with Barba and his actors.

184

3 This improvisation was not done while preparing a production. It was part of a special workshop Barba conducted with his actors in April 1981. Despite this, the format of the improvisation is identical to that used in the initial stages of developing a production.

4 Barba and his colleagues use videotape with a degree of skepticism. During the early stages of rehearsals for *Oxyrhincus Evangeliet* it was used extensively, but Barba and the actors decided that it hindered rather than helped the registering process. They felt that the human "warmth" of the improvisation was being replaced by a "cold" technology, because an electronic image was substituting for their memories and interaction with colleagues. As rehearsals progressed, the group returned to their traditional approach and used video less often.

5 Being a lecture/demonstration, this is not a normal rehearsal. But it gives an insight into Barba's dramaturgical approach.

6 During *Oxyrhincus Evangeliet* rehearsals, for instance, Barba wrote some original material based on the thematic sources from Brazil, Hasidism, and the ancient period of the Gnostic Gospels (Barba, 1985a:36).

7 This feedback is not limited to discussions with colleagues who come to see the work. Barba frequently asks these first audiences to respond to what they see in writing, and occasionally makes adjustments to the work based on these written responses (Barba, 1985h10).

8 Barba has developed two other approaches to creating performance texts. One uses training exercises as the original source material in rehearsals. In the other, intended for rehearsals with Odin off-shoot groups such as Farfa, the Canada Project, and solo performers like Carreri, the actors initiate and develop their own body of physical and vocal material prior to working with Barba. The major difference between these two methods and the more common thematic-based performance texts is the point of departure for rehearsals. The way in which the performance texts are created once the initial material is developed is essentially the same in all three methods.

9 Bowie's song-writing method possibly owes a debt to the automatic writing techniques of Dadaists such as Andre Breton who, in the 1920s, developed ways of writing poetry aimed at demonstrating how devalued language had become. One of these methods was identical to that used by Bowie in writing the lyrics for his songs. But, as with Barba, Bowie is interested in creating something (a song in this instance) rather than highlighting the limitations of language as a form of communication.

10 Barba has adapted the term "synesthetic" from its use in physiology in which it refers to a sensation felt in one part of the body when another part is stimulated. In Barba's use of the term, the performer provides the stimulation which is felt by the audience.

11 Sergei Eisenstein developed a theory of montage based on his editing work in the cinema which he also applied to the theatre (Eisenstein, 1974). And Meyerhold directed a number of productions, including *The Magnificent Cuckold* and *The Forest*, using the principle of what he called montage (Meyerhold, 1969:190–192).

12 To avoid over-simplification, it should be noted that traditional Eastern forms also contain non-symbolic codes (or conventions) that define the genres. The open-gait stance in which the performer stands on the outer soles of the feet in kathakali, and the bent knees, locked hips, and sliding feet movement of noh characterize their specific genres, but they do not convey narrative information.

5 PRODUCTIONS

1 Meyerhold developed a production esthetic that he referred to as the grotesque which, in essence, favored stylization of movement, voice, and design components over a theatre based on reproducing a facsimile of daily life (Meyerhold, 1969:141).

2 The notes and description of *Ornitofilene* and the other Barba productions dealt with in this chapter draw heavily on material published in Barba, 1986a:27–28; and Barba, 1979:179–182.

3 The relationship between Barba and these Italian scholars is material for a separate study. Suffice to say it is extensive in so far as these scholars were instrumental in developing ISTA and are all members of its permanent staff, in addition to which, most of them have published material on the Odin Teatret, ISTA, and/or the third theatre.

4 The script for *Ashes of Brecht* was published (see Barba, 1981b:13–36).

5 Barba's script of *Oxyrhincus Evangeliet* was published (see Barba, 1985a:33–80).

6 Coptic is a dead language. The Coptic used in the production was developed by the actors from a tape made by a Danish expert on Middle Eastern languages who recorded several speeches in the way in which it is thought Coptic was spoken. The actors used the phonetics of these speeches as the basis of their own Coptic, without considering questions of semantics, translation, or grammar.

6 THE INTERNATIONAL SCHOOL OF THEATRE ANTHROPOLOGY

1 There was a seventh ISTA session in Brecon and Cardiff, Wales, in April 1992, sponsored by the Cardiff-based Centre for Performance Research. The session is not included in this volume since it took place after the manuscript was submitted to the publishers.

2 The countries and number of participants from each were: West Germany, 11; Argentina, 6; Canada, 1; Denmark, 5; France, 4; India, 1; Lebanon, 1; Nicaragua, 1; Sweden, 1; Netherlands, 1, Venezuela, 1; England, 1; Belgium, 1; Colombia, 1; Spain, 3; Hungary, 1; Israel, 1; Japan, 2; Mexico, 1; Norway, 1; Switzerland, 2; USA, 1. This broad national representation is typical of all ISTAs.

3 The most important of these articles were the original versions of Barba's ISTA papers republished in *Beyond the Floating Islands* (1986a).

4 Two examples of this research are: a study done by Jean Pradier in which he worked with Michi Imafuji, a singer in Azuma's nihon buyo troupe, exploring the difference between the performer's daily speech and the voice used during improvisation; and a study of non-verbal communication by Ilse Hofer from the Department of Psychology at the University in Giessen, West Germany, in which she worked with Panigrahi, Azuma, and Ingemar Lindh, comparing how they express particular emotions (such as sorrow and love) physically, and how these expressions are interpreted by spectators with relatively little knowledge of the cultures the performers come from.

5 For more information on the "Theatre of Sources" see Robert Findlay's "A Necessary Afterword" in Osinski 1986, and Fowler 1985a.

6 Both Panigrahi and Azuma told me when I interviewed them that they had little reflexivity about their art until they worked with Barba. Both attributed this to the traditional training they had undergone in which one merely copied one's teacher without asking questions.

SELECT BIBLIOGRAPHY

Azuma, Katsuko (1986) Interview, Nordisk Teaterlaboratorium, Holstebro, Denmark, 16 September.

Barba, Eugenio (1965) "The Laboratory 13 Rzedow," *Tulane Drama Review* 9 (3): 153–171

——— (1967) "The Kathakali Theatre," *Tulane Drama Review* 2 (4) (T36): 37–50.

——— (1977) "An Offense Against Nature," *Rampelyset* (Denmark), interview with Per Moth.

——— (1979) *The Floating Islands*. Holstebro, Denmark: Odin Teatret Forlag.

——— (1981a) "Creating the Roles," *Canadian Theatre Review* 31 (Summer): 53–59.

——— (1981b) *Il Brecht dell'Odin*. Milan: Ubulibre.

——— (1982a) "The Way of Opposites," *Canadian Theatre Review* 35 (Summer): 12–37.

——— (1982b) "Theatre Anthropology," *The Drama Review* 26 (2) (T94): 5–32.

——— (1984) Seminar in Theatre Anthropology, New York University, New York, 10 January.

——— (1985a) *The Dilated Body*. Rome: Zeami Libre.

——— (1985b) "Interview With Gautam Dasgupta,"*Performing Arts Journal* (January):8–18.

——— (1985c) Interview, Nordisk Teaterlaboratorium, Holstebro, 5 September.

——— (1985d) Private conversation with the author, Nordisk Teaterlaboratorium, Holstebro, 6 September.

——— (1985e) "The Nature of Dramaturgy: Describing Actions at Work," *New Theatre Quarterly* 1 (1): 75–78.

——— (1985f) Private conversation with the author, Nordisk Teaterlaboratorium, Holstebro, 2 September.

——— (1985g) Lecture/seminar, Bond Street Theatre Coalition Interarts Center, Palenville, New York, 10 August.

——— (1985h) "The Dance of Faith on the Skeleton of the White Whale," *Tusind Oine* (Denmark), interview with Niels Olaf Gudne (all quotes from an English translation in the Odin archive. No translator cited).

——— (1986a) *Beyond the Floating Islands*. New York: Performing Arts Journal Publications.

——— (1986b) Lecture, New York University, New York, 10 November.

——— (1986c) Interview, Belgrade, Yugoslavia, 26 September.

——— (1986d) "The Female Role as Represented on the Stage in Various Cultures," program for the 1986 ISTA congress, Holstebro, Denmark, 17–22 September.

———— (1986e) "ISTA: Between the Face and the Mask," *Village Voice*, 25 November: 96 and 98.

———— (1987) "The Actor's Energy: Male/Female versus Animus/Anima," *New Theatre Quarterly* 3 (11): 237–240

———— (1988a) "The Way of Refusal: The Theatre's Body in Life," *New Theatre Quarterly* 4 (16): 291–299.

———— (1988b) "La Tercer Orilla del Rio," *Espacio* (Argentina) 2 (4): 15–24 (citations from an unpublished English translation in the Odin archives; translator not cited).

———— (1988c) "The Bridge," public lecture at the 8th International Gathering of Group Theatre in Chaclacayo, Peru, 26 November.

———— (1988d) "Eurasian Theatre," *The Drama Review* 32 (3) (T119): 126–130.

———— (1988e) "Eugenio Barba to Phillip Zarrilli: About the Visible and the Invisible in the Theatre and About ISTA in Particular," *The Drama Review* 32 (3) (T119): 7–14.

———— (1989) "The Fiction of Duality," *New Theatre Quarterly* 5 (20): 311–314.

———— (1990a) "Four Spectators," *The Drama Review* 34 (1) (T125):96–101.

———— (1990b) Interview, Bergamo, Italy, 16 July.

———— (1990c) "The University of Eurasian Theatre – Performance Techniques and Historiography," official program of the 6th ISTA session, 28 June–18 July, Bologna, Italy.

———— (1991) "The Third Theatre: The Legacy from Us to Ourselves," manuscript. (Forthcoming in *New Theatre Quarterly* 8(29).)

———— (1993) "Origins of Kaosmos," in the program for the Odin Treatret production of *Kaosmos: The Ritual of the Door.*

Barba, Eugenio and Ludwik Flaszen (1965) "A Theatre of Magic and Sacrilege," *Tulane Drama Review* 9 (3): 172–189.

Barba, Eugenio and Nicola Savarese (1991) *The Secret Art of the Performer: A Dictionary of Theatre Anthropology.* London, Routledge.

Basnett, Susan (comp.) (1989) *Magdalena: International Women's Experimental Theatre.* Oxford: Berg Publishers.

Bertani, Odoardo (1988) "E la sconfitta di un sogno," *Avvenire*, October 5.

Biner, Pierre (1972) *The Living Theatre.* New York: Avon.

Boal, Augusto (1979) *Theatre of the Oppressed.* New York: Urizen Books.

Bovin, Mette (1988) "Provocation Anthropology: Bartering Performance in Africa," *The Drama Review* 32 (1) (T117): 21–41.

Brook, Peter (1973) "Brook's Africa: An Interview by Michael Gibson," *The Drama Review* 17 (3) (T59): 37–51.

Carreri, Roberta (1985) Interview, Nordisk Teaterlaboratorium, Holstebro, Denmark, 26 August.

———— (1987) Lecture/demonstration at the 5th ISTA session, Salento, Italy, 8 September.

Chaillet, Ned (1980) "Odin Theatre: Cardiff," *The Times*, 11 August: 9.

Clifford, James (ed.) (1986) *Writing Culture.* Berkeley: University of California Press.

Coveney, Michael (1976) "Festival Under Fire," *Plays and Players* 24 (2): 12–14.

Daetwyler, Jean-Jacques (1980) *Tiers theatre.* Berne: Palindrome.

De Marinis, Marco (1987) "Dramaturgy of the Spectator," *The Drama Review* 31 (2) (T114): 100–114.

D'Urso, Tony and Eugenio Barba (1990) *Viaggi con – Voyages with – Odin Teatret.* Brindisi: Editrice Alfeo.

Eisenstein, Sergei (1974) "Montage Attractions for the Production of Ostrovsky's

Diary of a Scoundrel," in *Drama Theory and Criticism,* Bernard F. Dukore (ed.) New York: Holt, Rinehart & Winston (originally published in 1923).

Elsass, Peter, Jean Pradier and Franco Ruffini (1980) "Report on Work Undertaken in the First Public Session of ISTA," official report on the Bonn ISTA (unpublished).

Falke, Christoph (1985) Interview, Nordisk Teaterlaboratorium, Holstebro, Denmark, 3 September.

Farrimond, William (1981) "Actor Education: An Interdisciplinary Approach – An Analysis of the Training and Performance Principles Applied by Eugenio Barba and the Actors of the Odin Teatret in 1981," Ph.D. dissertation, University of Copenhagen.

Feingold, Michael (1984) "Die neue Brechtlichkeit," *Village Voice* 29, (19): 79.

Fowler, Richard (1985a) "The Four Theatres of Jerzy Grotowski: An Introductory Assessment," *New Theatre Quarterly* 1 (2): 173–178.

———— (1985b) "Odin Teatret: Twenty Years Old or a Fifth of a Century Young?" *Ant News* (Melbourne, Australia) 14: 2–4.

———— (1988) Personal letter to Eugenio Barba.

Fumaroli, Marc (1968) "Eugenio Barba's *Kaspariana,*" *Tulane Drama Review* 13 (1) (T41): 46–56.

———— (1969) "Funeral Rites: Eugenio Barba's *Ferai,*" *The Drama Review* 14 (1) (T45): 46–54.

Geertz, Clifford (1973) "Thick Description: Towards an Interpretive Theory of Culture," in *The Interpretations of Culture* by Clifford Geertz, pp. 3–30. New York: Basic Books.

Giacche, Piergiorgio (1989) "Memoire sociologique," *Bouffonneries* (France), nos. 22–23: 177–197.

Gordon, Mel (1974) "Meyerhold's Biomechanics," *The Drama Review* 18 (3): 73–88.

———— (1983) *Lazzi: The Comic Routines of the Commedia dell'Arte.* New York: Performing Arts Journal Publications.

Gough, Richard (1979) "Discovering One's Own Devil. ... Interviews With Toni Cots and Sylvia Ricciardelli," *Resources* 5–6 March, Cardiff Laboratory Theatre.

Grotowski, Jerzy (1964) "Doctor Faustus in Poland," *Tulane Drama Review* 8 (4) (T24): 120–133.

———— (1968) *Towards a Poor Theatre.* New York: Simon and Schuster.

Gussow, Mel (1984a) "*Brecht's Ashes 2*: A Man's Art," *New York Times,* 2 May: C21.

———— (1984b) "*Million* by Odin Group of Denmark," *New York Times,* 10 May: C25.

Hagested, Bent (1969) "A Sectarian Theatre: An Interview with Eugenio Barba," *The Drama Review* 14 (1) (T45): 56–56.

Hastrup, Kirsten (1987) *The Challenge of the Unreal.* Copenhagen: Museum Tasculanum Press.

Heilpern, John (1977) *Conference of the Birds.* Indianapolis/New York: Bobbs-Merrill.

Holms, Ingvar, Viveka Hagnall and Jane Rasch (1985) *A Model for Culture: Holstebro.* Stockholm: Almquist and Wiksell International (originally published in Swedish in 1976).

Innes, Christopher (1981) *Holy Theatre: Ritual and the Avant-garde,* New York: Cambridge University Press.

ISTA (1980) "Moon and Darkness," videotape of the performance made at the Bonn ISTA (no film maker credited).

Jenkins, Ronald (1977) "Bergamo International Theatre Workshop," *Mime News* 1 (11).

Jones, David Richard (1986) *Great Directors at Work.* Los Angeles: University of California Press.

Jovanov, Svetislav (1976) "Wedding with the Theatre," *Vecerne Novosti* (Yugoslavia),

September 27 (no page citation in the English translation in the Odin Teatret archives).

Kirby, Michael (1987) *A Formalist Theatre*. Philadelphia: University of Pennsylvania Press.

Klein, Stacy (1988) "Eugenio Barba, Master Craftsman and the Odin Teatret's 'Oxyrhyncus Evangeliet,'" Ph.D. dissertation, Tufts University.

Komparu, Kunio (1983) *The Noh Theatre: Principles and Perspectives*. New York: Weatherhill

Kumiega, Jennifer (1982) "Grotowski's Laboratory Theatre," in *The Director and the Stage* by Edward Braun pp. 191–200. New York: Holmes and Meier.

—————— (1985) *The Theatre of Grotowski*. New York: Methuen.

Larsen, Tage (1985) Interview, Nordisk Teaterlaboratorium, Holstebro, Denmark, 23 August.

Laukvik, Else Marie (1985) Interview, Nordisk Teaterlaboratorium, Holstebro, Denmark, 2 September.

Lewis, Robert (1970) "Emotional Memory," in *Actors on Acting*, Toby Cole and Helen Chinoy (eds), pp. 630–634. New York: Crown Publishers: 630–634.

Lundgren, Henrik (1984) "Odin Teatret: Theatre of Paradox," *Weekend Avisen* (Copenhagen), April:1–5.

Mairowitz, David Zane (1976) "Aarhus Festival and Beyond," *Plays and Players* 24 (3): 19–38.

Meyerhold, Vsevolod (1969) *Meyerhold on Theatre*, translated and edited by Edward Braun. New York: Hill and Wang.

Monti, Fanny (1989) "In scena a forli in 'viaggio suggestivo,'" *Romagna*, 16 April.

Munk, Erika (1986a) "Roles and Poles Apart," *Village Voice*, 11 November: 89–90.

—————— (1986b) "The Rites of Women," *Performing Arts Journal* 10 (2): 35–42.

Odin Teatret (1973) *Experiences*. Holstebro, Denmark: Odin Teatret Forlag.

—————— (1982) Production notes for *Brecht's Ashes 2* (unpublished).

—————— (1984) Program for *The Million* at La Mama, E.T.C., New York. Season: 8–13 May.

—————— (1985) Production notes for *Oxyrhincus Evangeliet* (unpublished).

—————— (1988) Program for *Talabot*.

Odin Teatret/Nordisk Teaterlaboratorium (1991) "The Danish Columbus," unpublished press release for the 1991 Festuge.

Osinski, Zbigniew (1986) *Grotowski and his Laboratory*. New York: Performing Arts Journal Publications.

Panigrahi, Sanjukta (1986) Interview, Nordisk Teaterlaboratorium, Holstebro, Denmark, 20 September.

Pardeilhan, Francis (1985) Interview, Nordisk Teaterlaboratorium, Holstebro, Denmark, 23 August.

Pavis, Patrice (1989) "Dancing With *Faust*: A Semiotician's Reflections on Barba's Intercultural Mise-en-scene," *The Drama Review* 33 (3) (T123): 37–57.

Pearson, Mike (1979) "Transforming into Gods ... A European Actor's Experience of Kathakali: An Interview With Tom Fjordfalk," *Resources*, 6 March, Cardiff Laboratory Theatre.

Peirano, Luis (1987) "Notas sobre la creacion teatral en America Latina," paper presented at the Seminario Regional sobre Creacion Teatral en America Latina y el Caribe, a UNESCO-sponsored conference on Latin American and Caribbean theatre held in Lima, Peru, 13–16 April.

Peyret, Jean Francois (1984) "L'Evangile d'Oxyrhyncus!" unpublished manuscript. This is an essay written by Peyret after attending final rehearsals prior to the first public performances of *Oxyrhincus Evangeliet*.

Pezin, Patrick (ed.) (1982) *Bouffonneries* (France), no. 4. Entire issue devoted to theatre anthropology.
—— (1986) *Bouffonneries* (France), no. 15/1. Entire issue devoted to theatre anthropology.
Phelan, Peggy (1988) "Feminist Theory, Poststructuralism, and Performance," *The Drama Review* 32 (1) (T117): 107–127.
Pradier, Jean-Marie (1986) Interview, New York University, New York, 16 July.
Rasmussen, Iben Nagel (1979) "Mutes in the Past," unpublished manuscript.
———— (1985) Interview, Copenhagen. 10 September.
———— (1986) Lecture/demonstration at the 4th ISTA congress, Holstebro, Denmark, 18 September.
Rasmussen, Iben Nagel, Eugenio Barba, Tony D'Urso and Ferdinando Taviani (1979) "Theatre Presence, Sea Lanes, Sardinia 1975," in *Theatre Papers*, Third Series (1979–1980), no. 7.
Ruffini, Franco (1981) *La scuola degli attori*, Milan: Casa Usher.
Scali, Mario (1985) "Le crie de Barba au bout de la lagune," *Liberation* (France), 21 October: 34.
Schechner, Richard (1973) *Environmental Theater.* New York: Hawthorn Books.
———— (1977) *Essays in Performance Theory: 1970–1976.* New York: Drama Book Specialists.
———— (1984) "Third Theatre: An Interview With Jerzy Grotowski about Eugenio Barba," *Village Voice* 29, (18): 103.
———— (1985) *Between Theater and Anthropology.* Philadelphia: University of Pennsylvania Press.
———— (1986) *The Drama Review* 30 (1) (T109): 52–99.
———— (ed.) (1990) *The Drama Review* 34 (3) (T127): 24–87.
Sciarrata, Patrick (1984) "A Visit From Signor Barba," National Mime News 1 (3):2–3.
Shoemaker, David (1990) "Report From Holstebro: Odin Teatret's *Talabot*," *New Theatre Quarterly* 6 (24): 307–317.
Simpson, Penny (1990) "Weaving Striking Images," *South Wales Echo*, 4 September.
Sklar, Deidre (1985) "Etienne Decroux's Promethean Mime," *The Drama Review* 29 (4) (T108): 64–75.
Smith, A. C. H. (1972) *Orghast at Persepolis.* New York: Viking Press.
Staniewski, Wlodzimierz (1977) "Gathering," in the program for the 1988 New York performances of *Gathering* and *Avvakum*.
Stanislavsky, Constantine (1967) *An Actor Prepares.* London: Geoffrey Bles.
Taviani, Ferdinando (1978) *Il libro dell'Odin.* Milan: Feltrinelli (1st edition 1975).
———— (1979) "Bird's Eye View," "A Point of View," and "Ways of Saying," in *The Floating Islands* by Eugenio Barba. Holstebro, Denmark: Odin Teatret Forlag.
———— (1986a) "Postscript: The Odin Story by Ferdinando Taviani," in *Beyond the Floating Islands* by Eugenio Barba. New York: Performing Arts Journal Publications.
———— (1986b) Talk given at the round table discussion following the 4th ISTA session in Holstebro, Denmark, 21 September.
Taviani, Ferdinando and Tony D'Urso (1977) *Lo straniero che danza.* Torino: Cooperativa Editoriale Studio.
Varley, Julia (1985) Interview, Nordisk Teaterlaboratorium, Holstebro, Denmark, 27 August.
Venza, Jac (producer and director) (1970) *Open Theatre: The Serpent*, documentary film on the making of *The Serpent.*
Volli, Ugo (1986) "The Gospel of Evil," *Teatrofestival* (Milan) 2: 10.
Wagner, Roy (1981) *The Invention of Culture.* Chicago: University of Chicago Press.

Watson, Ian (1985) "Odin Teatret: *The Million,*" *The Drama Review* 29 (3) (T107):131–137.

———— (1988) "Eastern and Western Influences on Performer Training in Eugenio Barba's Odin Teatret," *Asian Theatre Journal* 5 (1): 49–60.

———— (1989) "Eugenio Barba: The Latin American Connection," *New Theatre Quarterly* 5 (17): 67–72.

Wethal, Torgeir (director) (1972) *Vocal Training at Odin Teatret,* Produced by Odin Teatret Film and RAI, Italian television.

———— (1985) Interview, Nordisk Teaterlaboratorium, Holstebro, Denmark, 2 September.

Wichman, Elizabeth (1983) "Traditional Theater in Contemporary China," in *Chinese Theatre from its Origins to the Present Day,* Colin Mackerras (ed.). Hawaii: University of Hawaii Press.

Zahnd, Rene (1989) "La farce de la tragedie humaine," *Gazette de Lausanne,* 21 October.

Zarrilli, Phillip (1984a) "Doing the Exercises: The Transmission of In Body Performance Knowledge in a Traditional Martial Art," *Asian Theatre Journal* 1 (2):1-31.

———— (1984b) *The Kathakali Complex.* New Delhi: Abhinav Publications.

———— (1988) "For Whom Is the 'Invisible' Not Visible?: Reflections on Representation in the Work of Eugenio Barba," *The Drama Review* 32 (1) (T117): 95–106.

Zurowski, Andrezej (1985) "Pulling Faces at the Audience: The Lonely Theatre of Tadeusz Kantor," *New Theatre Quarterly* 1 (4): 364–368.

MAJOR FILMS AND VIDEOTAPES RELEVANT TO THE WORK OF EUGENIO BARBA

Antropologia Teatrale (1987) Videotape produced by Videoteam, Lecce, Italy. Eugenio Barba's open session on theatre anthropology at the Salento ISTA.

Ascent to the Sea (1978) Available on 16 mm film and videotape. Directed by Torgeir Wethal for Odin Teatret Film. The Odin production *Anabasis* in Peru.

Corporal Mime I and II (1971) Two films available on 16 mm film and videotape. Directed by Torgeir Wethal for Odin Teatret Film and RAI (Italian Television). Yves Lebreton, a pupil of Etienne Decroux, demonstrates and explains Decroux's "abstract mime" technique.

Dal Testo all'Azione (1987) Videotape produced by Videoteam, Lecce, Italy. A 30-minute edited version of Eugenio Barba's open session on theatre anthropology at the Salento ISTA.

The Female Role as Represented in Various Cultures (1986) Videotape produced by Odin Teatret Film. Two 30-minute tapes recorded during the Holstebro ISTA.

Ferai (1969) Available on 16 mm film and videotape. Directed by Marianne Ahrne for RAI. A filmed version of the Odin production.

In Search of Theatre (1974) Available on 16 mm film and videotape. Directed by L. Ripa di Meana for RAI. A documentary on the Odin's residency in southern Italy from May to October 1974.

The Million (1979) Available on 16 mm film and videotape. Produced by Odin Teatret Film. Film version of the Odin production.

Moon and Darkness (1980) Video tape produced by Odin Teatret Film. A taped version of Rasmussen's one-woman production.

On the Two Banks of the River (1978) Available on 16 mm film and videotape. Directed by Torgeir Wethal for Odin Teatret Film. A documentary of the Odin's 1978 tour in the Peruvian Andes during a period of martial law.

Oxyrhincus Evangeliet (1987) Available on 16 mm film. Directed by Torgeir Wethal for Odin Teatret Film. A filmed version of the Odin production.

Physical Training at Grotowski's Laboratory (1972) Available on 16 mm film and videotape. Directed by Torgeir Wethal for Odin Teatret Film and RAI. Ryszard Cieslak demonstrates some of the physical exercises developed at the Polish Laboratory Theatre in a workshop with two Odin actors.

Physical Training at Odin Teatret (1972) Available on 16 mm film and videotape. Directed by Torgeir Wethal for Odin Teatret Film and RAI. The Odin's physical training, with a commentary by Barba, showing its evolution from collectively learned skills to the actor's individualization of exercises.

Plastics Training at Grotowski's Laboratory (1972) Available on 16 mm film and video tape. Directed by Torgeir Wethal for Odin Teatret Film and RAI. Ryszard Cieslak

193

demonstrates some of the plastics exercises developed at the Polish Laboratory Theatre in a workshop with two Odin actors.

Puputan (1981) Videotape produced by Odin Teatret Film. A taped version of Cots' solo production.

Shakti (1987) Videotape produced by Videoteam, Lecce, Italy. A documentary on the Salento ISTA.

Theatre Meets Ritual (1976) Available on 16 mm film and videotape. Produced by Kurare (Venezuelan Television). Two barters organized during the Odin's 1976 tour of Venezuela, one in an urban negro village, the other among the Yanomami Indians of the Amazon.

Theatrum Mundi (1987) Videotape produced by Videoteam, Lecce, Italy. A filmed version of the Theatrum Mundi performance in Copertino Castle during the Salento ISTA. This piece, created by Barba for ISTA, included performers from India, Japan, Bali, and the Odin Teatret.

Vestita di Bianco (1974) Available on 16 mm film and videotape. Directed by Torgeir Wethal for Odin Teatret Film. The camera follows Rasmussen's solitary travels through several southern Italian villages, and her meetings with the local people.

Vocal Training at Odin Teatret (1972) Available on 16 mm film and videotape. Directed by Torgeir Wethal for Odin Teatret Film and RAI. A demonstration of the Odin's vocal training at the time, with a commentary by Barba.

Note: For rental and/or purchase information on these films and videotapes contact: Odin Teatret, Box 1283, DK-7500 Holstebro, Denmark.

INDEX